The Rich Man *and the* Kingdom

Series Editors for This Volume

Bernadette J. Brooten &

Francis Schüssler Fiorenza

The Rich Man *and the* Kingdom

John D. Rockefeller, Jr., and the Protestant Establishment

Albert F. Schenkel

Fortress Press
Minneapolis

The Rich Man and the Kingdom
John D. Rockefeller, Jr., and the Protestant Establishment

Harvard Theological Studies 39

This volume was prepared for publication by the staff of the *Harvard Theological Review* and appears in substantially the same form in which it was approved as a doctoral dissertation by the Committee on the Study of Religion, Harvard University.

Book design and typesetting at the *Harvard Theological Review*
Managing Editor: Tamar Duke-Cohan
Editorial Assistants: Ellen B. Aitken, Greg Schmidt Goering, Laura Nasrallah, Anthony Rivera, and Naomi Shulman
Cover Design: Evans McCormick Creative

The author and publisher gratefully acknowledge the kind permission of the Rockefeller Archive Center to reproduce images herein, and the University of Chicago to reproduce the photo of Frederick T. Gates.

Library of Congress Cataloging-in-Publication data

Schenkel, Albert F.
The rich man and the Kingdom : John D. Rockefeller, Jr., and the Protestant establishment / Albert F. Schenkel.
p. cm. — (Harvard theological studies)
Originally presented as the author's thesis (doctoral), Harvard University.
Includes bibliographical references (p.).
ISBN 0-8006-7092-2 (alk. paper)
1. Rockefeller, John D. (John Davison), 1874-1960.
2. Philanthropists—United States—Biography. 3. Stewardship, Christian. 4. Capitalism—United States—Religious aspects—Protestant churches. 5. Liberalism (Religion)—Protestant churches—History—20th century. 6. Liberalism (Religion)—United States—History—20th century. 7. United States—Church history—20th century. I. Title. II. Series: Harvard theological studies 39
HV28.R547S27 1995
361.7'4'092—dc20
[B] 95-2580
CIP

The paper used in this publication meets the minimum requirements of American National Standard for Information Sciences—Permanence of Paper for Printed Library Materials, ANSI Z329.48-1984.

Manufactured in the U.S.A. AF 1-7092
99 98 97 96 95 1 2 3 4 5 6 7 8 9 10

CONTENTS

Acknowledgments vii

Guide to Citations from the Rockefeller Archive Center ix

INTRODUCTION
Rockefeller Philanthropy and the Protestant Establishment 1

CHAPTER 1
Privilege and Duty: The Nurture of a Protestant Philanthropist 7

Evangelical Protestant Nurture 8

College Years: 1893–1897 15

Developments in Rockefeller's Theology and Social Thought: 1897–1910 23

CHAPTER 2
Guilt, Guidance, and Guardianship: A Protestant Philanthropist Comes of Age 31

John D. Rockefeller, Sr.: Lessons in Religious Philanthropy 33

Frederick T. Gates: Lessons in Scientific Giving and Religious Liberalism 36

William Lyon Mackenzie King: Lessons in Religious Social Ethics 44

Rockefeller's Mature Theology: 1917 and Beyond 51

CHAPTER 3
The Kingdom of God and the Welfare of Humankind: Religion and Rockefeller Philanthropy 63

Religion and Modern Philanthropy 65

Religion and Education 70

Religion and Medicine 84

Religion and Social Science 87

Religion and Internationalism 89

Evaluating Rockefeller Philanthropy 91

C H A P T E R 4
The China Medical Board: A Case Study in Religion and Rockefeller Philanthropy 97

C H A P T E R 5
The Religion of the Inarticulate: The Protestant Establishment and Common Religion 121
Rockefeller Interdenominational Work before the War 123
The Interchurch World Movement: The Inarticulate Say "No" 130
The Institute for Social and Religious Research 148
The Laymen's Report 155

C H A P T E R 6
The Reborn Church: Institutions of the Protestant Establishment 167
The Twilight Years of Traditional Voluntary Societies: 1920–1950 169
An Ambivalent Baptist 172
Riverside Church 174
Seminaries 179
Religious Cooperation and Protestant Federation: 1900–1960 181

C H A P T E R 7
The Rockefeller Connection: The Protestant Establishment as a Personal Network 197
The Rockefeller Network: Venues, Lineages, and Styles of Influence 198
The Rockefeller Network: Form and Substance 207

C H A P T E R 8
Conclusion: Secularization and Common Religion 237

I N D E X 241

Acknowledgments

I am grateful for the community of scholars who supported and challenged me as I wrote the dissertation now presented in this book. I offer special thanks to my patient and persistent mentor William R. Hutchison, who taught me much about how to treat ideas and how to treat people. The members of the American Religious History Colloquium at the Harvard Divinity School were a regular source of insight and encouragement. I am indebted to Diana L. Eck, Richard S. Tedlow, Conrad Wright, David D. Hall, and Ellen Fitzpatrick for their incisive comments at various stages of the work. Stephen Prothero, Richard Seager, and Nathan Showalter were especially good and honest friends.

The generous support of the Lilly Endowment made this project possible. I want to thank Robert W. Lynn and Craig Dykstra for their kind interest in my work and that of other young scholars of American religion.

The staff of the Rockefeller Archive Center, under the direction of Darwin H. Stapleton, was so kind and efficient that my memories of research there will always be pleasant ones. Tom Rosenbaum took special interest in my work and was a tremendous resource and guide with regard to the collections there. A timely research grant from the Center was a much needed boost in the midst of the journey.

The publication process has been ably handled by Tamar Duke-Cohan and Laura Nasrallah at the Harvard Theological Review and Michael West and Pam McClanahan at Fortress Press. My thanks to them for their patient cooperation.

My family and friends have sustained me with love and care beyond measure. The members of Covenant Church have been generous with their support and understanding. My mother, Betty Schenkel, and my children, David, Daniel, Andrew, Suzanne, and Rachel have inspired me constantly. There are no words to describe my gratitude and admiration for my wife Elizabeth. Without her constant support and tireless labors this project could never have been completed.

Guide to Citations from the Rockefeller Archive Center

The abbreviated titles listed below are used following the notation "Archives" to cite the collection of the Rockefeller Archive Center. For further explanation of the center's holdings, see Emily J. Oakhill and Kenneth W. Rose, comps., *A Guide to the Archives at the Rockefeller Archive Center* (New York: Rockefeller Archive Center, 1989)

Benevolences

Rockefeller Family Archives: Record Group 2, Office of the Messrs. Rockefeller, Series Z, John D. Rockefeller, Jr. Personal Papers, 1874–1961, 10. Benevolence Reports and Correspondence, 1938–1960, Rockefeller Archive Center, Tarrytown, NY.

Correspondence

Rockefeller Family Archives: Record Group 2, Office of the Messrs. Rockefeller, Series Z, John D. Rockefeller, Jr. Personal Papers, 1874–1961, 8. Correspondence, 1881–1936, Rockefeller Archive Center, Tarrytown, NY.

Davison II

Davison Fund, Inc., Records, 1930–1942, Davison II, Rockefeller Archive Center, Tarrytown, NY.

Educational Interests

Rockefeller Family Archives: Record Group 2, Office of the Messrs. Rockefeller, Series G, Educational Interests, 1896–1961, Rockefeller Archive Center, Tarrytown, NY.

Personal Education

Rockefeller Family Archives: Record Group 2, Office of the Messrs. Rockefeller, Series Z, John D. Rockefeller, Jr. Personal Papers, 1. School and College Records and Notebooks, Rockefeller Archive Center, Tarrytown, NY.

Fosdick Papers

Raymond B. Fosdick, Papers, (1919–1934)–1951, Rockefeller Archive Center, Tarrytown, NY.

Friends and Services

Rockefeller Family Archives: Record Group 2, Office of the Messrs. Rockefeller, Series H, Friends and Services, Rockefeller Archive Center, Tarrytown, NY.

Gates Papers

Frederick T. Gates, Papers, 1877–1939, Rockefeller Archive Center, Tarrytown, NY.

Religious Interests

Rockefeller Family Archives: Record Group 2, Office of the Messrs. Rockefeller, Series N, Religious Interests, 1894–1962, Rockefeller Archive Center, Tarrytown, NY.

Rockefeller Boards

Rockefeller Family Archives: Record Group 2, Office of the Messrs. Rockefeller, Series O, Rockefeller Boards, 1899–1961, Rockefeller Archive Center, Tarrytown, NY.

Rockefeller, Sr.

Rockefeller Family Archives: Record Group 1: John D. Rockefeller Papers, 1855–(1879–1894)–1942, Rockefeller Archive Center, Tarrytown, NY.

Addresses

Rockefeller Family Archives: Record Group 2, Office of the Messrs. Rockefeller, Series Z, John D. Rockefeller, Jr. Personal Papers, 1874–1961, 6. Addresses and Articles, 1891–1956, Rockefeller Archive Center, Tarrytown, NY.

Introduction

Rockefeller Philanthropy and the Protestant Establishment

John Davison Rockefeller, Jr., was this century's foremost religious philanthropist. He inherited not only his father's name but his father's staggering wealth and Protestant faith. The elder Rockefeller believed that God had given him his money; the younger Rockefeller believed that God wanted him to give the money away. Between 1917 and 1960, he gave away roughly a billion dollars.[1]

As a Protestant philanthropist, Rockefeller took seriously the mandate to extend the kingdom of God. The meaning of this endeavor changed drastically, however, during the years of his stewardship. In the late nineteenth century, evangelical Protestantism was firmly embedded in the constellation of values that comprised much of the culture of the United States. In the twentieth century, however, changing demographics, new material realities, and secular philosophies

1. Rockefeller's personal charitable giving reached five hundred and thirty-seven million dollars, and he played a major role in the disposition of an additional five hundred and forty million dollars of the fortune accumulated by his father. Authors have used numerous devices to avoid confusing the Junior and Senior Rockefellers. This study will use "Rockefeller" to refer only to John D. Rockefeller, Jr., and will always specify in some way when the discussion refers to the elder Rockefeller.

steadily displaced Protestantism as America's common religion. Rockefeller and many of his Protestant associates responded to these developments with ambivalence. They praised the aspects of modern culture that contributed to human well-being and saw them as products of God's providential care. At the same time they feared that the secularizing power inherent in many modern developments would erode the religious foundations on which civil order rested. They embraced Protestant modernism not primarily as a solution to theological problems, but as a religious expression fit for the task of building a new America in which Protestantism would continue to function as the common religion.

The hope of perpetuating Protestant hegemony is an underdeveloped theme in the scholarly treatment of Protestant modernism. The intellectual history of modernism has been clearly traced,[2] but its cultural dimensions have only recently begun to receive comparable attention. Martin E. Marty's exploration of modern American religion speaks of the need to take "transverse sections of history in as many directions as possible" in order to gain an understanding of the religious cultures of modernity. Marty describes a cosmopolitan outlook and an apologetic strategy toward the Bible as two aspects of modernist religious culture.[3] The attempt to preserve Protestantism as a common religion constituted yet another thread in the fabric of modernism. Rockefeller's philanthropic career brings this dimension of the modernist program into focus.

Rockefeller's philanthropy reflected enthusiasm over modernity's tools for serving humanity, as well as a desire to preserve Protestant moral governance in the affairs of the modern world. As many traditional charitable functions began to require modern expertise, Rockefeller worked with emerging experts, many of whom did not share his religious world view, in creating new scientific fields and applications. At the same time, Rockefeller gave more than one hundred million dollars toward explicitly religious causes, and the religious values he promoted were those designed to keep Protestantism fit for its ongoing

2. See William R. Hutchison, *The Modernist Impulse in American Protestantism* (Cambridge, MA: Harvard University Press, 1976).

3. Martin E. Marty, *Modern American Religion,* vol. 1: *The Irony of It All, 1893–1919* (Chicago: University of Chicago Press, 1986) 8–9, 17–24, 32–43.

guardianship. Rockefeller would have rejected the attempt to divide his charity into the categories "secular" and "religious," but the course of twentieth-century life guaranteed that scholars would utilize such divisions.

Many historians have written about Rockefeller's secular charity, especially about the role of Rockefeller and his associates in the development of scientific giving.[4] Nearly all of them have acknowledged that religion played an important part in the inception of modern philanthropy, but none has shown interest in the unique role of modernist religion—as distinguished from both traditional religion and modern secularism—in the development of this philanthropy.

Rockefeller's most recent biographers have portrayed him as a progressive, but he has not appeared in those treatments of progressivism that have focused on its relationship to Protestantism.[5] Yet Rockefeller's life provides important nuances to the story of that relationship. Instead of moving, like many others, from Protestantism to progressivism, he added one of these ideologies to the other and then adhered to both throughout the course of his career. He was a major creator of secular philanthropy who remained religious by adopting the modernist mode of religion.

Marxist historians of modern philanthropy have neglected to say much about Rockefeller's religion because it is of little interest to them. They have usefully elucidated many of the ways in which Rockefeller philanthropy contributed to the perpetuation and extension of capitalist hegemony.[6] The search for an adequate understand-

4. See, for example, Merle Curti, "Tradition and Innovation in American Philanthropy," *Proceedings of the American Philosophical Society* 105 (1961) 146–56; Robert H. Bremner, *American Philanthropy* (Chicago: University of Chicago Press, 1960) 1–75; Brian O'Connell, *America's Voluntary Spirit* (New York: Foundation Center, 1983) 1–44; Barry D. Karl and Stanley N. Katz, "Foundations and the Ruling Class," *Daedalus: Journal of the American Academy of Arts and Sciences: Philanthropy, Patronage, Politics* 116 (1987) 1–40.

5. John Ensor Harr and Peter J. Johnson, *The Rockefeller Century* (New York: Scribner's, 1988); Robert M. Crunden, *Ministers of Reform: The Progressive Achievement in American Culture* (New York: St. Martin's, 1983).

6. See especially Robert F. Arnove, ed., *Philanthropy and Cultural Imperialism: The Foundations at Home and Abroad* (Bloomington: Indiana University Press, 1982).

ing of Rockefeller's life and work, however, does not end here. Rockefeller consciously sought to model his life on religious principles. One has not understood Rockefeller until one has looked at how his philanthropic task fit into his religious world view.

If accounts of Rockefeller's secular philanthropy have given scant consideration to the religious dimension, historians have given even less attention to Rockefeller's specifically religious philanthropy. The hagiography of Rockefeller and his Protestant associates has preserved only a litany of the perceived summits of his religious charity, and the recent descriptions of the family dynasty have not chosen to pursue the issue any further.[7] Several articles have treated specific episodes, and critical biographies of contemporaries such as John R. Mott and Harry Emerson Fosdick have given us important parts of the story.[8] No one, however, has attempted an account of the whole, much less an interpretive treatment.

Rockefeller's religious charity was the counterpart of his secular charity. Both featured harmony between the religious and the secular; they were variations on the same theme. Together they expressed the conviction that the world needed a common religious devotion to the well-being of humankind, expressed in the modern idiom and served by modern science. Rockefeller envisioned a modernist Protestant America, and this vision was a major motivation for the whole of his philanthropic work.

Rockefeller and his associates failed to create a modernist Protestant America in the twentieth century. Fundamentalists and agnostics defected from the evangelical consensus to join Jews, Catholics, and

7. Foremost amid the hagiography is Raymond B. Fosdick, *John D. Rockefeller, Jr.: A Portrait* (New York: Harper & Brothers, 1956). Among the newer family histories, see, for example, Peter Collier and David Horowitz, *The Rockefellers: An American Dynasty* (New York: Holt, Rinehart & Winston, 1976) which devotes a mere five pages to recounting Rockefeller's religious philanthropy.

8. See the discussion and bibliography below, pp. 130-155, on Rockefeller's role in the Interchurch World Movement and the Institute for Social and Religious Research. See also C. Howard Hopkins, *John R. Mott, 1865–1955* (Grand Rapids, MI: Eerdmans, 1979); and Robert Moats Miller, *Harry Emerson Fosdick: Preacher, Pastor, Prophet* (New York: Oxford University Press, 1985).

hosts of others in opposing the perpetuation of any common religion based upon a liberalized Protestantism. Denominational Protestantism was forced to close its ranks and define its constituency in the midst of increasing religious diversity. Even liberal Protestants found the modernist sensibility difficult to maintain, and neoorthodox theology reinforced these reservations. Denominational Protestantism ceased to be America's church and became—in character if not in size—a sect.[9]

At the same time, Rockefeller's extensive contributions to American Protestantism and American society helped to insure that Protestantism would remain one of the dominant forces in America well into the twentieth century. A recent study of American mainline Protestantism in the years from 1900 to 1960 used the concept of "establishment" to describe the way in which Protestantism functioned in American culture in the years between the virtually unquestioned Protestant ascendancy of the late nineteenth century and the religious pluralism of the late twentieth century.[10] Rockefeller was part of this establishment. His nurture, training, and experience told him that Protestant hegemony was good for America. His philanthropic career represented a modern version of the unending Protestant quest both to establish the kingdom of God in America and to maintain Protestantism as the chosen instrument of this endeavor.

9. I refer here to Ernst Troeltsch's discussion of the differences in the characteristic interactions with society between a religious group that sees itself as coextensive with society and one that sees itself as small group within society. See *The Social Teaching of the Christian Churches* (1911; reprinted Chicago: University of Chicago Press, 1981) 328–43.

10. William R. Hutchison, "Protestantism as Establishment," in idem, ed., *Between the Times: The Travail of the Protestant Establishment in America, 1900–1960* (New York: Cambridge University Press, 1989) 3–13.

1

Privilege and Duty

The Nurture of a Protestant Philanthropist

Cleveland's Erie Street Baptist Church rejoiced with one of its stalwart couples in the birth of their first son on 29 January 1874, as Laura Celestia Spelman Rockefeller presented John D., Jr., to her proud husband. John D. Rockefeller, Sr., had joined the church in its early days, shortly after it was formed out of a protracted revival meeting that lasted one hundred and fifty nights. He had made the church the center of his social life for twenty years, and during those years he had become one of the richest men in Cleveland. Even after his move to affluent Euclid Avenue, however, he and his family continued to drive downtown to Erie Street Baptist. John D. Rockefeller, Sr., enjoyed the fruits of his work ethic, but he never forgot its roots.[1]

The Rockefellers believed that the same moral principles that created wealth were also essential in managing it. In their son, whom they saw as the primary heir of their rapidly growing fortune, they carefully nurtured the same asceticism that they had employed in obtaining it. They taught him the disciplines of evangelical devotional life and of giving to the church. They taught him familial duty and social responsibility. They provided strong guidance as he selected a

1. Allan Nevins, *John D. Rockefeller: The Heroic Age of American Enterprise* (New York: Scribner's, 1941) 88–89, 118. See also Collier and Horowitz, *The Rockefellers*, 30.

college that would reinforce these principles and as he chose a wife who shared them.

The younger Rockefeller internalized these lessons with unusual devotion. Although he adopted a liberal theology and found new means for expressing the old charitable impulse, he never abandoned the moral values of nineteenth-century Protestantism.[2]

Evangelical Protestant Nurture

Despite differences in their religious and cultural backgrounds, John D. and Laura Spelman Rockefeller agreed on the essentials of Christian nurture.[3] Both took religion and morality seriously and insisted that their children do the same. Senior's legendary iron will and self-discipline were inextricably entwined with religion. Of the pious Laura Spelman Rockefeller it has been said that "her life was built on the spirit and precepts of the New Testament, in unquestioning personal devotion."[4] Even when allowance is made for the idealization of later portraits, one must conclude that the elder Rockefellers were deeply religious parents in the style that we have come to see as typical of late nineteenth-century evangelicalism.

Senior was a product of nineteenth-century revivalism. He spent his first fourteen years in upstate New York. His mother, who saw in him the reflection of her own serious temperament, taught him the Baptist religion of the "burned-over district." Moving progressively westward from Oswego, New York, his family settled in Cleveland in 1853. Rockefeller was fourteen years old when he joined Erie Street Baptist Church. In the heat of revival he learned how to lead the

2. The standard biography of John D. Rockefeller, Jr., is Raymond B. Fosdick's *John D. Rockefeller, Jr., A Portrait*. John Ensor Harr and Peter J. Johnson's text, *The Rockefeller Century*, provides the first fresh research on Rockefeller, Jr.'s early life since Fosdick's work. Although Harr and Johnson are also Rockefeller "insiders," they consciously avoid the hagiographical tone of Fosdick.

3. Harr and Johnson, *Century*, 16–19. For a description of the family during Rockefeller, Jr.'s early years, see Allan Nevins, *Study in Power: John D. Rockefeller, Industrialist and Philanthropist* (2 vols.; New York: Scribner, 1953) 2. 1–19.

4. Frederick Taylor Gates, *Chapters in My Life* (New York: Free Press, 1977) 244.

kneeling congregation in prayer. He began to tithe to the church at age sixteen; as his biographer Nevins wrote, "he had not waited to become rich before he became generous."[5]

Rockefeller, Sr., also did not wait long to become rich. He decided against college and began work at the age of eighteen as a bookkeeper and clerk in a commission merchant's firm. Soon he joined a friend in starting a merchant firm. There he first dealt in petroleum, the commodity that made his fortune. In 1863 Rockefeller and his partners built a refinery, the first in Cleveland to produce kerosene commercially. In 1870 they founded Standard Oil Company, which within a decade acquired a virtual monopoly in the booming oil industry. Rockefeller, Sr., would be castigated by muckrakers as the archetypal robber baron of the era. Nevins portrayed him as a "one-track genius," a unique combination of visionary drive and disciplined precision.[6] In religious terms, he could be seen as the model of Max Weber's "inner-worldly ascetic."[7] Rockefeller, Sr., saw to it that the religious purpose evident in his pursuit of wealth was imparted to his son.

Although Rockefeller, Sr., was a model of self-discipline in his business practice and personal piety, he was not the primary disciplinarian in the family. Junior recalled him to a friend as "a beloved companion. He had a genius with children. He never told us what to do. He was one with us."[8] Increasingly during the first decade of Junior's life, Senior's business kept him in New York. The family began to spend winters there and finally moved there year-round in 1884. In both Cleveland and New York, the task of training the Rockefeller children fell largely to Laura Celestia Spelman Rockefeller.[9]

Laura grew up in Cleveland in a deeply religious Congregational family. The Spelmans had brought from Massachusetts and fostered in their children the same Protestant ethical seriousness that Rockefeller learned in Baptist circles. Cettie, as she was called, and John met in

5. Nevins, *Study in Power*, 2. 18.

6. Nevins, *Heroic Age*, 111.

7. Max Weber, *The Protestant Ethic and the Spirit of Capitalism* (New York: Scribner's, 1958) 149, 154, 193.

8. Fosdick, *Portrait*, 9.

9. Ibid., 13–23.

high school. While John, Sr., was beginning his commercial career in Cleveland, Laura went east to a respected finishing school in Massachusetts. Before her marriage she taught school, read widely, and listened to lectures from such thinkers as Henry Ward Beecher, Wendell Phillips, and Ralph Waldo Emerson. After she was married, she transferred her talents to home and children with enthusiasm and conviction. She bore four daughters before John, three of whom survived infancy: Bessie (1886), Alta (1871), and Edith (1872). Her sister, Lucy Spelman, later wrote of her, "I think she realized, as some mothers do, the prime importance of early environment and influences, and she worked for them and with them in their studies and all their activities. She knew how their future was wrapped up in the habits they formed early."[10]

The Rockefeller household performed devotional exercises daily before breakfast, including family prayers, Bible reading, and recitation of memorized Bible verses. They asked for God's blessing before every meal. Friday night was prayer meeting night, and the whole family always attended the meeting. Rockefeller later recalled that "at an early age, the children were encouraged by their mother to take part like the older people, either in a brief word of prayer or a word of personal experience."[11] The traditional taboos regarding such things as drinking, smoking, card-playing, dancing, theater-going were faithfully observed in the Rockefeller home.[12]

The Rockefellers routinely observed Sunday as a day of rest. They generally served a cold dinner, played no games, read only the Bible and "Sunday books," and rode only to church. There were no visitors. The children reviewed with their mother any ways in which they had sinned in the past week. She "would point out to them earnestly how in so doing they had sinned against God, Whose forgiveness she would lead them to seek in prayer."[13] Laura's Sunday "Home Talks" in-

10. Ibid., 15–17; the quotation is on p. 17.

11. John D. Rockefeller, Jr., "Duty, Service, Sacrifice," address at the fiftieth anniversary of the Men's Bible Class at Riverside Church, 29 February 1944, Archives: Addresses, box 4, folder 206. The notation "Archives:" indicates that the note provides an abbreviated reference to the Archival Guide that is located at the beginning of this volume. For a full citation of the archive, please see this guide.

12. Ibid.

13. Ibid.

cluded such homilies as "Prevailing Prayer," in which she urged that before one can pray one must be entirely committed to the Holy Spirit, and if one is so committed "one must be in the expectant attitude, waiting and watching with assured hope for its fulfillment, for it is through prayer that one learns God's purpose and will in one's life."[14] Church activities on Sundays included morning worship, Sunday school (in which both parents served as superintendents), young people's afternoon prayer meetings, and evening prayer services or hymn sings. Rockefeller played in the church orchestra and learned, along with his sisters, to substitute as a teacher for the younger children.[15] Rockefeller reflected later, "A day with such limitations as this would simply appall the modern child. And yet I have only the happiest recollections of the Sundays of my childhood. . . . The day was a happy day, for it was a family day."[16]

There is no indication that Laura Rockefeller encouraged her children to seek a conversion experience. Although all three were baptized in the Baptist church by immersion, she seems to have viewed their baptisms in a way more characteristic of her own Congregational tradition. Writing to friends shortly after the event, she reported that Alta, Edith, and John, aged twelve, eleven, and nine, had been baptized on the same day. The baptisms had come as a result of the friends' query as to why they had not yet been baptized, since they clearly evidenced faith. She had been unable to answer the question, and it haunted her, so she had the children baptized. Clearly, however, she regarded Christian nurture as the important matter and did not seek to induce in her children a crisis of conversion.[17]

In an unpublished article Rockefeller later wrote:

> At the age of nine I joined the church—the Baptist Church because my parents were Baptists. I was brought up in a Christian home. . . . I had always attended church, Sunday school and the prayer-meeting too, when so young that I recall falling asleep before the service was over. It would have been unnatural for me under the circumstances to have done anything else than join

14. Fosdick, *Portrait*, 18–19.

15. John D. Rockefeller, Jr., "Why I Am a Church Member," unpublished article, March 1920, Archives: Religious Interests, box 39, folder 321.

16. Rockefeller, "Duty, Service, Sacrifice."

17. Fosdick, *Portrait*, 19–20.

> the church. Conversion in the ordinary sense of the term, as used in a revival meeting, was unknown to me. Only he who has been leading a sinful life and is suddenly brought up with a round turn and like the soldier receives the order "About face," really knows the full significance of the word conversion. Under normal circumstances in a Christian home conversion in this sense would be abnormal.[18]

Memorable times spent in swimming, skating, riding, and playing "blind-man's bluff" with their father added the requisite levity to a potentially dreary family regimen. Senior was known to have a "soberly mirthful" disposition around the family; he seldom laughed loudly.[19] The few things Senior did enjoy, such as riding, landscaping, and golf, he pursued fanatically, but his cultural horizons were not expansive. "Always a narrow man," wrote his biographer, "he remained narrow."[20] Junior inherited his father's quiet intensity, but also his mother's appreciation for music and literature. As the mother explained to her son, "It is not selfish to sometimes do the things that one loves best to do. It makes for others' good also sooner or later."[21]

Although life was not dour in the Rockefeller household, it was certainly earnest. The most frequent visitors to the Rockefeller home were preachers and social reformers, including Augustus H. Strong, president of Rochester Theological Seminary; Edward Judson, the son of famous pioneer missionary parents; and Frances E. Willard, the temperance leader. Laura Rockefeller actively participated in the temperance movement, as she reminded her son on his twenty-third birthday:

> Twenty-three years old—born in 1874! That is the date of the Woman's Temperance Crusade in Ohio, when Mrs. Duncan marched through the streets, and talked and sang and prayed in the saloons, with many other ladies as intelligent. I might have joined them, if a wee baby-boy had not claimed me."[22]

Laura's moral earnestness was reinforced by her husband in the one area in which he did undertake to train their son—finance. Detailed

18. Rockefeller, "Why I Am a Church Member."
19. Fosdick, *Portrait*, 28.
20. Nevins, *Study in Power*, 1. 641–42.
21. Fosdick, *Portrait*, 16.
22. Ibid., 30; see also 27–30.

account books from his thirteenth year show that the young Rockefeller was trained by the man who produced the famous "Ledger A," the journal in which Rockefeller, Sr., as a young accountant, had established the practice of recording every cent earned, spent, or given away. The combined effort of mother and father left an indelible imprint: "My mother and father raised but one question: Is it right, is it duty?" As Rockefeller told his biographer, "I took responsibility early and, like my parents, I was serious."[23]

When the Rockefellers moved to New York City, they seem to have continued their religious disciplines in much the same fashion. They joined the Fifth Avenue Baptist Church, the congregation that would remain Rockefeller's church home for the next seventy-six years. Called Fifth Avenue Baptist in 1884, the church was actually located on West Forty-Sixth Street. In 1922 it moved to Park Avenue; in 1931, under the leadership of Harry Emerson Fosdick, it became the Riverside Church. When Rockefeller was in his teens, William H. P. Faunce became pastor of Fifth Avenue Baptist and began the tradition of liberalism that marked the church ever since.[24]

An essay written by Junior at the age of eleven, entitled "One Hundred Years Hence," reflected both his unusual seriousness and the prevailing morally progressive tone of the Protestant culture in which he was raised:

> I think that, in a hundred years, balloons will be made so large and strong that people will travel in them instead of in cars and steamboats; and that they will go twice as fast. Women will have the right to vote, and may be presidents. There will be no manufacture of liquor as a drink, throughout the United States, and consequently fewer jails and policemen. . . . Wars will be no more. Foreigners will be educated before they can vote. Indians will become civilized and intelligent. . . . It is hoped and expected that the people of our country will be wiser and better and therefore happier than now."[25]

Rockefeller preached his earliest surviving sermon shortly before his eighteenth birthday. It indicated that he had learned well the lessons of his childhood. The potential curse of his father's wealth had

23. Ibid., 43, 32.
24. Ibid., 10–27.
25. Ibid., 30.

been neutralized by training in asceticism. As the young Rockefeller considered the question, "What is the kernel of Christianity?" he found the answer in the words of Jesus: "If any man would come after me, let him deny himself and take up his cross, and follow me" (Matt 16:24). He was using the tools of his nurture to grapple with the issue that would remain important to him throughout his life—how the rich man can be truly religious. "We all know how much happier we are when we have something definite to do, and are not idle. Just so our happiness will be increased ten-fold when we take up some practical work for Christ, and do not live solely for our own pleasure."[26]

The social context in which Rockefeller came to maturity was a far cry from that of the revivalism in which his father had been reared. What could it have meant to John D. Rockefeller, Jr., to be saved from sin? Probably his deepest religious need was to be saved from his inherited wealth. Certainly those who knew Rockefeller recognized the existential burden that the family wealth represented for him and the sincerity with which he sought a transcendent purpose for its disposition.

Max Weber, whose characterization of the Protestant work ethic fits Senior so well, quoted John Wesley's maxim about wealth in his discussion of the link between asceticism and capitalism:

> I fear, wherever riches have increased, the essence of religion has decreased in the same proportion. . . . For religion must necessarily produce both industry and frugality, and these cannot but produce riches. But as riches increase, so will pride, anger, and the love of the world in all its branches. . . Is there no way to prevent this—this continual decay of pure religion? We ought not to prevent people from being diligent and frugal; we must exhort Christians to gain all they can, and to save all they can; that is, in effect, to grow rich.[27]

Weber, however, did not give Wesley's solution to the problem of riches: "If those who 'gain all they can' and 'save all they can,' will

26. John D. Rockefeller, Jr., "The Kernel of Christianity," speech at the Young People's Meeting at Fifth Avenue Baptist Church, 16 November 1891, Archives: Addresses, box 1, folder 1.

27. Quoted in Weber, *The Protestant Ethic*, 175.

likewise 'give all they can,' then the more they will grow in grace."[28] Rockefeller, Sr., espoused Wesley's maxim in its entirety. The same asceticism that made possible modern capitalism also made possible modern philanthropy. Rockefeller's parents gave him the problem of riches, but they also gave him spiritual resources designed to solve this problem.

College Years: 1893–1897

Rockefeller began his college career in the eventful year 1893. During most of this year the World's Columbian Exposition was thrilling thousands with the sights and sounds of modernity. At the same time, one hundred thousand of Chicago's inhabitants were homeless throughout the winter. Financial panic brought on a prolonged depression. Populists and premillennialists railed against modernity as Jacob Coxey's army of the unemployed waited in the wings for its march on Washington the following spring. Frederick Jackson Turner pronounced the frontier closed, while immigrants flooded the Atlantic coast. New solutions were needed, and new social sciences offered them. Junior entered college in a turbulent time, but a time full of promise.[29]

Rockefeller's early education had been quite uneventful. He had been tutored at home until the age of ten. Over the next six years he had attended four schools and taken a rest one winter in order to recuperate from illness. Evidently Rockefeller applied himself to his studies conscientiously, although he described himself later as "shy, ill-adjusted, and not very robust."[30] He undertook college preparation in yet another school, the Browning School, which was founded in 1889 as a tutorial program for John and four friends. John A. Browning, whom Rockefeller would later call his only memorable precollege

28. John Wesley, *The Works of the Reverend John Wesley* (4th ed.; 14 vols.; London: John Mason, 1840–42) 13. 246–47, quoted in ibid.

29. Rockefeller visited the Exposition in the summer of 1893, but said only that he developed "a very good idea of its vastness and immensity" (Harr and Johnson, *Century*, 35). Harr and Johnson (pp. 32–50) portray Rockefeller as Henry Adams's "new man," rooted in the old yet equipped by the new to deal with the new age.

30. Fosdick, *Portrait*, 39.

teacher, worked with Rockefeller over the next four years, excluding a second winter's break because of ill health. Rockefeller credited Browning with teaching him to concentrate and to make notes and outlines in the meticulous fashion that he would continue to follow throughout his life. John's exposure to the fine arts was limited to music, which "in our home took the place of theater and was an offset for our limited social life."[31]

In 1891 Rockefeller began to think about college. He took preliminary examinations for entrance into Yale and managed to pass every section but one. Browning assured him that one additional year of preparation would suffice, but Rockefeller stayed two more years with Browning. By the time he was ready to leave for college, his mind had changed about Yale. Rockefeller's correspondence with Dr. William Rainey Harper, with whom his father had founded the University of Chicago, provides a glimpse of the decision-making process. Rockefeller wrote to Harper, confiding that since he did not make friends readily, he feared he might be "lost in the crowd" at Yale and therefore was considering Brown as well.[32] Harper responded with a ringing endorsement of Brown on three counts: the personal ability and accessibility of President Elisha Benjamin Andrews, the Baptist affiliation of the school, and its smaller size.[33] Rockefeller's young pastor, W. H. P. Faunce, a Brown alumnus who would himself one day preside over the institution, added his strong recommendation both for the school and for President Andrews, whom he called "one of the most stimulating minds of this country."[34] Rockefeller's father is known to have respected Andrews and had consulted him in connection with the founding of the University of Chicago. With these persuasions and those of three close friends who had also chosen Brown, Rockefeller headed for Providence, Rhode Island, in the fall of 1893.

31. Ibid., 39, 42.

32. John D. Rockefeller, Jr., to William R. Harper, February 1893, quoted in Fosdick, *Portrait*, 46–47.

33. William R. Harper to John D, Rockefeller, Jr., 11 February 1893, quoted in Fosdick, *Portrait*, 46–47.

34. William H. P. Faunce to John D. Rockefeller, Jr., 1 April 1893, quoted in Fosdick, *Portrait*, 46–47.

The young Rockefeller's social ineptitude seems to have preoccupied him during the days of decision and initial adjustment. Rockefeller lived in Slater Hall during his Brown years. It was the newest dormitory, and although his bath was a quarter mile away in the gymnasium, Slater was complete with a general water faucet in the hall and a gas stove in his bedroom, which provided him the means to make hot chocolate. Rockefeller found an entree to his fellows by keeping his cupboard stocked with Whitman's instant chocolate and Borden's Eagle Brand condensed milk.[35] Music also provided John with additional social contacts, as he participated in the Glee Club, Mandolin Club, and later a string quartet. Relationships with women were more difficult for him. He was shy and diffident and thus found the social events of college life challenging. In his sophomore year, John decided that the way to overcome his awkwardness was to master the essential social skill of dancing. On the night of his very first dance, he met the popular and attractive Abby Aldrich, daughter of Senator Nelson Aldrich. By his senior year John was attending as many as four dances a week and had added theater attendance and football games to an active social life in which Abby Aldrich often played a part. Rockefeller served as class president his junior year, and during senior year he held the even more coveted position of manager of the football team.[36]

During his college years, Rockefeller did not violate the spirit of his parents' moral code, although he held less strictly to the letter of it. He maintained strict personal disciplines with regard to Sabbath observance and alcohol consumption, even when some among his broadening circle of associates concluded that he was excessively inhibited. He maintained regular church attendance at a Baptist church in Providence and occasionally spoke at Christian gatherings. At the same time, he added considerable tolerance to his religious outlook during his college years. Confronted for the first time with the plethora of Protestant denominations, with irreligion and massive alcohol con-

35. Mary Ellen Chase, *Abby Aldrich Rockefeller* (New York: Macmillan, 1950) 17–19.

36. Fosdick, *Portrait*, 52–57, 71.

sumption, Rockefeller held nimbly, if still firmly, to his original convictions. As he wrote to his Grandmother Spelman in 1896:

> One sees all sorts and conditions of men here viewing life, duty, pleasure and the hereafter so differently. My ideas and opinions change, I find, in many ways. I would stickle less for the letter of the law, now, more for the spirit. There are certain fundamental distinctions between right and wrong, and these must be observed and followed. But this is only one small part of the experience of life. Day by day I shall learn, and day by day I pray that I may ever stand firm for the right.[37]

The challenge that Brown offered to Rockefeller's narrow world was not only moral, but also intellectual. In a YMCA address during his freshman year, Rockefeller grappled anew with the same text he had used to elucidate the kernel of Christianity three years earlier. Rockefeller clearly stated that although some creedal specifics might have become less important, religion was as indispensable to him as before. Reciting the efforts of secular social scientists about whom he was learning, he commented, "Their idea is to do good because it is good, to be virtuous because it is right, to aid the unfortunate for the love of mankind. This is a praiseworthy motive, but infinitely more noble is it to do right for Christ's sake, to help our brothers for the love of Christ." The religious motive was the only one that would overcome discouragement, that would valorize effort even when it might fail. This sermon closed with an altar call: "You cannot serve God and mammon."[38] Thus, although the conservative roots of his faith were shaken, Rockefeller found a way to conserve what was most important to him in Christianity—its strong religiously based sense of duty and its direction concerning how he should spend his life and substance.

Rockefeller continued throughout his college years to be a serious student, performing well enough to win election to the Phi Beta Kappa Society by the end of his career. As Harper and Faunce had hoped when they recommended Brown to their young friend, Rockefeller came under the spell of President Elijah Benjamin Andrews.

37. Ibid., 63–82, 76.

38. John D. Rockefeller, Jr., "Then Said Jesus," address to the YMCA, 18 January 1894, Archives: Addresses, box 1, folder 3.

Andrews was a colorful and controversial social scientist whose incisiveness and integrity inspired tremendous loyalty from his students and often elicited an equally potent negative response from the business community. He had joined with other progressive economists in founding the American Economics Association in 1885, with the goal of understanding and mastering the chaos of the industrial age. During the nineties, Andrews advocated numerous reforms antithetical to laissez-faire doctrine and was embroiled in a controversy with the university trustees over his support for William Jennings Bryan and free silver coinage. In addition to his intellectual vigor, Andrews was revered by students for his intense spirituality. His searching stare was enhanced by a glass eye which replaced an eye lost in the Union cause. For Rockefeller, Andrews provided a model of uncompromising spirituality which was not tied to personal taboos or a conservative social outlook. Not surprisingly, Rockefeller told his biographer that Andrews was a great influence on his life.[39]

Andrews made his impact on Rockefeller indirectly through his revised curriculum, heavy in social sciences taught by like-minded young faculty members. Junior took three courses in political economy from Henry B. Gardiner, a disciple of Richard T. Ely. One was listed: "Socialism. Based on a Study of Karl Marx's *Capital*." In this course Gardiner pointed out the failure of capitalism to distribute equitably the gains of industrial progress and argued that a socialistic ethic was more in harmony with Christian thought than was an individualistic one. In another course taught by Gardiner, Rockefeller was examined with questions that included:

> To what does the anarchist attribute existing economic evils? What remedy does he propose? What would be the function of government under his scheme? . . .
>
> What is the justification of government control of monopolies? Does it necessarily follow that government should control all monopolies? In the case of what monopolies is government control most necessary? What forms may it take? . . . .
>
> Outline and criticize Henry George's analysis of the influences governing the distribution of products under the existing economic organization, by which he seeks to show that the owner of natural opportunities reaps the full benefit of economic

39. Harr and Johnson, *Century*, 45–46; Fosdick, *Portrait*, 79.

> progress. Discuss the justice and expediency of George's proposed remedy.[40]

In an introductory anthropology course, Rockefeller noted that "man differs absolutely only in one respect from apes. That difference [is] the power of speech."[41] He noted this as "proof of evolution." In a course entitled, "Social Problems and Conditions," offered by George Wilson, he heard the insights of anthropology and ethnology applied to the family, marriage, divorce, immigration, charity, pauperism, criminology, penology, intemperance, education, and social legislation. One can even see the impact of the social science emphasis on his work for a class in the rhetorical art of persuasion. Among his speeches were "The Dangers to America Arising from Unrestricted Immigration" and "Profit Sharing as a Remedy for Industrial Ills." In the latter, one finds material that could well be dismissed as merely sophomoric rhetoric were it not echoed in Rockefeller's later career:

> It is hardly necessary to enumerate these ills. . . the oppression of Labor by Capital is a brief summary of the whole matter. Now, as always, the employer seeks to get all that he can out of the employed, regardless of his well-being. . . . By adopting the profit sharing system. . . these machines of flesh and blood can be made men in the true sense of the term, with self-respect and a purpose in life. . . . Is there any so deaf to the cry of the oppressed laborer as to stand in the way of such a system which would ameliorate their condition? May the day soon come when labor and capital shall have one aim and one interest.[42]

40. *Brown University Catalogue 1895–1896* (Providence, RI: Remington, 1895) 76; *Brown University Catalogue 1896–1897* (Providence, RI: Remington, 1897) 56, 73, 76; Rockefeller's Brown grade reports in Archives: Personal Education, box 3, folder 30; Henry B. Gardner, "Examination in Political Economy VII, December 22, 1896," Archives: Personal Education, box 4, folder 39. See also Harr and Johnson, *Century*, 46–50; and Fosdick, *Portrait*, 79.

41. John D. Rockefeller, Jr., class notes for Anthropology 1, Archives: Personal Education, box 3, folder 31.

42. John D. Rockefeller, Jr., "The Dangers to America Arising from Unrestricted Immigration," and "Profit Sharing as a Remedy for Industrial Ills," pp. 1–5; both in Archives: Personal Education, box 3, folder 29.

Although the mature Rockefeller never advocated profit sharing, he did espouse the view that labor and capital shared common interests.

It was President Andrews's philosophy and phrasing that appeared several years later in Rockefeller's pronouncements on Christianity and culture. The impressionable college senior must have thought that Andrews's course in practical ethics was tailored to prepare him to enter the offices of his father. Andrews rested his ethical system on the universal rule that one must act always in accord with moral reason. His first subrule was the Golden Rule: "Do unto others as you would have them do unto you." In elaborating this rule, however, Andrews did not merely parrot individualistic orthodoxy; he stressed the need for both moral imagination and "representation" in understanding others in their social situation.

Not only must other individuals be genuinely understood and respected, but the progress of society as a whole must be considered in moral decision making. According to Andrews, socialism and individualism in their pure forms were both inadequate ethical systems. Personal idealism and scientific study must be yoked together. Andrews issued this missionary call:

> The world painfully needs two more classes of missionaries still—social missionaries to the rich and political missionaries. Where are the young men and women of means and leisure who will duly study the social problems of our time and help to create their solution?[43]

Such exhortation reinforced the moral seriousness of Rockefeller's family training.

The task of Andrews's missionaries may have sounded more secular than orthodox, but to Andrews such a distinction between the secular and the sacred was "pernicious." Andrews defined religion as "an attitude of the self toward the ultimate worth of the universe." Human duties were seen as divine. Without this religious sanction, moral principles could not be upheld; history proved this, according

43. John D. Rockefeller, Jr., class notes for Practical Ethics (Philosophy 67), spring 1897, pp. 8–10, Archives: Personal Education, box 3, folder 31; Harr and Johnson, *Century*, 48.

to Andrews. Spencer and his ilk, who argued for the withering of religion as a passing phase of ethics, were simply wrong. Religion was the indispensable foundation of ethics, just as science was its indispensable tool.[44]

Andrews offered a unique way of combining the social with the individual, and the religious with the secular, in an age that produced many such combinations. In the year that Rockefeller heard him lecture, Charles Sheldon published the novel *In His Steps*, an eloquent plea for social reform through individuals committed to ask always the question, "What would Jesus do?"[45] Such counsel would have seemed to Andrews to lack the requisite scientific specificity. At the same time, Andrews did not, in 1896, go as far as Walter Rauschenbusch later would go in calling for a "new evangelism" and a clear-cut choice for socialism. He was a religious progressive who drew his ethical imperative from individualistic moral reflection, but who also acted on the basis of scientific study. "Idle trust in God and the so-called laws of social growth" were not sufficient, Andrews believed:

> More than ever manifest in our day is the need of a conscious human guidance to society in its evolution. . . . If given efforts to reform, shape, and manage society suffer shipwreck, the proper inference is not that a let-alone policy is best, but that we need in the field deeper study and a more consummate art.[46]

Andrews's social gospel was individualistic, scientific, and activistic.

President Andrews's missionary call may well have been ringing in Rockefeller's ears as he read these questions on one of George Wilson's examinations in the spring of 1897: "Explain (a) the charity organization idea. (b) What are its (1) advantages, and (2) disadvantages? What are the hopeful tendencies in modern charities? Discuss—'Intelligent giving and intelligent withholding are alike true charity.'"[47]

44. Rockefeller, class notes for Practical Ethics, 11–15.

45. Charles Sheldon, *In His Steps* (New York: Burt, 1896).

46. Harr and Johnson, *Century*, 46. See Walter Rauschenbusch, "The New Evangelism," in William R. Hutchison, ed., *American Protestant Thought in the Liberal Era* (Lanham: University Press of America, 1985) 108–16.

47. George Wilson, "Examination in Social Sciences 2," March 1897, Archives: Personal Education, box 4, folder 39.

During his college career, the young Rockefeller broadened with regard to his social skills, his understanding of society, and his conceptions of religion. At the same time, his sense of religious calling to a careful stewardship of his family's fortune was reinforced not only by moral exhortation but also by the weight of scientific verification.

Developments in Rockefeller's Theology and Social Thought: 1897–1910

Rockefeller continued to move in a liberal direction theologically during his early adult years without any major spiritual crisis. His family, work environment, courtship, and church involvement all served to reinforce the basics on which his faith was built while allowing or encouraging theological adaptations.

Rockefeller brought new ideas home from college, but his family was quite open to them. Senior's faith had never been narrowly dogmatic. He had long been willing to overlook particularities of creed and included churches of various Protestant denominations, as well as Catholic charities, in his giving. The ministry of Fifth Avenue Baptist had kept the Rockefellers abreast of the progressive theology and social thought offered at Baptist colleges like Brown. Rockefeller's religious development did not distance him from his family.

Upon returning home, Rockefeller went to work in his father's office, ready to be trained by his father to care for the family's affairs. As it turned out, it was not his father, but the Reverend Frederick Gates who became his mentor. Gates provided the young Rockefeller with an additional model of Baptist liberalism.[48]

Rockefeller married Abby Aldrich in 1901. Her father was a Republican senator from Rhode Island whom Lincoln Steffens called "The Boss of the United States."[49] Rockefeller professed to have prayed daily for four years over whether or not to marry Aldrich. The deci-

48. Gates's extensive influence on Rockefeller will be discussed in the next chapter.

49. Lincoln Steffens, "Rhode Island: A State for Sale," *McClure's Magazine* 24 (1905) 344.

sion was a significant spiritual event for Rockefeller, if not a terribly romantic one.

> I believe profoundly in the power of prayer, nor could it be otherwise in view of my personal experience. In early manhood I prayed regularly and specifically morning and night for divine guidance in making one of the greatest decisions of my life. Awakened from a sound sleep one night before the first sign of the coming of dawn had made its appearance in the eastern sky, I had a feeling of such perfect assurance as to what my decision should be that without a moment's delay I got out of bed, turned on the light and wrote a letter committing myself to the course of action thus made clear to me. In the light of that personal experience, no one could shake my belief in the answer to prayer.[50]

Although Rockefeller did not mention it in this account, his mother had counseled him the night before his dawn of assurance, "Of course you love Miss Aldrich. Why don't you go at once and tell her so?"[51]

Abby proved to be an invaluable counterbalance to John's extreme seriousness and conscientiousness. She was an extrovert—warm, witty, and intuitive. She established her independence from John's obsessive attention to detail and never hesitated to speak to him frankly. John's Christian service pleased her; she shared his commitment to the welfare of others and the principle that life consists of more than possessions. The Aldriches were Congregationalists, and although religion had not been the center of her home, Abby joined her husband in daily prayer and weekly attendance at church and Sunday School. At the same time, she was known to prefer "slightly worldly ministers" and to be annoyed by "heavy-hearted ones"; she also hated voluble piety.[52]

The newly married Rockefellers attended Fifth Avenue Baptist Church, where Rockefeller had become one of the most active members. The Young Men's Bible Class—under the leadership of Charles Evans Hughes, who would later serve as Chief Justice of the United States—proved to be a major influence in his life. For two years

50. Rockefeller, "Why I Am a Church Member."

51. John D. Rockefeller, Jr., to Raymond B. Fosdick, quoted in Fosdick, *Portrait*, 100.

52. Chase, *Abby Aldrich Rockefeller*, 31–32, 47.

Rockefeller was a devoted member of the class, several times filling in as teacher. When Hughes stepped down in 1900, Rockefeller was asked to become leader of the class. For the next eight years, the rich young man taught the principles of Jesus each week, much to the glee of New York newsmen who were hostile to his family. Under Rockefeller's conscientious leadership the class grew from fifty to two hundred.

For Rockefeller, the class was an opportunity to apply his collegiate ideals to practical problems. The notes that remain from these Bible studies indicate a desire on Rockefeller's part to help his class apply the ethics of Jesus to their lives.[53] The lessons were biblical, thematic, and practical, often using the parables of Jesus and the life of Paul to illustrate moral principles. Rockefeller frequently covered topics such as giving, friendship, opportunity, Christianity in business, and "high standards."

Rockefeller's personal religion was not totally without contemplative content. He spoke of the necessity of prayer, especially in times of crisis. His overriding concern, however, was ethical action. He consistently enjoined the stock virtues of turn-of-the-century individualistic Protestantism. The triad of related terms that figured most prominently in Rockefeller's view of the Christian life consisted of duty, service, and giving.

Rockefeller passed on to his class the Victorian principles in which he had been nurtured. "The key to happiness. . . is a well-trained will, self-control, self-mastery," he told his Bible class.[54] There was an undeniable conservatism to this concept of duty, an implicit obligation to conform to family and culture. In one Bible lesson, Rockefeller lectured the class on "Four Fundamentals of Good Citizenship: work, thrift, respect for authority and law, and reverence for things that are sacred and holy."[55]

53. John D. Rockefeller, Jr.'s dated notes for thirty-four of these classes as well as undated notes that probably correspond to other classes are preserved in Archives: Addresses, boxes 1–3, 5.

54. John D. Rockefeller, Jr., "Liberty or License," Bible Class, 5 November 1911, Archives: Addresses, box 1, folder 29.

55. John D. Rockefeller, Jr., "Four Fundamentals of Good Citizenship," Bible Class, 5 November 1922, Archives: Addresses, box 2, folder 111. See also idem, "Bible Talks, misc.," Archives: Addresses, box 5, folder 252.

Rockefeller's sensitivity to the opinions of others, turned into religious principle, provided another dimension to the concept of duty. A favorite scripture was, "Let your light so shine before men that they may see your good works, and glorify your father who is in heaven" (Matt 5:16).[56] It has been suggested that his earthly father's reputation, not his heavenly father's, was the primary motive in Rockefeller's philanthropy. Rockefeller never publicly acknowledged wrongdoing on his father's part, despite evidence of Senior's ruthless business practices in the building of the Standard Oil monopoly. It does seem, however, that guilt over his family's wealth and grief over his father's reputation as a villain were emotions that ran deep within Rockefeller. These emotions may have helped to create the religious devotion to humanity that emerges in his exposition of biblical texts. Rockefeller showed a profound ability to empathize with the characters in these texts and to interact with them in a way that shaped his response to the circumstances that life dealt him. An example was Rockefeller's treatment of Gen 4:1–15:

> How many men there are now days who assume a perfect indifference regarding their fellow men; who claim that they are not their brother's keepers. They say, "Am I not independent and free to do as I like? Are you not the same? Then why do you keep talking about responsibility and one's duty toward others? . . . A truce then with this everlasting question as to what others will think of my actions, as to how the course of my life will affect someone else." Like Cain, they shake off this responsibility, but in vain.
>
> Every man stands in such a relation to every other man that he has no right to say, "I will be absolutely independent." Our lives are interrelated and interdependent to such an extent that they may well be compared to a tangled mass of threads, so interwoven and related that one cannot be touched or affected in any way without touching many of the others. . . . Therefore it becomes the duty of an earnest Christian to be ever so watchful of word and deed that through him a weaker brother may not be made to fall.[57]

56. John D. Rockefeller, Jr., "Let Your Light So Shine," Bible Class dated between 1900 and 1908, Archives: Addresses, box 5, folder 257.

57. John D. Rockefeller, Jr., "Genesis IV: 1–15," Bible Class dated between 1900 and 1908, pp. 5, 10, Archives: Addresses, box 5, folder 254. For

Rockefeller was never content to let a person's duty rest with mere avoidance of evil; one must serve others. "We do not try to make a man just good," Rockefeller quipped, "but good for something. . . [otherwise] he is good for nothing." Only through serving could one develop what was highest and best in oneself. Giving must always involve the giving of self and time as well as money.[58]

It was, of course, in the giving of money that Rockefeller excelled. Rockefeller's teaching on giving always contained the caveats necessary to good Protestant stewardship. One could not be naive or indiscriminate in giving; Jesus's counsel, "give to him who asks of you" (Matt 5:42), was not to be taken literally. One must give scientifically, but one must give—for one's own sake as well as that of others. Rockefeller's stock message on giving would later be enhanced by material from none other than Bruce Barton, whose controversial best seller, *The Man Nobody Knows*, depicted Jesus as an entrepreneur.

> There are two seas in Palestine. One fresh. . . . It laughs in the sunshine. . . . Every life is happier because it is there. There is another sea. . . . The air hangs heavy above its waters and neither man nor beast nor fowl will drink.
>
> What makes this mighty difference in these neighbor seas? The Sea of Galilee receives but does not keep the Jordan. For every drop that flows into it another drop flows out. . . . The other sea is shrewder, hoarding its income jealously.
>
> The Sea of Galilee gives and lives. This other sea gives nothing. It is named the Dead.[59]

a treatment of the "guilt motivation motif," see Harr and Johnson, *Century*, 87. Nelson W. Aldrich, Jr. (*Old Money: The Mythology of America's Upper Class* [New York: Knopf, 1988]) suggests the related argument that philanthropy was a necessary component of the Rockefeller family ascension into "old money" status.

58. John D. Rockefeller, Jr., "Service," Union Church, Northeast Harbor, Maine, 1916, Archives: Addresses, box 1, folder 46; idem, "Giving," Bible class, winter 1904; Archives: Addresses, box 1, folder 9.

59. John D. Rockefeller, Jr., "Matthew 5:42," Archives: Addresses, box 5, folder 252; idem, "The Will to Win the Peace: an address delivered in Detroit, Michigan, September 11, 1945, at a meeting of four hundred business and industrial leaders called by the Community Chest Corporate Gifts Committee," Archives: Addresses, box 5, folder 219. See also Bruce Barton, *The Man Nobody Knows* (Indianapolis: Bobbs-Merrill, 1925).

In its distilled essence, Rockefeller's religion was activist, liberal Protestantism. It made strong ethical demands and few doctrinal ones. It satisfied Rockefeller's need for purpose and direction in life. There is no evident hypocrisy; one rich man exhorted other rich men to live according to the teachings of Jesus that he found pertinent. At the same time, there was apparently little social analysis in Rockefeller's class. What is evident is naïveté and insensitivity to the culture-bound nature of the Christianity being taught. The teachings of Jesus and Paul as seen through the eyes of John D. Rockefeller, Jr., may have been inspiring to the men of Fifth Avenue Baptist, but to critical outsiders the Bible class lacked ample consideration of the problems of poverty and exploitation from the point of view of the poor and exploited.

Quite simply, before 1908 Rockefeller lacked the empathy and dialogue with those outside his own social class necessary to activate the ethical principles of teachers like President Andrews. This lack of empathy was especially evident in a 1902 address to the Brown University YMCA entitled "Christianity in Business." Speaking as part of a celebrity lecture series called "Life Work Talks," Rockefeller confirmed the worst stereotypes of the social Darwinism practiced by the Rockefellers by likening business success to the growing of an American Beauty rose, stating that the destruction of some businesses was necessary to the success of a few.[60]

One should note that the analogy of the American Beauty rose embodied precisely the theistic evolutionary philosophy espoused by John Fiske. Rockefeller had read Fiske's *Through Nature to God* and made copious notes on its historical and theological treatment of the nature of evil and the evolution of moral consciousness. Fiske's theodicy claimed that despite appearances of evil consequences an ethical force was guiding the cosmic process of evolution:

> Below the surface din and clashing of the struggle for life we hear the undertone of the deep ethical purpose, as it rolls in solemn music through the ages, its volume swelled by every victory, great or small, of right over wrong, till in the fullness of time, in God's own time, it shall burst forth in the triumphant chorus of Humanity purified and redeemed.

60. John D. Rockefeller, Jr., "Christianity in Business," speech at the Brown YMCA, 5 February 1902, Archives: Addresses, box 1, folder 8.

Fiske acknowledged that "on its industrial side the struggle has been. . . fierce; the evolution of higher efficiency through merciless competition is a matter of common knowledge." Fiske, nonetheless, argued that because we accept "that the attainment of higher life is in itself desirable," we must acquiesce in the "universal strife and slaughter" as part of the machinery of God's providence.[61]

During the early years of the century, events were pressing Rockefeller toward the changes in his social outlook for which his college years had prepared him. This was the era of the muckrakers. Ida Tarbell's *History of the Standard Oil Company* (1902), Thomas W. Lawson's *Frenzied Finance* (1904), and other exposés forced Rockefeller to look at the family business from new perspectives.[62] Outwardly he continued to represent his attitude toward his father with an appropriate piety, but there were indications that he would not follow in his father's footsteps in the business world. In 1904 he suffered a nervous collapse brought on by his distress over the revelations about his father's business practices, and he spent the better part of a year abroad. Rockefeller had already successfully collaborated with Gates in the founding of the Rockefeller Institute for Medical Research and the General Education Board. By 1910 he had withdrawn from nearly all the family business interests to devote his full attention to philanthropy.[63]

61. John D. Rockefeller, Jr., "The Mystery of Evil," ca. 1900, found by the author in Rockefeller's copy of John Fiske, *Through Nature to God* (Boston: Houghton, Mifflin, 1899); now in Archives: Addresses, box 1, folder 5A; in *Through Nature to God*, see pp. ix, 130, 68–69.

62. Ida M. Tarbell, *History of the Standard Oil Company* (New York: Macmillian, 1904); Thomas W. Lawson, *Frenzied Finance* (1905; reprinted New York: Greenwood, 1968); see Nevins, *Study in Power*, 2. 328–55 for an account of Rockefeller's defenders and opponents.

63. This period is treated in very different ways by Fosdick (*Portrait*, 98–142) and Harr and Johnson (*Century*, 51–88). The latter places importance on Junior's nervous collapse (see p. 85) while the former ignores it entirely.

2

Guilt, Guidance, and Guardianship

A Protestant Philanthropist Comes of Age

In the fall of 1917 the Baptist Social Union of New York asked Rockefeller if he would address their next monthly luncheon on a topic of his choosing. With characteristic modesty, Rockefeller agreed to speak before the Union only if expectations were kept at a minimum: "Please do not expect an important address from me, for you know I am in no sense a public speaker. What I may say will be more or less informal and will doubtless not occupy more than fifteen, at the outside twenty, minutes."[1] Rockefeller did keep his remarks brief, but they proved to be far from unimportant. The speech, entitled "The Christian Church—What of Its Future?" became one of the best-known popular articulations of liberal Protestantism.[2] For Rockefeller, moreover, it became something of a manifesto. So consistently did he hold to this distillation of his mature thought that he used virtually the same text when he addressed the Protestant Council of the City of New York in 1945.

1. John D. Rockefeller, Jr., to H. N. McKinney, 1 November 1917, Archives: Religious Interests, box 38, folder 315.

2. John D. Rockefeller, Jr., "The Christian Church—What of Its Future?" stenographic notes, 1918, Archives: Religious Interests, box 38, folder 315; published in the *Saturday Evening Post*, 9 February 1918, pp. 16, 37.

Three powerful personalities influenced Rockefeller profoundly in his theological, ethical, and professional development during the years between his return from Brown in 1897 and his declaration of religious principles in 1917. These men were John D. Rockefeller, Sr., Frederick Taylor Gates, and William Lyon Mackenzie King.

From his father, Rockefeller learned about the power and the problems inherent in giving largely to religious groups. He watched Senior seek to exert influence on those to whom he gave and then suffer from public condemnation—both deserved and undeserved—for doing so. Rockefeller learned both positive and negative lessons from his father's example.

Gates was the commanding presence in the Rockefeller offices during Rockefeller's early years there. He was the senior partner as Rockefeller developed as a philanthropist amid the creative ferment that produced the principles of scientific philanthropy and the Rockefeller family of foundations which incorporated them. Gates also articulated so powerfully and creatively the Protestant liberalism that he and Rockefeller shared that the younger man kept many of these ideas as his own long after he himself became the leading figure in Rockefeller philanthropy.

One important way in which the mature Rockefeller differed from Senior and Gates was that he took a more progressive view of labor relations. It is safe to say that had he not done so, many of the doors of cooperation essential to his philanthropic enterprise would never have opened to him. Mackenzie King was the person who helped Rockefeller find his way out of the fortress that his father's generation had built around the family's corporate empire and into a new degree of public responsibility.

When he gave his address on the future of the Christian church, Rockefeller was forty-three years old. The contours of his thought were fully formed. He was in the midst of the five-year process of receiving the bulk of his inheritance.[3] He had fully emerged from Gates's shadow as the leader of the secular Rockefeller philanthropies, ready to take his place as a major religious philanthropist.

3. With Laura Spelman Rockefeller's death in 1916, Senior began to transfer the bulk of his wealth to his son, a process which was complete by 1921. See Harr and Johnson, *Century*, 120.

John D. Rockefeller, Sr.: Lessons in Religious Philanthropy

During Rockefeller's recovery from nervous collapse in the winter of 1905, his father was embroiled in a famous controversy over his one hundred thousand dollar gift to the American Board of Commissioners for Foreign Missions (A.B.C.F.M.). Washington Gladden, basing his judgment on Ida Tarbell's exposé, branded Senior's contribution as "tainted money."[4] Gladden was subsequently embarrassed to find that the contribution had been solicited by James L. Barton, the secretary of the board.

Barton's first encounter with the Rockefeller family had been in the spring of 1902, when Rockefeller, Jr., had contacted Barton at the urging of John R. Mott for his help in understanding the foreign missions enterprise. A year later Barton approached the younger Rockefeller to arrange a meeting for the purpose of soliciting a major contribution from his father and was graciously but firmly rebuffed. Six months later Barton met Gates, and on Gates's recommendation Rockefeller, Sr., made a contribution to the A.B.C.F.M. This contribution of one hundred thousand dollars was not as large as had been requested and was made in order to "try them," by shaming the "rich Congregational Church" into contributing to their own work.[5]

Barton received Rockefeller's gift on 13 February, but waited a month before announcing its receipt as a joyful surprise. Only after Gates stated his willingness to go public with the relevant correspondence did Barton fully relate the chronology of his relationship with the Rockefellers, lamely implying that the younger Rockefeller's 1902 contact with Barton had constituted approaching Barton about the eventual gift.[6]

During the spring of 1905 Rockefeller, Sr., felt Gladden's words as salt in the wounds inflicted by Tarbell. He frequently communicated

4. Washington Gladden, "Tainted Money," *Outlook* 52 (1895) 886–87.

5. John D. Rockefeller, Jr., to James L. Barton, 17 April 1902; Barton to Rockefeller, Jr., 14 April 1903; Frederick T. Gates to John D. Rockefeller, Sr., 31 January 1905; Rockefeller, Sr., to Gates, 11 February 1905; Archives: Religious Interests, box 1, folder 1.

6. Frederick T. Gates, *Chapters in My Life* (New York: Free Press, 1977) 201–4.

with his associates, asking how the public was perceiving various accusations and suggesting public relations strategies. During the months of April and May, Senior's anxiety was at a peak. He questioned the loyalty of Faunce, who in the elder Rockefeller's opinion had failed to take a sufficiently strong stand in his defense. He and his staff, along with William Rainey Harper, considered launching a counterattack against Gladden based on a scandalous rumor concerning a man in Gladden's church who was involved in selling peruna—a "medicine" made from poor whiskey. The young Rockefeller was learning that philanthropy could be as unpleasant as business.[7]

Senior's primary religious giving went to Baptists, who seemed more than willing to be tainted by it. As William D. P. Bliss wrote in the *Independent* in 1906,

> The fifty-two Baptist churches in Manhattan and the Bronx, with their 19,738 members and their property valued at $6 million, present almost the one sensational instance in New York City of a denomination largely ruled by one wealthy man. The well-known Bible class. . . led by Mr. J. D. Rockefeller Jr., shows what money can do. . . . The Bible class, aided by perhaps one billion dollars worth of advertising, is known throughout the United States. Mr. John D. Rockefeller agrees to double each year the amounts raised by the Baptist City Mission and the New York State Baptist Convention. The result is that it is more than whispered that if any Baptist city missionary or State preacher pleases Mr. Rockefeller, he remains; if he does not, he goes. However it be with his money, the church of Mr. Rockefeller certainly has a taint in the eyes of the world.[8]

Although Bliss overstated the case, there was substance to the concern that Rockefeller, Sr., might be influencing the Baptist denomination. In business, the elder Rockefeller was willing to put his money in the hands of trusted businessmen without interference, and he tended to view his giving to religious organizations with the same

7. John D. Rockefeller, Sr., to Starr Murphy, 17 April 1905; William Rainey Harper to Frederick T. Gates, 14 April 1905; Archives: Religious Interests, box 1, folder 1; Rockefeller, Sr., to Gates, 25 and 27 May 1905, Archives: Religious Interests, box 1, folder 2.

8. William D. P. Bliss, "The Church in Social Service: A Study of Denominations in New York," *The Independent* 60 (1906) 141–42; this article also can be found in Archives: Religious Interests, box 1, folder 2.

attitude. Unfortunately, the Baptist boards to which he contributed were often short on businessmen whom Senior trusted.

In May 1908 the Northern Baptist Convention was formed, and Harry Pratt Judson, president of the University of Chicago, was elected as its president. Rockefeller, Sr., trusted Judson's business sense. He supported Judson's proposal of a united financial committee for the Home and Foreign Mission Societies, which was accepted. A month later, Senior was writing to Gates about a number of matters. He asked, referring to a business matter, "Have we put anybody into the Linseed Company as accountant or in other confidential positions, and if not, should we not carefully keep this in mind and introduce our men on whom we can rely?" He then moved on without hesitation to the Baptists, "By the by, I notice that Applegarth and Mabie are both leaving the mission organization. . . . I wonder if we ought to employ a man by the year to represent us in those bodies. We put a large amount of money there, and it might be best for us to have a thoroughgoing reliable businessman."[9] Gates tactfully responded,

> I will bear in mind your suggestion of a paid representative. It is novel and attractive. How welcome such a man would be I am not sure. He would need to be a very wise man, for no Board or Executive Committee or Secretary would be likely to take a position that might antagonize him in fear that they might alienate you. He would undoubtedly dominate the policies of the Societies, and the responsibility of choosing him would be great. The suggestion, while attractive, therefore, has its serious side.[10]

A week later, Judson wrote to Gates to get his counsel on a list of proposed members for the financial committee. Gates communicated to him the Rockefeller opinion that the old guard, especially on the foreign board, had not been fiscally responsible. He recommended several persons, including James C. Colgate of Fifth Avenue Baptist, Wallace Buttrick of the General Education Board, and Rockefeller, Jr. Rockefeller was invited to join the board and conferred with his father about the position. Rockefeller reported to Gates that his father

9. John D. Rockefeller, Sr., to Frederick T. Gates, 8 June 1908, Archives: Religious Interests, box 2, folder 14.

10. Frederick T. Gates to John D. Rockefeller, Sr., 9 June 1908, Archives: Religious Interests, box 2, folder 14.

thought perhaps the Rockefellers ought to have more than one representative on the board and suggested both Gates and Junior. Rockefeller felt that perhaps the size of his family's gifts to the denomination merited as many as three representatives and that Judson would be happy to make such an arrangement.[11]

Upon further consideration, Rockefeller declined service on the committee for himself and family representatives, fearing that such an arrangement would lead to the expectation that the Rockefellers would fund the whole budget themselves or at least be responsible for raising the whole amount. Rockefeller influence nonetheless hung heavy over the committee. It seems, in this sense, appropriate that the very stationery on which Judson corresponded with the Rockefellers was adorned with the letterhead, "University of Chicago Founded by John D. Rockefeller."

Rockefeller was by temperament far more sensitive to the interests of others than was his father. He nonetheless learned from his father's experience with religious philanthropy that both awesome power and unpleasant accusation would always accompany the disposition of his family fortune.

Frederick T. Gates: Lessons in Scientific Giving and Religious Liberalism

When Rockefeller entered the family offices in 1897, his father gave him no specific directions about what aspects of the Rockefeller empire he ought to master. Senior was already in semiretirement. The family offices were under the direction of Gates, and he became Rockefeller's primary mentor. Rockefeller recalled years later that "no father could have been more kindly or helpful to his own son than Mr. Gates was to me."[12]

11. Harry Pratt Judson to Frederick T. Gates, 17 June 1908; Gates to Judson, 22 June 1908; Judson to John D. Rockefeller, Jr., 30 June 1908; Rockefeller to Gates, 28 July 1908; Archives: Religious Interests, box 2, folder 14.

12. John D. Rockefeller, Jr., "Addresses to the Honor of Frederick Taylor Gates: A Meeting at the Rockefeller Institute for Medical Research," 15 May 1929, Archives: Gates Papers, box 3, folder 69.

Gates had begun working for Rockefeller, Sr., six years earlier, after a brief career in the Baptist ministry. He had attended the University of Rochester, which was at that time a Baptist college under the direction of theological moderate Martin B. Anderson, and Rochester Theological Seminary, from which he graduated in 1880. For eight years he had served a Baptist church in Minneapolis before being elected as the executive secretary of the newly formed American Baptist Education Society.

In 1889 William Rainey Harper, a Baptist educator serving as professor of Hebrew at Yale, transferred to Gates the responsibility of improving the negotiations that he and other leading Baptist educators had been fruitlessly pursuing with Senior concerning a proposed Baptist college to be situated in Chicago. The elder Rockefeller immediately "came out of his shell" in response to Gates's direct approach.[13] In 1891 Rockefeller, Sr., invited Gates to assist him in his charitable giving. Gates also proved a sagacious business counselor and was employed by Rockefeller in reviewing his non-oil-related investments. Gates described himself in 1891 as "eager, impetuous, insistent, and withal exacting and irritable." He quickly placed his distinctive mark on Rockefeller family affairs, particularly in the field of philanthropy.[14]

When Gates came into the Rockefeller office, Rockefeller, Sr., was accustomed to sifting through thousands of requests for charitable assistance each year in order to find the few to which he would respond. Senior claimed nearly to have had a nervous breakdown trying to keep up with the volume of appeals. When Gates took charge, he refused as a matter of principle all personal and local requests, instead channeling Rockefeller's giving through municipal, national, and international agencies with expertise in the field. Gates then worked with the executives of these agencies to rationalize requirements and procedures for the highest effectiveness. Whereas, for example, Rockefeller had been considering hundreds of appeals from Baptist churches and groups, Gates referred all such requests to the Home and

13. Gates, *Chapters*, 106.

14. Ibid., 56–120. Letter Press Book of the American Baptist Education Society, 1891, 467–73, quoted in Raymond B. Fosdick, *The Story of the Rockefeller Foundation* (New York: Harper, 1952) 1.

Foreign Mission Boards and carefully oversaw the use of Rockefeller's vast gifts to these organizations.[15]

Even these principles, however, were not sufficient to insure the profitable use of so great a fortune as that of elder Rockefeller. In 1905 Gates approached Rockefeller, Sr., with his suggestions for the disposition of his fortune, proposing that Rockefeller, Sr., seek to ascertain the most prominent areas of human need and the best-qualified experts in these fields to guide his giving. He further suggested a series of trusts for the promotion of such fields as higher education, medical research, fine arts, scientific agriculture, Christian ethics, and civic virtue. "Your wealth is rolling up, rolling up like an avalanche! You must keep up with it! You must distribute it faster than it grows! If you do not, it will crush you and your children and your children's children," Gates urged.[16]

These ideas were eventually refined into the Rockefeller Foundation and the other Rockefeller charitable trusts. At a 1923 board meeting, Gates summed up his feelings about the foundation:

> When you die and come to approach the judgment of Almighty God, what do you think He will demand of you? Do you for an instant presume to believe that He will inquire of your petty failures or your trivial virtues? No! He will ask just one question: "What did you do as a trustee of the Rockefeller Foundation?[17]

Gates approached every decision for the Rockefeller Foundation with this degree of seriousness.

Rockefeller, the young heir, served an apprenticeship under Gates, the charismatic employee, for the first several years of their association. By 1901 Gates announced that Rockefeller had acquired "a postgraduate degree in business and benevolence."[18] From 1901 to 1917 they collaborated in the founding of the Rockefeller benevolent empire, with Rockefeller's reserve and attention to detail proving the

15. John D. Rockefeller, Sr., *Random Reminiscences of Men and Events* (New York: Doubleday, 1933) 156; Gates, *Chapters*, 161–64.

16. Frederick T. Gates to John D. Rockefeller, Sr., 3 June 1905, quoted in Gates, *Chapters*, 207–9. See also Nevins, *Study in Power*, 2. 291.

17. Fosdick, *Foundation*, 1.

18. Gates, *Chapters*, 242.

perfect balance for Gates's visionary schemes and pronouncements. From 1912, when Gates began the process of retiring, Rockefeller was increasingly in command of the family's philanthropy. Gates retired fully from the foundation's board in 1923.[19]

Religion was one area in which Gates had a profound influence on Rockefeller. Gates was a consistent and articulate liberal, and although he was not the only such influence in Rockefeller's life, he was undoubtedly an important one. Gates carried on a spiritually grounded attack against Protestant orthodoxy, the animus of which he attributed to the religious setting of his childhood, particularly the home of his father, who had been a Baptist pastor in upstate New York and Kansas during Gates's youth. A "Puritan" nurture such as he experienced, Gates believed, tended to "thwart and crush in the young the natural impulses of the being whom God made and pronounced good." The orthodoxy of Calvin and Knox, Gates wrote later, destroyed one's best and most noble impulses and tended "to suppress the natural instinct of right-minded persons to be friends with God, to serve society, and cheerfully and faithfully to discharge the duties of life." It was not religion at all, but "a travesty of religion utterly false and not genuine," according to Gates.[20]

Despite his hatred for Calvinist orthodoxy, Gates professed a lively Christian faith. His positive experience of religion, Gates reported, began during his adolescence, apart from the revivalistic atmosphere of his home. Gates recalled,

> I felt no overwhelming need of a crucified Savior, whose blood must procure forgiveness. I suppose that a sense of moral beauty had begun to develop with my awakening physical and social sensibilities. I began to see the wondrous beauty of the character and words of Jesus: his teachings, particularly his social and moral teachings, became attractive, and I was drawn to his person and character, and felt that throughout my life I wanted to side with him and his friends against the world and his enemies. Such, frankly, was the only "conversion" I ever had. This experience of religion, as I now see it, was the usual awakening in right-minded young men and women at the dawn of the fuller life, of the sense of the good, the true, and the beautiful, and the

19. Harr and Johnson, *Century*, 51–65.
20. Gates, *Chapters*, 17–18.

> dedication of themselves to a life of disinterested human service. This was and is my religion. It has never changed, and is wholly dissociated from all doctrinal speculation.[21]

Gates elaborated on his philosophy of religion in a similar statement, which he entitled "The Spirit of True Religion." Gates understood the essence of both morality and religion to be "the love of the good, the true, and the beautiful in conduct." When one expressed such love out of a sense of duty, one acted in the realm of morality; when one expressed this love in a "warm and enthusiastic" way, one acted in the realm of religion. Love that was out of "the hope of reward or fear of punishment," was not really love at all, Gates believed, because true love was always "instinctive, spontaneous, natural."[22]

Upon moving to New York City, Gates joined the Memorial Baptist Church, which was under the ministry of Edward Judson, but he preferred the Congregational Church of Montclair, of which Amory Bradford was pastor. Bradford's church required no doctrinal assent from its members beyond a commitment to follow the spirit of Jesus.

Perhaps because his own childhood religious experience had been unpleasant, Gates took special care with his own children. In a letter to Charles W. Eliot, he agreed with Eliot's recently published reflection that "all our best ideas of God and of religion are rooted in family life and come to us through the family life—not handed down out of Heaven in a volume."[23]

At the same time, Gates maintained an interest in the study of the Bible. Throughout his life, Gates read portions of the Bible to his family and characterized his view of the Bible as critical, yet reverent. He was consulted as an authority on biblical scholarship by young Baptist scholars and was especially thrilled by Harnack's reconstruction of the "Logia" or "Q" document, which, Gates wrote, "has to do with eternal principles, is absolutely sane and there is scarcely a claim

21. Ibid., 49.

22. Frederick T. Gates, "The Spirit of True Religion," Archives: Gates Papers, box 3, folder 67.

23. Frederick T. Gates to Charles W. Eliot, 1 November 1910, Archives: Gates Papers, box 1, folder 21.

in it that modern science or modern reason would not allow to faith."[24] As a result of his studies, Gates's religious views continued to move in the direction of modernism. He decided that the distinctive practices of the Baptists were "foreign to the mind of Christ." Gates concluded that the love for humanity exemplified by Jesus was the vital permanent aspect of Christianity and that such Christianity was the only hope of the human race.[25] Gates wrote to Rockefeller associate Simon Flexner after Flexner had sent him Joseph Klausner's *Jesus in Nazareth*, "The ethics of Jesus are the realization of all messianic ideals in a way infinitely more glorious and universal than any dreamed by any of the religions. Its ultimate triumph will be the utter extinction of exclusiveness, and science and religion will move forward hand in hand."[26]

One of the major obstacles to this "ultimate triumph" was the sectarianism of the Protestant churches. Gates saw the Protestant churches of America—small, struggling, impoverished, yet continuing to compete—as an affront to both his religious and his progressive sensibilities.

> Sectarianism is the curse of religion at home and abroad: a blight upon religion, whether viewed from an economic, intellectual, or spiritual standpoint. The union of evangelistic denominations would solve more problems of human progress than any other single reform.

Gates stated that he would not expect great things from the American churches until he saw "the churches uniting four or five into one, Baptist, Methodist, Presbyterian, Congregationalist, Episcopalian all over the land." He also saw the need for such mergers in foreign missions.[27]

24. Frederick T. Gates to David Houston, 27 January 1911, Archives: Gates Papers, box 2, folder 35.

25. Gates, *Chapters*, 131, 205.

26. Frederick T. Gates to Simon Flexner, 23 February 1926, Archives: Gates Papers, box 1, folder 23.

27. Frederick T. Gates to John D. Rockefeller, Jr., 30 July 1911, Archives: Religious Interests, box 2, folder 5; Gates to Rockefeller, 23 July 1991, Archives: Religious Interests, box 46, folder 365.

Although Gates's social views were quite conservative, he showed some measure of sympathy for the social gospel. After reading Walter Rauschenbusch's *Christianity and the Social Crisis* in 1909, he wrote to Rauschenbusch professing "unalloyed delight" at the book's incisive analysis of the state of the church. Rauschenbusch responded cordially, stating that he respected Gates's breadth of experience and appreciated his praise for the book.[28]

The most prominent public statement of Gates's theological views came during the "tainted money" controversy. In an attempt to explain Rockefeller, Sr.'s motivation for the A.B.C.F.M. gift, Gates released for publication a lengthy letter to Senior in which he had enumerated fourteen reasons for making the contribution. The letter reflected Gates's long-term thinking about foreign missions. It was striking in its neglect of the evangelistic motive and its promotion of the secular benefits of missions: the many services of modern science were being made available to other lands that were in turn becoming new markets for American commerce. The benefits were mutual.

The letter was widely reprinted and was attacked by conservatives for its omission of evangelism. Gates defended himself lamely on this point by saying that he felt it inappropriate to press Senior with evangelistic arguments that he had heard since his youth. Second, Gates stated that because the Rockefellers had observed that the Congregational missions were less successful than Baptist missions in winning converts—a fact that earlier had deterred Rockefeller from contributing to the A.B.C.F.M.—Gates had sought to demonstrate in the letter that there were adequate reasons for carrying on foreign missions even without the evangelistic motive.[29]

Gates needed no defense in the eyes of his friends. Faunce wrote that Gates's letter was a most refreshing apologia for missions since

28. Frederick T. Gates to Walter Rauschenbusch, 20 November 1909; Rauschenbusch to Gates, 27 November 1909; Archives: Gates Papers, box 23, folder 63. See also Walter Rauschenbusch, *Christianity and the Social Crisis* (New York: Macmillan, 1907).

29. Frederick T. Gates to John D. Rockefeller, Jr., 31 January 1905, Archives: Religious Interests, box 1, folder 1; Frederick T. Gates, "Gates' Letter to Rockefeller," *Boston Herald*, 17 April 1905; Gates to Thomas B. Barbour, 20 April 1905; Archives: Religious Interests, box 1, folder 1.

"without sentimentalism, without cataloguing the number of heathen that are dropping into perdition each second, you set forth arguments so cogent, and considerations so broad, that they must strike the hard sense of the American people and do lasting service."[30] Lyman Abbott wrote that he intended to keep the "very striking letter" for possible publication in a missions issue of the *Outlook* "when the present controversies have gone by."[31]

In Gates's own notes regarding the letter, he commented that the letter marked his "denominational and religious emancipation." He further reflected,

> In the letter the motives urged are purely humanitarian, largely even secular. But in my religion there was no distinction between the sacred and the secular. All things had become sacred. God loves Monday quite as much as Sunday. It was with reason that he made six times as many secular days as sacred. The utter obliteration of this false distinction belongs to the very essence of the teachings of Jesus. My letter did not exaggerate my feeling. At the time I was full of the subject. I even broke forth into song in my evenings at home.

To the file copy of his letter bearing these comments, Gates appended two short verses:

> My Prayer
> All bonds, oh God, of creed and race
> Help me to break, and set me free
> To love and seek and work, with Thee
> The God of all before thy face.
>
> Mr. Rockefeller
> If Paul of old could owe a debt
> To all, he more. All lands, the near the far
> The great, the small, and all the isles that dot
> The seas, have sent him gold.
> If he were now to reach his hand to bless
> Each spot from which has come some gift to swell
> The mass of his great store, what race,

30. William H. P. Faunce to Frederick T. Gates, 21 April 1905, Archives: Religious Interests, box 1, folder 1.

31. Lyman Abbott to Frederick T. Gates, 18 April 1905, Archives: Religious Interests, box 1, folder 1.

What land, what home, nay, hut in far off wild,
That would not feel his touch to help and heal?[32]

Gates reinforced in the younger Rockefeller the three main ideas contained in these poems: the breadth of God, a desire to do good to all, and the responsibility of the Rockefeller family to all humankind. On important points of application, however, Rockefeller would diverge from Gates. By the time Rockefeller was becoming the leader in the partnership, Gates suspected Rockefeller of being too liberal on social and political issues. The person primarily responsible for Rockefeller's social liberalism was Mackenzie King.

William Lyon Mackenzie King: Lessons in Religious Social Ethics

In the same year that Rockefeller withdrew from most of his father's business interests to devote himself to philanthropy, he had his first experience as a reformer. The judge charged with investigating the alleged Tammany Hall traffic in prostitutes appointed him foreman of the "White Slave Grand Jury." Tammany Hall may well have favored the Rockefeller appointment, viewing him as an ineffectual representative of the monied aristocracy. To the surprise of the public and the judge—who sought to prevent the jury's report from being presented—the tenacious investigation yielded fifty-four indictments. When the public was slow to act on the jury's findings, Rockefeller himself acted, joining with Jewish business leaders Jacob Schiff and Paul Warburg to form a watchdog committee to combat prostitution on the Lower East Side.[33]

Earlier, Rockefeller had shown progressive inclinations by supporting the Bureau of Municipal Research, founded in 1906 to apply scientific principles to city management. In the related search for municipal administrators with management talent and reform zeal, Rockefeller met Raymond Fosdick, who would be his lifelong associate and authorized biographer.[34]

The Ludlow Massacre of 1915 was the most important episode ending Rockefeller's social and ethical innocence. Ironically, this tragic

32. Frederick T. Gates, "The Letter on Missions," 17 April 1905, Archives: Gates Papers, box 2, folder 48.

33. Harr and Johnson, *Century*, 108–11.

34. Ibid., 112–13.

incident involved the Colorado Fuel and Iron Company (C.F.I.), one of the few businesses in which Rockefeller had retained nominal involvement (in this case as an inactive member of the board of directors).[35]

A violent labor dispute between Colorado miners and thirty mining companies raged throughout the winter of 1913–1914. In April 1914 Rockefeller was called before the House Committee on Mines and Mining as it sought to mediate the struggle. With unthinking loyalty, Rockefeller parroted the management line, professing complete trust in the western directors of the company and standing by their anti-union position. Two weeks later, fighting between C.F.I. employees and the National Guard at Ludlow, Colorado, resulted in the inadvertent deaths of two women and eleven children. The resulting public outcry focused on the Rockefellers.

The incident brought shame and anguish to the young Rockefeller, who had not previously felt the full force of the attack on his father's business practices. Two larger-than-life figures entered Rockefeller's life as he attempted to respond to the public outcry surrounding the Ludlow tragedy: Ivy Ledbetter Lee, an industrial public relations expert from Georgia, and William Lyon Mackenzie King, leader of the Liberal Party in Canada.

Lee was a Princeton-educated, Southern Methodist minister's son whose recent public relations campaign had won a rate hike for the railroad industry. Lee's contribution on this occasion was simple: he persuaded Rockefeller to communicate with the public. This change constituted a break with Gilded Age business management, which ignored public opinion. This is not to say that everything Lee told the public was true. Bulletins circulated by Lee about the situation in Colorado were based on reports from field management. The serious distortions and errors they contained led his biographer to call the campaign "one of the greatest errors in his career." Others used stronger language: Carl Sandburg wrote of "Ivy L. Lee—Paid Liar," and Upton Sinclair called Lee "Poison Ivy."[36]

35. Ibid., 125–49. See also Fosdick, *Portrait*, 143–66.

36. Ray E. Hiebert, *Courtier to the Crowd: The Story of Ivy Lee and the Development of Public Relations* (Ames: Iowa State University Press, 1966) 100. Carl Sandberg, "Ivy L. Lee—Paid Liar," *New York Call*, 7 March 1915; Upton Sinclair, *The Brass Check: A Study of American Journalism* (Pasadena, CA: privately printed, 1915), quoted in Hiebert, *Courtier*, 298.

There is no evidence that Rockefeller condoned lying in presenting his case; he seems to have believed that the truth would vindicate him. His moral reasoning did not go beyond assessing conscious motives. Since he had not meant to hurt anyone, Rockefeller assumed that he was guiltless. Because he was not aware of any known biases, he assumed that his view of the truth was accurate. Like any good progressive, Rockefeller was sure the truth would clear the matter. This did not, however, preclude his attempting to suppress versions of the affair that he deemed false, including one sponsored by the Federal Council of Churches.[37]

The person who sought to help Rockefeller to step outside the confines of his privileged class and genuinely to encounter the situations of others was Mackenzie King. King, like Rockefeller, was a religious person, a devout Presbyterian who read the Bible daily and adhered to strict personal disciplines. King had done graduate work in sociology at the University of Chicago and spent time at Hull House, Jane Addams's pioneer settlement house. After completing an economics program at Harvard, King had become recognized as a prodigy in the field of industrial relations. He had served as labor minister in the Liberal government from 1908 until the Liberals fell from power in 1911. When Rockefeller called on him for assistance in 1914, King needed a challenge and found himself intrigued by the possibilities involved in influencing a Rockefeller with regard to labor relations.

To his surprise, King found the the younger Rockefeller quite compatible. In addition to having similar religious convictions, Rockefeller and King were the same age, and they shared the same convictions about the need for moderate social reform—reform that would eschew both the intransigence of the older generation and the statist tendencies of socialism. The two seemed to share a spiritual affinity that King described in his diary as "a perfect sympathy in all things as we talk together."[38] Confiding in a friend, King wrote,

37. Howard M. Gitelman, *The Legacy of the Ludlow Massacre: A Chapter in American Industrial Relations* (Philadelphia: University of Pennsylvania Press, 1988) 16, 35–37.

38. F. A. McGregor, *The Rise and Fall of Mackenzie King* (Toronto: Macmillan, 1962) 190.

> I have found in Mr. John D. Rockefeller, Jr., one of the best of men and most welcome of friends. . . . Whatever his father may have done or is, that man I have found to be almost without exception the truest follower of Christ. . . . His humility, his sincerity, his fearlessness, his simple faith, his fidelity to principle—so far as he has horizon at all his one purpose is to serve his fellow men.[39]

Years later, when the two were reunited after a decade apart, King would find it to be "as if our association in the years that preceded had known no break. How true it is that the things of the spirit know nothing of time."[40]

Rockefeller was equally generous in his assessment of King. Deflecting praise for his enlightenment about labor relations to his mentor, Rockefeller said that he was merely King's mouthpiece. King possessed, thought Rockefeller, not only an enormous wealth of experience, but also "an intuitive sense of the right thing to do—whether it was a man who ought to be talked with or a situation that ought to be met."[41]

King's impact on Rockefeller first became evident in his February 1915 performance before the United States Commission on Industrial Relations, chaired by Frank P. Walsh, a progressive attorney from Kansas City. Rockefeller's concessions to the legitimacy of unions and collective bargaining won the applause of the public, and even the momentary admiration of "Mother" Jones, who greeted him appreciatively on the occasion even though she later recanted her endorsement. There was still much to be desired by Walsh and others, who, having heard Rockefeller carefully disavow knowledge of the actual situation in the mine fields, felt that such ignorance was inexcusable.[42]

Walter Lippmann's account of "Mr. Rockefeller on the Stand," written for his new progressive weekly, *The New Republic*, was particularly insightful. He saw Rockefeller not as the imperial capitalist

39. Harr and Johnson, *Century*, 133.

40. William Lyon Mackenzie King to John D. Rockefeller, Jr., 30 September 1930, Archives: Religious Interests, box 48, folder 387.

41. Fosdick, *Portrait*, 161.

42. Gitelman, *Legacy*, 68–89.

who ruled with an iron hand, but as an inept heir who had been "thrust by the accident of birth into a position in which he rules but does not reign." Walsh sought to paint Rockefeller as a grand nefarious figure; but Lippmann thought that "in John D. Rockefeller, Jr., there seemed to be nothing but a young man having a lot of trouble, very much harassed and very well-meaning."[43]

Rockefeller's performance raised the ire of old-timers like Gates, who objected to his conciliatory "attempt to parry the blows, but not return them." Gates's anger was no doubt fueled by the fact that L. M. Bowers, one of the field officers of C.F.I., was Gates's uncle. Concluding that Rockefeller had become too liberal, he countered, "It may be urged that this policy is the Christian policy. I do not understand Christ [as one who] adopted any spirit of conciliation toward those who came to him in the spirit of these unionists."[44]

The culmination of King's tutelage of Rockefeller came in the spring of 1916, when he accompanied King on a visit to the Colorado mine fields. The rich young man was exposed to the life of a mining community for two weeks. He visited with miners on the job and their families in their homes. He held rounds of meetings and personal conferences and even attended a dance, at which he danced with practically every woman in the room. On the last day of the visit, which he called "a red-letter day in my life," Rockefeller addressed a joint meeting of officers and employee representatives. Buoyed by his sense of personal satisfaction, Rockefeller stated,

> Had this meeting been held two weeks ago, I should have stood here as a stranger to many of you, recognizing few faces. Having had the opportunity last week of visiting all of the camps in the southern coal fields and of talking individually with practically all of the representatives,. . . having visited your homes, met many of your wives and children, we meet here not as strangers but as friends, and it is in that spirit of mutual friendship that I am glad to have this opportunity to discuss with you men our common interests.[45]

43. Walter Lippmann, "Mr. Rockefeller on the Stand," *New Republic* 1 (1915) 12–13.

44. Fosdick, *Portrait*, 158.

45. Ibid., 162.

This statement reflected both the appeal and the limits of Rockefeller's new approach to class conflict. Rockefeller's accessibility was disarming, and his pledge of friendship brought hope. Rockefeller yielded no real power, however, to his new "friends."

Over the next few months Rockefeller publicly articulated what he called his "Colorado Plan" for industrial relations. The plan called for the establishment of representative councils of employees who would do the collective bargaining with company management. Such company unions were rendered illegal by the Wagner Act of 1935, but over the intervening years Rockefeller made the promotion of this model of industrial relations a pet project. Public criticism of his use of the Rockefeller Foundation in promoting the plan forced him to organize his labor relations activities separately from the foundation. He established a company in order to market his labor relations program and supported universities that agreed to teach it.[46]

Rockefeller's industrial representation plan has been seen variously as a genuine attempt at progressive labor relations, a public relations hoax, and a sop thrown to labor to stave off unionization. There can be no doubt that Rockefeller valued the promise of social stability and the control inherent in its structure. There is also no question that guilt played a part in moving Rockefeller to embrace a program that he considered to be just. The plan also fit well with Rockefeller's understanding of religious ethics.

Harking back to Andrews's social ethics, Rockefeller's idea relied upon the ability of individuals to act ethically by an empathic application of the Golden Rule. To four thousand businessmen gathered at Cornell University in January 1917, Rockefeller gave this advice:

> If I were to sum up in a few words what I have been endeavoring to say to you in regard to the personal relation in industry, I should say, apply the Golden Rule. . . . If in the days to come, as you have to do with labor, you will put yourself in the other man's place and govern your actions by what you would wish done to you, were you the employee instead of the employer,. . . strife and discord as between labor and capital will give place to co-operation and harmony, the interests of both will be greatly furthered, the public will be better served, and through the es-

46. Gitelman, *Legacy*, 333.

> tablishment of industrial peace, a great stride will have been taken toward the establishment of peace among nations.[47]

Once Rockefeller had satisfied himself as to the fairness of his own plan, he distanced himself from his earlier support of unions. He confided in King that he had changed the name of his pamphlet on industrial relations from "Brotherhood in Industry" to "The Personal Relation in Industry" out of fear that it might be construed as support for the railroad brotherhoods. In December 1920 the Federal Council of Churches (F.C.C.) publicly stated its opinion that the "open shop" campaign then being waged by management amounted to a "closed shop" for members of labor unions. Rockefeller expressed his disagreement to Robert E. Speer, president of the F.C.C., citing a statement by President Faunce of Brown in support of his position. Speer responded, professing to be in agreement, in principle, and to have said as much in his book *The Principles of Jesus*. At the same time, Speer alluded to differences over how one ought to apply such principles as love for neighbor, the sacredness of human life, and the command, "Thou shalt not steal." He questioned whether the fundamental inequities in the capitalist system were really in keeping with the spirit of Christ. Not all Protestants were reading the Golden Rule as Rockefeller did.[48]

With the return of Mackenzie King to Canada in 1920, Raymond Fosdick became Rockefeller's primary counselor for industrial matters. In 1922, for the purpose of spreading Rockefeller's industrial relations plan through research and consulting, Rockefeller and Fosdick initiated a group that grew into Industrial Relations Counselors, Inc. Fosdick also inherited the job of public relations that had always been entwined in the endeavor:

> One of my jobs, through the industrial relations bureau which Mr. Rockefeller set up in my office, is to try to protect him

47. John D. Rockefeller, Jr., *The Personal Relation in Industry* (New York: privately printed, 1917) 42–43.

48. John D. Rockefeller, Jr., to William Lyon Mackenzie King, 10 April 1916, quoted in Gitelman, *Legacy*, 210. See "Open Shop Move as Blow to Unions," *New York Times*, 27 December 1920; John D. Rockefeller, Jr., to Robert E. Speer, 27 December 1920; Speer to Rockefeller, 5 January 1920; Archives: Religious Interests, box 31, folder 246. Robert E. Speer, *The Principles of Jesus* (New York: Fleming H. Revell, 1899).

> from any storms that may be developing on the horizon in regard to labor conditions in the industries in which he is interested. . . . My only point is that Mr. Rockefeller should not be exposed to a sudden blow without warning and without having a chance to build up an adequate defense.[49]

Fosdick wrote to Rockefeller, "Your work and your reputation ought not to be jeopardized by you being forced into a position where to the public, you seem to be supporting the wrong side of an industrial dispute."[50]

Under King's tutelage, Rockefeller was able to present himself in a way that won the admiration, or at least the sympathy, of some part of the public. Although Gates was displeased that Rockefeller accomplished this by a departure from past practice, Senior did not seem to mind. He saw the beginnings of a kind of mastery in his son that Lippmann failed to see. Junior was learning to make his own way and showing resourcefulness and determination in doing so. The family legacy would not destroy him; he would adapt it for a new generation.

Rockefeller's Mature Theology: 1917 and Beyond

The Protestantism that Rockefeller espoused by 1917 did more than afford him the opportunity to absolve himself from guilt; it provided a visionary program for the salvation of America and the world. Rockefeller money would play an essential part in this program. The public image of the Rockefeller family was an enduring issue in Rockefeller's public service, but it was neither the only issue, nor the defining one. Rockefeller learned, despite his sensitivity, to roll with the punches of public opinion. His remorse over the sins of his father was real. From the materials of his Protestant faith, however, he constructed for the situation a solution that did much more than assuage his conscience. It served as a blueprint for the disposition of his resources.

49. Raymond Fosdick to Bertram Cutler, 5 February 1926, quoted in Daryl L. Revoldt, "Raymond B. Fosdick: Reform, Internationalism, and the Rockefeller Foundation" (diss., University of Akron, 1982) 346–47.

50. Raymond Fosdick to John D. Rockefeller, Jr., 24 April 1926, quoted in Revoldt, "Raymond B. Fosdick," 346–47.

Rockefeller began to take a major role as a religious philanthropist during the First World War. When the United States entered the war in 1917, Rockefeller was forty-three, too old to fight. He threw himself into various forms of public service, including YMCA morale-building work. His major wartime charitable project, the United War Work Campaign, was a precursor to his later religious charity. The sectarian rivalry among the seven major Protestant, Catholic, and Jewish groups working among the troops was offensive to Rockefeller. The biggest offender was the YMCA, whose constituency included a conservative wing opposed to a united effort. Rockefeller personally convinced George W. Perkins of the YMCA to join in a United Campaign that raised one hundred and seventy million dollars, the largest voluntary offering in American history.[51]

It was this theme of cooperation that Rockefeller most often elaborated in his wartime addresses. Antagonisms among nations, classes, business interests, and denominations were being broken down in the Allied cause, and this cooperation could be preserved and extended through personal relationships and mutual understanding. As in his industrial relations plan, Rockefeller attributed the idea of brotherhood to Jesus of Nazareth, who had modeled it when he had encountered the woman taken in adultery, when he had associated with publicans and sinners, and when he had reached out to the physically and spiritually sick. International relations would improve when they were conducted on this model of personal relationship and mutual commitment to good will. In addressing issues of social ethics, Rockefeller had settled on a working principle that was both personal and progressive, and he would continue to repeat it in his interdenominational religious work and internationalist projects after the war.[52]

This "personalist" approach was not unique to Rockefeller and his mentors. As Rockefeller's theological sophistication increased, he began to express himself through the idiom of the liberal Protestant discourse about social problems that was prominent at places like Union Theological Seminary of New York and the University of Chicago Divinity School, two institutions with which he was closely associ-

51. Fosdick, *Portrait*, 404–7.

52. John D. Rockefeller, Jr., *Brotherhood of Men and Nations* (Denver, CO: privately printed, 1918) 41.

ated as a major donor and a friend of faculty members. Borden Parker Bowne was chief among those who developed a personalist theology under the influence of German scholars like Hermann Lotze. Bowne elaborated the social application of personalist philosophy, viewing society as a "world of persons" in which each person's action made its impact on all others. Others, like Union's William Adams Brown, developed Albrecht Ritschl's teaching about the kingdom of God into a call for individual social action. Liberals like Rockefeller were thus afforded a theological basis for an enlightened social ethic which stressed responsible personal action while avoiding a sharp focus on the "super-personal forces of evil" addressed by Rauschenbusch and more radical proponents of the social gospel.[53]

A related project within the liberal theology of this period was the attempt to verify Christianity by appealing to spiritual and moral experience, rather than to reason or revelation. In *The Essence of Christianity* (1902), Brown wrote, "What the theoretical reason cannot afford, the conscience and religious experience provide us."[54] In this ethicized brand of modernist theology, Rockefeller found not only a way of verifying his own religious experience, but also a religious expression that was fit for the ongoing task of molding culture. Rockefeller used this kind of apologetic strategy as he emerged as a popular exponent of liberal Christianity.[55]

In "The Christian Church—What of Its Future?" Rockefeller argued that Christianity was alive and well in the lives of common people and lacked only a reborn church that would reflect this fact. He acknowledged that the outbreak of the war and its barbarity had been a blow to claims of Christian efficacy. As the tragedy wore on,

53. According to Dana Creel, within his lifetime John D. Rockefeller, Jr., gave three million and three hundred thousand dollars to the University of Chicago and three million and seven hundred thousand dollars to Union Theological Seminary. See Dana Creel, "Charitable, Educational, Religious, Scientific and Public Contributions by Mr. John D. Rockefeller, Jr., From January 1, 1917 to December 31, 1959," Archives: Benevolences, box 25. Rockefeller's personal network of theologians is discussed below. See Hutchison, *Modernist Impulse*, 122–32, for a discussion of personalist theology.

54. William Adams Brown, *The Essence of Christianity: A Study in the History of Definition* (New York: Scribner's, 1902) 256.

55. Hutchison, *Modernist Impulse*, 127. Rockefeller, "The Christian Church."

however, another picture was becoming evident: "a spirit of self-sacrifice and unselfishness" was animating the efforts of allied people in all stations of life. One must concede that "these people are living the Christ life, their inspiration comes from God," Rockefeller declared. He called such people followers of the "Religion of the Inarticulate." Their existence demonstrated that "never in the history of the world was Christianity a more vital force in human life than it is today."[56]

What would happen to the "Religion of the Inarticulate" after the war? Rockefeller gave three alternatives: it would die out; it would develop its own church; or it would find its home in a reborn Christian church that had laid aside its sectarian agenda to embody the ideals of the broad masses of people.

This reborn church would be called the "Church of the Living God" and would require those who wished to be members to confess a "love for God, as He is revealed in Christ. . . and the vital translation of this love into a Christian life." The warmth and acceptance of this church would draw the spiritually inarticulate—those who quietly lived Christ-like lives—into its fellowship. Although it would maintain the two Christian ordinances of baptism and the Lord's Supper, it would declare their form—and even participation in them—as nonessentials. Borrowing a phrase from his friend Ernest D. Burton, Rockefeller declared that "a life, not a creed," would be the test of faith for members of the reborn church:

> Its object would be to be to promote applied religion, not theoretical religion. This would involve its sympathetic interests in all the great problems of human life; in social and moral problems, those of industry and business, the civic and educational problems; in all such as touch the life of man.[57]

56. Rockefeller, "The Christian Church."

57. The phrase, "a life, not a creed," used by Fosdick (*Portrait*, 202) to epitomize Rockefeller's spiritual life, was borrowed by Rockefeller from University of Chicago President Ernest D. Burton. Rockefeller himself used the phrase as early as 1913. See Archives: Addresses, box 1, folder 24. Notes from Ernest D. Burton's lecture, "The Religion of the Bible—The Religion of Experience," were filed by Rockefeller along with his own Bible lesson entitled, "Rambling Thoughts of a Fellow Worker," 9 February 1909, Archives: Addresses, box 1, folder 22. In his notes, Rockefeller summarized Burton as saying, "*Christianity* is *not* the affirmation of a dogma about the Book or the Church, not the acceptance of any series of propositions approved by a council—*but a life*."

Rockefeller's chief concern was that this church be the "church of all the people, of everyone who is fighting sin and trying to establish righteousness." His words echoed those of his friend and advisor Charles W. Eliot, President of Harvard University, who had written of "an all-saints religion" that would honor the simple goodness of common persons.[58]

The major obstacle to Protestantism's becoming the "Church of the Living God" was denominationalism. Rockefeller, reflecting the influence of Gates, called for the merger of churches in small communities and cooperation in "great religious centers" in large cities. The resources saved by cooperation could finance the churches' home and foreign mission. Such a church would enter an unprecedented period of influence. "I see it literally establishing the Kingdom of God on earth," Rockefeller proclaimed. After pointing to the great struggle between good and evil, the outcome of which hung in the balance, Rockefeller closed with this challenge:

> If the various divisions of the church as it is organized today catch the vision, have the breadth, the tolerance, the courage, and setting aside all non-essentials, all barriers, will stand upon the bed-rock principles of God's love and Christ's living spirit, "not satisfied until the church is the church of all good men and women, until all good thoughts and deeds are laid at the feet of the Lord of all good life," the Church of the Living God will come into being, ushering in a new era of Christian unity.[59]

The *New York Herald* published the major part of the speech, obtained without knowledge of Rockefeller or his staff, and Rockefeller was immediately deluged with requests for repeat performances and further publication. Friends to whom Rockefeller sent it for comment expressed delight. "Mrs. Woelfkin is ready to vote for your ordination. I'll do the same. It is a gem," responded Rockefeller's pastor, Cornelius Woelfkin. "Your vision is your own, and prophets need no endorsement, but will catch the consent of the minds and hearts feeling for the truth."[60] Not all Baptists were so kind. Frank Goodchild,

58. Charles W. Eliot, "The Religion of the Future," in idem, *The Durable Satisfactions of Life* (New York: Thomas Y. Crowell, 1910) 173–74.

59. Rockefeller, "The Christian Church."

60. Cornelius Woelfkin to John D. Rockefeller, Jr., 6 December 1927, Archives: Religious Interests, box 38, folder 315.

a well-respected New York City Baptist pastor, blasted the speech in a highly publicized sermon. By the time Rockefeller disposed of ordinances, creeds, and membership requirements, Goodchild insisted, what he had left was not a Baptist church. "That reduces the whole thing to a merely ethical basis. That would not come up to the requirements of a Jewish synagogue. It would not make a recognizable Unitarian Church. It would be a Society for Ethical Culture, simply that and nothing more."[61]

Rockefeller's former pastor, Dr. Faunce, joined Woelfkin in sending to Rockefeller the names of Baptists who agreed with Rockefeller, along with encouragement toward wider circulation. Rockefeller revised the piece to remove references to the Baptist church, and after taking further counsel with Faunce and friends like John Douglas Adams of the Hartford Theological Seminary, he submitted it to the *Saturday Evening Post*, which gratefully accepted it for publication. Ivy Lee oversaw the reprinting of the speech in pamphlet form and sent it to "every one of the 125 thousand clergymen in the United States."[62]

Many Protestant leaders were glad to have a celebrity endorsement for modernism. Those who sent congratulations included William B. Millar, general secretary of the Laymen's Missionary Movement; Cleveland H. Dodge; Shailer Mathews, dean of the Chicago Divinity School; James L. Barton, secretary of the A.B.C.F.M.; Francis G. Peabody of Harvard; and dozens of ministers from around the country.[63]

Objections, also, were heard from pulpits around the country, and many of these were reprinted for the edification of various constituencies. Fundamentalist responses ranged from careful rebuttal to spirited denunciation. Curtis Lee Laws reasoned that Christianity could make no lasting gains by altering its message to the modern temper:

61. Frank M. Goodchild, "The Future of the Baptist Church," 9 December 1917, Archives: Religious Interests, box 38, folder 315.

62. William H. P. Faunce to John D. Rockefeller, Jr., 13 December 1917; Rockefeller to John Douglas Adams, 18 December 1917; Adams to Rockefeller, 26 December 1917; Ivy Lee, Jr., to Rockefeller, 1 February 1918; Archives: Religious Interests, box 38, folder 315.

63. Letters from those listed are found in Archives: Religious Interests, box 38, folder 314.

"Nothing is ever gained by doing a wrong thing because it is expedient."[64] C. Mckay Smock provided a more virulent attack:

> Mr. Rockefeller would have the church that God organized, that God endowed, that God commissioned, that God purchased and stamped for His own, stand before the bar of men, who are dead in trespasses and sins, blinded by Satan, dominated by "the lust of the flesh, the lust of the eyes, and the pride of life," and meekly submit herself to their criticism, and if they so will, cast aside her divine distinctiveness and throw herself on man's mercy. . . . As for Mr. Rockefeller and his church, the church "of all good (but 'Inarticulate') men and women," I face him with these solemn words of Paul, dictated by the Holy Spirit of God, "But though we, or an angel from heaven, preach any other gospel unto you than that which we have preached unto you, let him be accursed."[65]

Some Protestants to the theological left of Rockefeller also expressed reservations. Sydney Stron of Queen Anne Congregational Church in Seattle, although generally favorable to Rockefeller's ideas, raised questions about the ability of capitalism to beget the kingdom of God:

> Can the Reborn Church, which is to be full of good will, without competition and strife, come out of the heart of the business world of America—which is very close to 26 Broadway—until that heart has been changed? . . . I am asking myself as well as Mr. Rockefeller—since every clergyman belongs to the privileged capitalistic class quite as definitely as Mr. Rockefeller.[66]

Many Roman Catholics were offended by Rockefeller's dismissal of the Christian church as a failure. Joseph P. Conroy, S.J., noting that Rockefeller used as an example of selfless service the noble wartime toils of a Belgian woman, pointed out what never would

64. Curtis Lee Laws, "The Social Union and Mr. Rockefeller's Address," *The Watchman-Examiner* 5 (1917) 1602, Archives: Religious Interests, box 38, folder 316.

65. C. Mckay Smock, *A Reply to Mr. Rockefeller* (Weston, WV: First Baptist Church, 13 July 1918), Archives: Religious Interests, box 38, folder 316.

66. Sydney Strong, *Mr. Rockefeller's "Re-Born Church"* (Seattle: Queen Anne Congregational Church, 3 May 1918), Archives: Religious Interests, box 38, folder 316.

have occurred to Rockefeller: if asked, this woman would have confessed herself a Catholic. Conroy concluded that although the church of Christ had seemed to fail, "in reality it had sent its roots ineradicably deep into the hearts of men. The rock upon which Christ had built His Church was still there."[67]

It was not primarily Belgium that concerned Rockefeller, but America, where Rockefeller saw public religious renewal as a necessity. When called upon as a celebrity to address the American public in times of crisis, Rockefeller could be counted on to plead for a return to religious faith. In 1945, as Rockefeller exhorted the American public to demand a peace "on terms that shall be Christian, not pagan," he insisted that civilization would not survive without belief in a "supreme being in harmony with whose all-wise laws and high purposes man is progressing, however slowly and haltingly, toward an ultimate and lofty destiny."[68]

Whenever he cited the promise of progress, Rockefeller invariably balanced it with a jeremiad, lamenting the fact that religion had not fully mastered modernity. Speaking at the University of Chicago in 1941, Rockefeller suggested that world events were once again demonstrating that "ruin awaits a civilization, however advanced its scientific and material frontiers, that is not guided and motivated by moral and spiritual power." Advancing technology was dangerously outrunning its spiritual resources as advanced troops might outdistance their support. "The spiritual life of man must dominate and direct his intellectual and material achievements," or doom was certain.[69]

Rockefeller consistently identified the enemy of religion as "materialism," by which he meant a focus on temporal values rather than transcendent ones. While on a trip to Egypt in 1928, he mused,

> I have stood under the shadow of the colossal pyramid tombs and lofty temples of Egypt. . . built. . . in the frantic effort to

67. Joseph P. Conroy, S.J., *A Religion—With a Minus Sign: An Open Letter to Mr. Rockefeller, Jr.* (Chicago: Loyola University Press, 1918) 5–6.

68. John D. Rockefeller, Jr., "The Power to See It Through," 29 January 1945, Archives: Addresses, box 4, folder 191.

69. John D. Rockefeller, Jr., "Education—Research," delivered at a luncheon held on the occasion of the fiftieth anniversary of the University of Chicago, 25 April 1941, Archives: Addresses, box 4, folder 184.

> make the human form of man and his material surroundings eternal. Today they lie in ruins. . . . I have walked also by the Sea of Galilee and have trod the valleys and hillsides whence came the carpenter of Nazareth, who, unaided by any of the trappings of materialism, but by the sheer force of his spiritual idealism alone, has moved the world to its foundations. Is it strange, then, that this vivid demonstration of the impotence of materialism, of the abiding power of spiritual values, leads me with renewed conviction to the belief that only that nation or civilization that exalts above materialism the spiritual values of honor, integrity, justice, service, sacrifice, love, can survive?[70]

Rockefeller's anthropological concept of religion became well known to the Christian public. For example, a definition of religion that he used in the 1930s was reprinted on mass-produced calendars: "Religion in essence is the inborn longing of the human soul for God. . . . It is as fundamental as life itself, as enduring as the human race."[71]

Perhaps Rockefeller's gospel could best be called a "gospel of religion." In the thirties, when foreign missionary executives like John R. Mott began to understand the mission enterprise as part of an ecumenical religious struggle against materialism, Rockefeller was quite in agreement. The Laymen's Inquiry of 1932, funded by Rockefeller, was a product of this point of view. Furthermore, Rockefeller interpreted both world wars as battles between the spiritual and material forces in the world.[72]

Rockefeller's desire to define the specifics of religion was born out of his sense that religion was the necessary guardian of culture and required public acceptance. Rockefeller believed that religion was public, and thus he also believed that it had to be defined broadly. He was convinced that liberal Protestantism was superior to other forms

70. John D. Rockefeller, Jr., "'Spiritual Values: Egypt,' paragraph dictated by Mr. JDR, Jr., when in Egypt—winter of 1928," Archives: Addresses, box 3, folder 139.

71. John D. Rockefeller, Jr., "Definition of Religion," Archives: Addresses, box 5, folder 259; idem, "Christianity Today," Lenten service at Christ's Episcopal Church, Tarrytown, NY, 7 March 1937, Archives: Addresses, box 3, folder 162.

72. C. Howard Hopkins, *John R. Mott, 1865–1955: A Biography* (Grand Rapids, MI: Eerdmans, 1979) 569–74; Rockefeller, *Brotherhood of Men and Nations*, 3. See also a speech which Rockefeller gave several times, *Why I Believe in the U.S.O.* (New York: U.S.O. War Fund Campaign, 1942).

of religion. At the same time, because the public function of religion was his chief concern, Rockefeller viewed Catholicism, Judaism, and other religious traditions as fellow belligerents in the fight to save America. In an address given in connection with the New York World's Fair Temple of Religion, Rockefeller clearly articulated the connection between religious tolerance and the public function of religion. "I believe profoundly that the permanent progress of this nation, or of any nation, is dependent upon the extent to which the lives of its people are ordered by a vitalizing faith in God." Reminding his audience of the religious faith of the nation's founders, Rockefeller announced that the nation needed to make a fresh decision for faith in God over "the sordidness of materialism." The American people, however, would not "give its allegiance to any religion that is narrow or divisive," only to one that exalted truth, justice, and love exemplified in daily living. "To such a faith," he proposed, "let us unite irrespective of race or creed. . . as a witness. . . that we hold religion to be the supreme authority and guide of life; that we have kept faith with the founders of our country and their God."[73]

Rockefeller's religion was not without personal devotional expression. In an article written just after the war he professed to avail himself of "the privilege of daily intercession and communion with God."[74] Despite his tolerance for the views of others, Rockefeller enforced the strictest Protestant virtues within his growing family. Abby ("Babs") was born in 1903; John Davison III in 1906; Nelson in 1908; Laurance in 1910; Winthrop in 1912; and David in 1915. John, Jr., was an authoritarian father, expecting meticulous performance and lacking in his father's playfulness. Abby was the understanding mother, whose sense of humor countered her husband's seriousness. The family emulated the religious regimen of Rockefeller's youth. Daily family Bible reading and prayer were mandatory for all the children, as were Sunday school and church on Sundays. Rockefeller maintained to the end his strictures against drinking, smoking, and gambling, although—at the urging of Abby and Pastor Fosdick—he

73. John D. Rockefeller, Jr., "Christian Ideals: Address of JDR, Jr. in behalf of New York World's Fair Temple of Religion, Bankers Club, November 9, 1938," Archives: Addresses, box 4, folder 172.

74. Rockefeller, "Why I Am a Church Member."

loosened his views about what was acceptable Sabbath behavior. As the children developed, Babs struggled most under her father's overbearing scrupulosity and later remembered family prayers only for stolen glances at the undignified poses of family members as they knelt in a row.[75] John III most deeply imbibed his father's moral seriousness and sense of responsibility. Nelson inherited his mother's carefree ease, and Laurance became Nelson's adoring companion. Winthrop was the "odd man out," too young to keep up with the older boys and too old for his younger brother. David, born after his father's obsessive parenting style had mellowed, enjoyed more serene nurture.[76]

Earlier, I suggested that Rockefeller's primary religious need was to be saved from his wealth. It may also be suggested that his peculiar kind of religious zeal was designed to last as long as his wealth did. As long as new evils remained to be conquered and as long as the family fortune had not disappeared, Rockefeller's soul was satisfied. To Rockefeller, the obvious religious need in most local communities was interdenominational unity, which would allow for a more efficient use of religious resources and the maintenance of a religious foundation beneath modern American culture. Rockefeller's religious liberalism also caused him to consider the resources of modern science as new means to be used in the work of "applied Christianity." Between 1917 and 1960, Rockefeller used these principles to wage a Christian philanthropic campaign of unprecedented size and scope.

Gates's assessment of the mature Rockefeller serves as a good snapshot. In response to Charles Eliot's 1925 inquiry about "JDR, Jr.'s character and habits of mind,"[77] Gates crafted, but did not send, this reply:

> As to John Jr.: 1. He is thoroughly conscientious. 2. He is profoundly religious. In earlier life his religion was accompanied with what you and I would characterize as pure superstition. The preaching of Fosdick has made him a modernist. He accepts

75. Abby Rockefeller, interview by Laura Chasin, 10 November 1973, quoted in Harr and Johnson, *Century*, 102.

76. Harr and Johnson, *Century*, 90–95, 102.

77. Charles Eliot to Frederick T. Gates, 29 June 1925, Archives: Gates Papers, box 4, folder 78.

> pretty fully modern science, and will do much to liberalize the Baptist faith along the Fosdick lines. 3. He is on principle I think trying to dispossess himself and his children of his father's fortune. I mean, that of itself is an end. . . . 4. John is passionately loyal to his father and much of his writing, his giving and his whole conduct of life is governed by the purpose hardly at all concealed of rehabilitating his father's public reputation. . . . 5. The influence of his most excellent wife and children and the experiences of the last twenty years have greatly developed John intellectually, and not less in breadth and catholicity of feeling. 6. Altogether he is the most admirable very rich man to my mind that history records.[78]

Although Gates overstated Fosdick's contribution to Rockefeller's modernism, as well as Rockefeller's place in history, this statement represents an incisive summary of Rockefeller's character, motivation, and development.

78. Frederick T. Gates to Charles W. Eliot, from an abstract of Gates's papers prepared in 1939–40 by Beatrice Buse. The letter is no longer in the collection. See Archives: Gates Papers, boxes 4, 78. Gates did not send this letter; he filed it with this note: "This draft was deemed variously objectionable by me and was not sent, though Aunty [Gates's sister-in-law, who lived in his home] liked this and disliked the one actually sent." I have not seen the letter that he did send.

3

The Kingdom of God and the Welfare of Humankind

Religion and Rockefeller Philanthropy

On a Sunday morning in the fall of 1924, Rockefeller presented a lesson to the Young Men's Bible Class at the Park Avenue Baptist Church; it was entitled, "Has Civilization Outgrown Religion?" As proof that it had not, he alluded to a vast array of religious expressions "never dreamed of one hundred years ago." The advances of religion were manifest in the medical field: more and better hospitals; the availability of medical and surgical care for rich and poor alike; curative and preventative breakthroughs related to diseases like pneumonia, spinal meningitis, yellow fever, typhoid fever, hookworm, and malaria; an increase in public health services. Religious charity was also flourishing in new forms, with modern charitable foundations offering hundreds of millions of dollars for education, social service centers, day nurseries, and other altruistic purposes; moreover, Christians were performing more personal service in these fields as well. The living and working conditions of humankind, moreover, were improving in such areas as sanitation and labor practices.

Rockefeller divined that "back of and underlying all these manifestations, whether conscious or not" was "the Christ spirit—the religious motive." Modern progress represented not only "the products of man's brains," but also "the fruit and flower of religious idealism." Although rigid creedal orthodoxy was waning, the genuine religion of the New Testament was alive and well. The letter had given way to the spirit; the focus had shifted from heaven to human society. While church services might be fewer and shorter, "meetings of a social, educational, recreational character in the secular rooms of the church, in the parish hall, and in settlements are infinitely more numerous."

Civilization had not outgrown—in fact, could not outgrow—religion, Rockefeller assured his class; its claims on the human heart were timeless. He conceded, however, that despite the many advances of modernity, material civilization had "temporarily outstripped religion." The products of human intellect had outrun the development of human character and spiritual values. Western civilization stood at a crossroads. History had proven that civilizations built on materialism destroyed themselves. The products of the human mind were more durable than those crafted by the hand, but also lacked permanence. "Spiritual values only are enduring, eternal. Upon them alone can a lasting civilization be built. . . . Religion must quicken its pace. . . . Nothing else but true religion, God's spirit working through man, can save our civilization or the civilization of the world."[1]

These two themes—the religious dimension of modern cultural progress and the ongoing need of modernity for religion—were entwined at the core of Rockefeller's understanding of religion and society. One reflected God's immanence; the other stressed God's transcendence. One constituted an affirmation of God's sovereignty; the other reminded the audience of the need for prophetic vigilance. Rockefeller shared this social stance with Baptists like Shailer Mathews and Harry Emerson Fosdick. Although chastened by the social and political failures of the West, these Protestants continued to work for a better future in the name of Christ by the use of modern means. They sought to govern and direct secular "progress" even as they affirmed it. Although modernity might temporarily outstrip them, they affirmed, with some anxiety, that it could not ultimately do so. These

1. John D. Rockefeller, Jr., "Has Civilization Outgrown Religion?" lesson to the Young Men's Bible Class at Park Avenue Baptist Church, 30 November 1924, Archives: Addresses, box 1, folder 120.

two religious themes constantly recur when one examines the motivation and shape of Rockefeller philanthropy.[2]

Rockefeller invested hundreds of millions of dollars in endeavors not understood as religious by many of his peers. Rockefeller's good works included nearly all the expressions of religion he listed in his 1924 Sunday School lesson. These projects were usually marked by a drive for organization, professionalization, and efficiency—the complex of values that lay at the heart of many of the important developments in early twentieth-century America. At the same time, they were motivated and directed by religious sensibilities and often insisted on the importance of religion for civilization as a whole. Rockefeller sought to build a modern Protestant civilization.

Religion and Modern Philanthropy

Scholars of American philanthropy have generally recognized that religion was an important factor in the formation of modern philanthropy. The importance of almsgiving and charity in the Hebrew scriptures and the New Testament provided an encouragement for charitable practice. Protestantism, combined with English law and experience, lay at the foundation of the American charitable tradition in such classic appeals as John Winthrop's *A Modell of Christian Charity* and George Whitefield's call for contributions for his orphan asylum in Georgia. A number of American peculiarities molded the expression of these values through the eighteenth and nineteenth centuries. According to Merle Curti these peculiarities included the following: separation of church and state, the federal system, frontier conditions, immigration, slavery, love for voluntary associations, and the democratic repudiation of the idea of a structured society with a hereditary class of needy poor.[3]

2. For a discussion of Protestant modernism in this period, see Hutchison, *Modernist Impulse*, 254–56, 274–82.

3. Curti, "Tradition and Innovation," 146; see also Bremner, *American Philanthropy*, 1–75; and O'Connell, *Voluntary Spirit*, 1–44. John Winthrop, "A Modell of Christian Charity," in Perry Miller and Thomas H. Johnson, eds., *The Puritans* (2 vols.; New York: Harper & Row, 1963) 1. 195–98. Whitefield's efforts are detailed in Bremner, *American Philanthropy*, 21–23.

Modern philanthropy of the type engaged in by the Rockefellers involved more than these traditional Christian and democratic elements. It was built on the progressive ideal that the world's ills could be overcome through science and education. Modern philanthropy was directed not toward the alleviation of symptoms, but toward the eradication of the causes of human suffering. It diverged from the traditional ethic of charitable resignation: "the poor you have always with you" (Matt 26:11a). Modern philanthropy was a product of the progressive ethos that pervaded early modern America.[4]

The relationship between secular and religious elements of the progressive ethos is a matter of lively debate among cultural historians. The institutional school of American historians has stressed the new secular values of rationalization and scientific management. It has focused on the "shift from small-scale, informal, locally or regionally oriented groups to large-scale, national, formal organizations" in the years between 1890 and 1920. It has understood the essence of the progressive impulse as the widespread emergence of complex organizations dependent on specialized knowledge and concomitant bureaucracies. This phenomenon not only dominated business development, but was also a major factor in the shaping of modern social work, modern religion, and modern philanthropy. Robert Wiebe and others have argued convincingly that both the new secular values of rationality, functionality, regularity, continuity and their application by a new class of bureaucratic administrators are the keys to understanding the progressive attack on the world's ills.[5]

Other historians, including Clyde Griffen, have seen progressive reform before the First World War as an extension of the traditional nineteenth-century Protestant crusade to realize the kingdom of God on earth. Robert Crunden has used the phrase "innovative nostalgia" to describe the complex mix of traditional religious and modern secu-

4. For a discussion of modern philanthropy and the ideal of progress, see Karl and Katz, "Foundations," 5–7. See also Bremner, *American Philanthropy*, 89–142.

5. Robert Wiebe, *The Search for Order, 1877–1920* (Westport, CN: Greenwood, 1967) vii–ix; see also Louis Galambos, "The Emerging Organizational Synthesis in Modern American History," *Business History Review* 44 (1970) 279–90, esp. 280.

lar impulses that made up American cultural style in the years between 1889 and 1920; he has also described a process by which mother Protestantism gave birth to secular democratic values that succeeded her in ruling American life. This approach has brought back into focus what seemed obvious from progressive rhetoric, namely, that a religious world view was an important element of progressivism. By focusing on the passing of Protestantism and the advance of secularism, however, this approach does not squarely undertake the task of illuminating what Protestants thought they were doing in the first two decades of the century, nor does it explain the continuity between the Protestantism that passed away and the one that maintained a powerful existence well into the century.[6]

Modern philanthropy of the type engaged in by the Rockefellers required the existence of one other factor as well—the accumulation of gaudy fortunes by a few industrialists of the Gilded Age. The sheer size of the Rockefeller fortune, which rose to one billion dollars within the patriarch's lifetime, demanded a more systematic approach to charity. Senior could not begin to respond to all requests that were sent to him for funds, much less adequately evaluate their worthiness. The solution crafted by Gates, with the assistance of the younger Rockefeller, was the concept of "wholesale philanthropy" based on "scientific giving" in which a wealthy person placed his or her charity in the hands of experts for broad-ranging and scientific consideration of its best use.[7]

John D. Rockefeller, Jr., became the principal agent for the five hundred and thirty-one million dollars given by his father for social betterment. Much of the family benevolence was carried out through boards founded by the family. These included the Rockefeller Institute for Medical Research (established 1901) to which he gave sixty-one million dollars; the General Education Board (established 1902)

6. Crunden, *Ministers of Reform*, ix–xii; Clyde Griffen, "The Progressive Ethos," in Stanley Coben and Lorman Ratner, eds., *The Development of an American Culture* (New York: St. Martin's, 1983) 144–80. See also Jean B. Quandt, "Religion and Social Thought: The Secularization of Postmillennialism," *American Quarterly* 25 (1973) 390–409.

7. Fosdick, *Portrait*, 134–35. See Robert Shaplen, *Toward the Well-Being of Mankind: Fifty Years of the Rockefeller Foundation* (New York: Doubleday, 1964) 1–8.

to which he gave one hundred and twenty-nine million dollars; the Laura Spelman Rockefeller Memorial (established 1918) to which he gave seventy-four million dollars; and the Rockefeller Foundation (established 1913) to which he gave one hundred and eighty-three million dollars. These foundations constituted the primary vehicles for Rockefeller giving in the fields of education, social science, and medical research. Junior helped to create all of these boards and maintained significant interest and influence in them throughout his lifetime.

Between 1917 and 1960 Rockefeller gave four hundred and seventy-four million dollars from his personal wealth in addition to his involvement in the family's boards. Of his personal philanthropy, twenty-one percent was directed toward explicitly religious causes. Educational organizations received about eighteen percent; social welfare and relief agencies, seventeen percent; restoration and preservation projects, fourteen percent; public parks and roads, nine percent; museums, laboratories, and libraries, seven percent; and medical research and practice, five percent.[8] This breakdown does not represent a straightforward expression of Rockefeller's charitable priorities, since he often chose to direct his personal giving into areas not primarily benefited by his father. It does, however, accurately reflect the breadth of vision evident throughout Junior's career as a philanthropist.

A look at the Rockefeller philanthropic enterprise both takes us to the heart of the complex process of secularization and religious persistence and calls attention to an aspect of the process that has often been slighted by political historians—the importance of Protestant modernism in providing a cultural outlook that held Protestantism and secular thought together in the minds of many. Rockefeller promoted modern science, supported the modern university, and responded to the findings of modern research not because he thought that religion should yield the task of cultural leadership to science, but because he saw no conflict between the two. Science did not represent a harbinger of secularity; it represented a new and better set of tools in the

8. Creel, "Contributions."

time-honored Baptist tradition of "the use of means." Conservatives would argue that the religion of Rockefeller's theologians of choice was no longer recognizably Protestant. To the degree that the Protestant establishment embraced modernism and embodied it, however, modernism provided a theological justification for powerful Protestants to form the culture with the best tools they had at hand.

Rockefeller's giving was influenced by modernism's ability to affirm the works of God in nature and the works of humanity. This "healthy-minded" brand of spirituality was essential to Rockefeller's vision for the preservation of nature, history, and the arts. Rockefeller's father never gave as broadly, and, given the starkness of his aesthetic sense, he was probably not able to do so. Senior's Baptist religion preserved a primitive plainness; modernism opened new avenues to Junior. Furthermore, modernist notions of God and religion enabled Rockefeller to hope that an acceptable common religion might be maintained that would serve the traditional role of moral guardianship for the rapidly changing modern world.

The objection may be raised that Protestant modernism was nothing more than the capitulation of nineteenth-century religion to the norms of twentieth-century secularity and hence offered no unique ingredients to the cultural milieu of the early part of the century. The fact is, however, that modernists genuinely believed that God was immanent in the cultural process as it progressed toward the telos of manifesting God's kingdom. The impassioned discussions underlying Rockefeller philanthropic undertakings are impressive because of the sincere religious fervor of many of those involved. The belief that God was present in history, working through events both sacred and secular, is key to understanding Rockefeller's philanthropic vision. Likewise, the sense of impending crisis, should religion loose its grip on modern culture, explains the urgency with which much of Rockefeller's ideas were implemented.[9]

It is widely accepted that modernist confidence in immanence and progress was greatly shaken by the First World War and subsequent

9. Hutchison, *Modernist Impulse*, 1–11. Hutchison explains (pp. 9, 171) that modernists could also speak of religion as standing over against culture, as Rockefeller did, especially when taking a prophetic social stance.

political failures in the West. Although profoundly disappointed by these events, Rockefeller held to a basic modernist affirmation until his dying day. This was due in part to the fact that Rockefeller philanthropy concentrated in the fields of medicine, education, and the natural sciences. The political failures of the early twentieth century only served to strengthen the major principles of Rockefeller philanthropy—that religious values needed reaffirmation and that an international corps of research scientists held the key to uplifting the mass of humanity. Wars were mere political interruptions in the great work of scientific progress carried out under God's inspiration.

This is not to say that all who worked in Rockefeller philanthropic enterprises shared a common religious perspective. Many varieties of belief and unbelief were represented among the administrators and scientists around Rockefeller. The tensions caused and the issues raised in the course of their working together are exemplary of the complex and incomplete process of secularization in modern America.

Religion and Education

In the religious and progressive culture of Rockefeller's young manhood, many of the proposed solutions to the problems of humanity involved education. Rockefeller associate Edwin A. Alderman was representative of many of his contemporaries in holding to what his biographer called "The Gospel of Popular Education": "I believe in the dignity and in the conquering power of knowledge."[10] This gospel was not antithetical to the Christian gospel in the minds of Rockefeller and his closest advisors; rather, education both depended on Christianity and complemented it. "Jews are the only class of people in the community outside of church members who habitually, and as a class, foster the higher education of their youth. Religion is the foster-mother of education," Gates asserted.[11] Elisha Benjamin Andrews wrote in his textbook on economics: "The economic elevation of the poor will

10. Dumas Malone, *Edwin A. Alderman: A Biography* (New York: Doubleday, Doran, 1940) 260, 103; the quotation is from inaugural address at Tulane University, 12 March 1901. Alderman later served as president of the University of Virginia.

11. Frederick T. Gates to General Education Board, 23 January 1906, Archives: Rockefeller Boards, box 19, folder 198.

prove to be *ultimately* an *ethical* and an *educational* work," to be accomplished by "(i) the Christian *religion*, which, rightly understood, includes all true *morality*, (ii) *sympathizing public opinion*, and (iii) *compulsory education*."[12]

Rockefeller's educational philanthropy embodied the Christian religion "rightly understood." At the same time, it often came into conflict with the sort of Christianity that was, to Rockefeller's way of thinking, incorrect. In education, as elsewhere, the Rockefeller project of seeking the welfare of humankind often meant superseding the work of benighted Christians.

Especially important in Rockefeller's vision of educational philanthropy was the implementation, at each level of education, of a comprehensive nonsectarian plan that could win broad popular support. With historical hindsight, one may argue that the Rockefeller combination of religion and science did not always produce an improvement over the work of sectarian predecessors. One can also see how the Rockefeller program led to secularization in all kinds of ways. This investigation will, however, seek first to understand the programs as Rockefeller and his staff understood them.

Edwin A. Alderman had the privilege of acknowledging on behalf of the General Education Board "the largest sum ever given by a man in the history of the race for any social or philanthropic purposes"—the thirty-two million dollars given by Senior in 1907. This unprecedented investment in the "conquering power of knowledge" had its origin in a train ride taken by Rockefeller in 1901. Robert Ogden, a successful northern merchant and evangelical Sunday School teacher, devised a tour of the South to introduce prominent guests to the educational needs of that region, especially the needs among African Americans. Rockefeller made the inaugural run of the "millionaires' special," along with a group of fifty northern reformers including New York magazine editors Walter Hines Page and Albert Shaw; William H. Baldwin, Jr., president of the Long Island Railroad; New York banker Morris Jesup; William C. Doane, the Episcopal bishop

12. Elisha Benjamin Andrews, *Institutes of Economics: A Succinct Textbook of Political Economy for the Use of Classes in Colleges, High Schools and Academies* (Boston: Silver, Burdett & Co., 1889) 226.

of Albany; and reformer Lyman Abbott. Rockefeller later described the trip as "one of the outstanding events in my life."[13]

Concern for African American education was already well established in the Rockefeller family. Throughout Rockefeller's childhood his father served as the primary benefactor of Spelman Seminary in Atlanta and several other schools, including Morehouse College. At the age of ten Rockefeller had accompanied Grandmother Lucy Henry Spelman, who had been a participant in the underground railroad, to the seminary that bore her name. There he was called upon to give a short speech for the third anniversary celebration.[14]

In the late nineteenth century the education of African Americans was a major undertaking of northern Protestants who realized that the southern "public" was not ready to take African American education seriously. Prior to Ogden's venture, the northern presence consisted almost exclusively of Baptist, Methodist, and Congregationalist home missionaries. They worked on the assumption that African Americans were to be full participants in the republic and therefore ought to receive classical liberal education.

The efforts of these missionary educators paled in contrast to the need. During the years of Rockefeller's young adulthood, however, the criticism of the missionaries' efforts was not that they had done too little, but that they had attempted too much. William H. Baldwin, a regular speaker at Protestant education conferences, was one such critic. He spoke of the northern missionaries as a "new army" which had invaded the south "armed with the spelling-book and Bible" and had inflicted casualties on whites and blacks alike. Baldwin argued that it would have best for all concerned if African Americans had been taught "the dignity of manual labor" instead of "the fruits of liberal education." The results of the missionary policy, according to

13. John D. Rockefeller, Jr., to Raymond B. Fosdick, quoted in Raymond B. Fosdick, *Adventure In Giving: The Story of the General Education Board, A Foundation Established by John D. Rockefeller* (New York: Harper & Row, 1962) 5.

14. Taylor Branch, *Parting the Waters: America In the King Years, 1954–63* (New York: Simon & Schuster, 1988) 28.

Baldwin, were a stagnant southern economy and a bitter white population.[15]

In January 1902 the General Education Board (G.E.B.) was founded at Rockefeller's initiative. Unlike the northern missionary teachers, the G.E.B. avoided giving offense by accommodating itself to the racially based distinctions regarding education upheld by southerners. Vocational education, not liberal arts education, was the norm for African Americans. Several in the original board who were experienced in southern education, especially the secretary of the Baptist Home Mission Society, Wallace Buttrick, convinced Rockefeller that the white South would accept education of African Americans only along with an effort to educate poor whites. The board consequently stated as its purpose "the promotion of education within the United States without distinction of race, sex, or creed."[16]

Certainly a case could be made for the need to educate rural whites as well as blacks. As Gates observed in 1905, "From the point of view of rigidly orthodox Puritan Christianity, these communities have been made Christian statistically in larger percentage than any other equal portion of mankind," yet the educational system was "unrelated directly or in any effective way even indirectly to the earthly life or needs of those for whom it exists." To support his contention, Gates referred to pictures taken by the Rockefeller Sanitary Commission of rural schools in session, showing teachers and pupils alike suffering from hookworm—emaciated, pale, and listless. To Gates, practical Christianity demanded the supply of food, shelter, clothing, and education. If they failed in this ministry, modern university-educated

15. William H. Baldwin, "The Present Problem of Negro Education, Industrial Education," in *Proceedings of the Second Capon Spring Conference the Education in the South* (Raleigh, NC: Edwards & Broughton, 1899) 94–95. See also Fosdick, *Adventure*, 80–81.

16. For a statement of the rationale of late nineteenth-century denominational private education for blacks, see D. J. Satterfield, "The Relation of Denominational Schools to the Public School," in *Proceedings of the First Capon Springs Conference for Christian Education in the South, June 29–July 3, 1898* (Raleigh, NC: Edwards & Broughton, 1898) 26–29; Fosdick, *Adventure*, 5–8.

Christians made themselves like the scribes criticized by Christ—they wore academic gowns to seek prestige, but lacked the social compassion to help the downtrodden. Gates closed an early G.E.B. memo with one of his apocalyptic challenges:

> When the colleges shall studiously employ themselves in carrying civilization, with all its blessings, downward to the people on the soil. . . then, behold, the heavens shall suddenly open, and a voice from on High shall say to them, "Come, ye blessed of My Father, inherit the kingdom prepared for you from the foundation of the world. For I was an hungered, and ye gave Me meat; I was thirsty, and ye gave Me drink; naked, and ye clothed Me; sick, and ye visited Me; imprisoned, and ye came to Me. For inasmuch as ye did it unto the least of these, My brethren, even these least, ye did it unto Me."[17]

The nature of the "civilization" that Rockefeller-funded colleges carried "downward to the people of the soil" during this period depended on whether the people were white or black. The directors of the G.E.B. lent their support to the institutional and agricultural approach to black education propagated by Booker T. Washington and epitomized by institutions like Hampton and Tuskeegee. This educational philosophy was espoused by scientific progressives and could be made to sound sage out of the mouths of advocates like Harvard President Charles W. Eliot, who served as one of Rockefeller's primary educational advisors. The scientific orthodoxy to which it was related was laced with social Darwinism, economic pragmatism, and theories of racially based distinction. This educational philosophy also fit neatly with thinly veiled expressions of racial bigotry. Baldwin, who became the first president of the G.E.B., felt himself to be squarely within the ranks of Bostonian progressivism when he said:

> The potential economic value of the Negro population properly educated is infinite and incalculable. In the Negro is the opportunity of the South. Time has proven that he is best fitted to perform the heavy labor in the Southern states. "The Negro and the mule is the only combination so far to grow cotton." The South needs him; but the South needs him educated to be a

17. Frederick T. Gates to members of the General Education Board, "The Colleges and Rural Life," 1905, p. 5, Archives: Rockefeller Boards, box 19, folder 198.

> suitable citizen. Properly directed he is the best possible laborer to meet the climatic conditions of the South. He will willingly fill the more menial positions, and do the heavy work, at less wages, than the American white man or any foreign race which has yet come to our shores. This will permit the Southern white laborer to perform the more expert labor, and to leave the fields, the mines, and the simpler trades for the Negro.[18]

Baldwin also challenged the hypocrisy of the northern missionaries who pressed for social recognition of African Americans in the South, but failed to speak out against racism in the North. He pointed out that "the ordinary Negro would have as much difficulty in obtaining room and board in a hotel in Boston as he would have in the City of Atlanta."[19] Efficiency and the social good were Baldwin's stated motives. The social implications, however, of Baldwin's yoking of "the Negro and the mule" are unmistakeable.

Even balder statements of racism can be found in Rockefeller circles during this period. Wallace Buttrick, the first director of the G.E.B., knew how to give his audience of Tennessee school superintendents what they wanted to hear from a northern Baptist: "The Negro is an inferior race. . . the Anglo-Saxon is superior. There cannot be any question about that."[20]

When James L. M. Curry, who served as a charter member of the board, spoke to a group of southern educators, he built on the foundation of white supremacy his case for the responsibility of whites to provide education for their African American sisters and brothers. History had demonstrated that whites would and should rule. This did not, however, necessarily mean hostility toward African Americans, Curry maintained, if the "more refined class of white people" would

18. William H. Baldwin, "The Present Problem of Negro Education in the South," *Journal of Social Science* 37 (1899) 52–60, quoted in James D. Anderson, "Philanthropic Control Over Black Higher Education," in Robert F. Arnove, ed., *Philanthropy and Cultural Imperialism: The Foundations at Home and Abroad* (Bloomington: Indiana University Press, 1982) 155.

19. Baldwin, "The Present Problem of Negro Education," in Arnove, *Philanthropy*, 23.

20. Wallace Buttrick, *Proceedings, Conference of Tennessee School Superintendents*, Nashville, TN, 8–9 April 1903, Southern Education Collection, University of North Carolina, quoted in Fosdick, *Adventure*, 11.

come forward to lead the way in properly educating them. Curry presented paternalism as the only road to African American advancement.[21]

The denominational missionaries whom Baldwin and others maligned found this kind of reasoning unchristian. The principal of a southern seminary, when pressed by northern philanthropists with the argument that African Americans ought not be "measured by the same standard, either morally or mentally as white people," responded with indignation, "We know of only one standard of scholarship and morals. We put before the colored people the same ideal we are keeping before ourselves."[22]

There is no indication that Rockefeller shared or assented to the more blatant racism of some of his associates with regard to the education of African Americans. There is even some indication that he was not satisfied with the board's work among blacks. He wrote to Buttrick in 1914, "I have felt for some time that possibly the Board was not performing its full duty to the Negroes and that we should consider the situation fully and seriously."[23] In an address at Fisk University, he praised Washington as "far-seeing, wise, a veritable statesman," while also extolling African American poets James Weldon Johnson and Countee Cullen, as well as businessman Charles C. Spaulding among those "winning a growing respect for and appreciation of the Negro race."[24] Nonetheless, he contented himself that the General Education Board was doing all that southern sentiment would allow, leaving himself open to the charge that social stability and the southern agricultural economy were his real concerns. As late as 1927, Rockefeller reportedly orchestrated the dedication of Sisters Chapel at

21. James L. M. Curry, "Education in the Southern States," in *Proceedings of the Second Capon Springs Conference*, 38.

22. Satterfield, "The Relation of Denominational Schools to the Public School," 28.

23. John D. Rockefeller, Jr., to Wallace Buttrick, 2 February 1914, General Education Board files, quoted in Fosdick, *Adventure*, 99.

24. John D. Rockefeller, Jr., "The Negro's Contribution to Civilization: Part of an Address at Fisk University," 6 June 1928, Archives: Religious Interests, box 31, folder 247.

Spelman College in such a way as to assure onlookers that African American education posed no threat to the status quo of the South.[25]

If the progressive blend of religion and science did much to reinforce the racist social order in the South, this does not mean that it did not also sow some of the seeds of the destruction of that order. In his celebrated history of the King era, Taylor Branch included an exploration of the connections between Rockefeller benevolence and Martin Luther King, Jr.'s career. From Spelman College (where King's parents met) to Crozier Seminary and Riverside Church, King's ideals and career were nurtured in institutions built by Rockefeller money in accordance with a white modernist Protestant blueprint.[26]

Whatever evaluation may be made of its racial policies, the G.E.B. did provide a major infusion of energy for the lagging system of education in the South. By 1911, nearly one thousand new public high schools had been founded, forty-one African American schools had received contributions of nearly a million dollars, and the principles of scientific farming had been demonstrated on over twenty thousand farms in programs that were in the process of being turned over to the United States Department of Agriculture. Gates wrote to the elder Rockefeller, encouraging him that the hand of God was in all his endeavors,

> As Divine Providence has smiled on your labors in the financial world and brought in to you very rich returns, so Divine Providence is using you as an instrument for the advancement of civilization and the amelioration of conditions of human life as Providence has never before used a commercial man, if you will pardon me for speaking so boldly, since the foundation of the world.[27]

Having embarked on the sacred duty of southern education, the Rockefeller plan, with Gates and Rockefeller in leadership, then undertook the ambitious project of reforming American higher education

25. Anderson, "Philanthropic Control," 153–58; Branch, *Parting the Waters*, 38.

26. Branch, *Parting the Waters*, 27–39, 52, 69–104.

27. Frederick T. Gates to John D. Rockefeller, Sr., 30 October 1911, Archives: Rockefeller Boards, box 19, folder 198.

as a whole. The project involved a competition with Andrew Carnegie, whose advisors held ideas about higher education that Gates felt were inferior to his own vision for developing a national strategy. Gates persuaded Rockefeller to hasten his plans to set up a ten million dollar endowment for the benefit of American higher education before a rumored Carnegie gift could "catch the public eye and fasten itself in the public thought."[28] In 1905, the elder Rockefeller responded with a twenty million dollar gift, which was administered by the G.E.B.

Ironically, the major thrust of Gates's educational philosophy was nearly identical with that of Carnegie: the organization of the patchwork arrangement of colleges and universities that dotted the landscape of the United States at the turn of the century. In Gates's words,

> The purpose is not merely to encourage higher education in the United States, but is mainly to contribute, as far as may be, toward reducing our higher education to something like an orderly and comprehensive system—to discourage unnecessary duplication and waste, and to encourage economy and efficiency.[29]

In Gates's view, one of the major obstacles to a coordinated national effort in higher education was the denominational college. Gates noted in one policy memorandum that nine-tenths of the four hundred and fifty colleges and universities in the United States were founded and then controlled either directly or indirectly by denominations. He believed that eighty to ninety percent of those in colleges and universities had been reared in the homes of church members. Gates was a committed interdenominationalist who saw no reason for Protestants to duplicate one another's efforts. At the same time, he was a realist who recognized that the denominations were the embodiment of the religious sentiment that he saw as a necessary motive for education.[30]

With regard to denominational colleges, Gates proposed that the board "use them gladly and fearlessly—they are for good and not

28. Frederick T. Gates to John D. Rockefeller, Sr., 13 June 1905, Archives: Rockefeller Boards, box 18, folder 185.

29. Frederick T. Gates to General Education Board, 30 June 1905, p. 6, Archives: Rockefeller Boards, box 18, folder 185.

30. Frederick T. Gates to General Education Board, 23 January 1906, p. 7, Archives: Rockefeller Boards, box 19, folder 198.

harm." The first plank of Gates's educational policy was to "operate sympathetically and helpfully with the religious denominations." In presenting his plan to the members of the G.E.B., Gates wrote,

> Several of the denominations have influential and useful education boards of national scope. It is believed that these various denominational boards will be ready to cooperate with this Board in the direction of systematizing their own schools, and perhaps at the same time of correlating them, where possible, with the schools of other denominations so as to avoid unnecessary duplication.[31]

Gates did not state the basis of his belief that denominational colleges would cooperate with the board; perhaps he believed they would have no choice.

Gates's policy toward denominational schools was less friendly in the implementation stage. When evaluating the state of higher education in Nebraska, he was faced by a situation in which denominational schools competed against one another and against a state university that they regarded as "godless." Gates recommended that the General Education Board show disapproval of the sectarian squabbling by refusing to support denominational schools. Gates found similar instances of denominational mismanagement in South Dakota, Washington, Texas, Colorado, Kansas, "and elsewhere both west and south." The board decided, on the basis of Gates's research, to support denominational colleges only when they were needed as part of a comprehensive regional system. Even then it would support only those colleges that evidenced "a reasonable promise of growth, permanence and power."[32]

Gates blamed real estate promoters for the proliferation of unneeded and underfunded denominational schools. The promoters often gave land in boom towns to denominational pastors. These pastors

31. Ibid., 7–9, 27; Frederick T. Gates, "The Purpose of the Rockefeller Foundation" (marked "Shd be G.E.B.?") with "Suggestions as to the Policy of Administration," Archives: Rockefeller Boards, box 19, folder 198; Gates to General Education Board, 30 June 1905, pp. 3–4, Archives: Rockefeller Boards, box 18, folder 185.

32. Frederick T. Gates, "Memorandum on Educational Conditions and Prospects in the State of Nebraska," 23 January 1908, p. 7, Archives: Rockefeller Boards, box 19, folder 198.

came east to raise money for new schools without investigating whether or not such schools were needed. They relied, Gates reasoned, on "the Pearsons, the Carnegies, and at present less confidently the Rockefellers of the East" to develop their schools. Gates believed that Carnegie's policies toward small colleges were exacerbating the problem of duplication of effort among Protestants. Little Rockefeller money went to denominational schools in the West; Gates preferred to support the state schools, most notably the University of Iowa. On the other hand, his analysis of Minnesota led to the recommendation that several denominational colleges be supported in order to take the burden from the state university. In numerous other instances, denominational colleges that met Rockefeller guidelines received favorable consideration.[33]

The policy of the Carnegie Foundation for the Advancement of Teaching, formed to administer a gift of ten million dollars given by Carnegie for teachers' pensions, was in reality more hostile to denominational colleges than the Rockefeller board. It required the trustees of participating colleges to state that no distinctly denominational tenet influenced admission, instruction, or the choice of trustees, officers, or faculty. Historian Dorothy Bass has found fifteen instances of denominational colleges disaffiliating in order to qualify. In contrast, she has suggested, the Rockefeller practice of supporting strong denominational colleges actually freed denominational money for strengthening the weaker ones. It is noteworthy that the philanthropy of Protestant modernists and that of secular modernists shared the objective of standardization according to the canons of science. The Rockefeller board, however, affirmed that religious schools could be a part of a modern educational system and was willing to accept the reality of sectarian particularity where the Carnegie Foundation was not.[34]

33. Frederick T. Gates, "Minutes on Higher Education in South Dakota and the Newer States, Anent the Application of Yankton College," pp. 3–11; idem, "Memorandum on Educational Conditions and Prospects in the State of Minnesota with Suggestions Regarding Policy," 24 March 1908, pp. 9–13; Archives: Rockefeller Boards, box 19, folder 198. The last memorandum especially commended Hamline University (Baptist), Macalester College (Presbyterian), St. Thomas College (Roman Catholic), and Carleton College (Congregational).

34. Dorothy Bass, "Ministry on the Margin: Protestants and Education," in Hutchison, *Between the Times*, 51–55. Gates thought that the Carnegie pen-

In this and other philanthropic enterprises, Rockefeller followed Gates's lead. As discussed in the previous chapter, Gates functioned as a theological mentor for Rockefeller. In the period before the First World War, Rockefeller generally allowed Gates to speak for the team and was content to join his father in paying and working to implement Gates's vision. The Colorado Fuel and Iron incident (1914) marked the first sign of Rockefeller's independence from Gates. The degree to which Rockefeller had been influenced by Gates was even more apparent as Rockefeller began to take the role of spokesperson late in the second decade and into the 1920s.

Not everyone in the Rockefeller team shared the religious vision of Rockefeller and Gates. Coexisting with their religious idealism were various brands of pure secularism. The philosophy of Wickliffe Rose, for example, stood in an interesting contrast to Rockefeller's. Rose was the son of a Tennessee clergyman, a professor of philosophy at Peabody College, and a trustee of the G.E.B. In 1923 he agreed to accept the presidency of the board on the condition that Rockefeller initiate an additional fund—one that would recognize that education and research should be assisted without regard to geographical boundaries. In response to Rose's urgings, the Rockefellers founded the International Education Board and subsequently granted twenty-eight million dollars to such scholars as Niels Bohr and Werner Heisenberg and to such facilities as the reflecting telescope at Mount Palomar. Raymond B. Fosdick wrote that Rose was "possessed by the faith of Aristotle that the salvation of mankind lay in the extension of knowledge. . . [that] it is the avenue that leads to the ultimate unity of the world."[35] Rose, like Rockefeller, believed that ethical principles should reign over the physical sciences, but he had no appreciation for the necessity of religion or even an ethics based on the social sciences. Writing after the outbreak of the Second World War, Raymond Fosdick reflected on Rose's career:

---

sion fund was an act of "extraordinary folly" since teachers should be models of thrift and should not need pensions (Frederick T. Gates to John D. Rockefeller, Sr., 24 April 1905, Archives: Rockefeller Boards, box 18, folder 185.)

35. Raymond B. Fosdick, "Introduction," in George W. Gray, *Education on an International Scale: A History of the International Education Board, 1923–1938* (New York: Harcourt, Brace, 1941) v–vi. See also Fosdick, *Adventure*, 230–33.

> He almost seemed to feel that there was some process of osmosis by which the aims and something of the mood of the fundamental sciences would by diffusion be transferred to the problems of social control. . . . As one surveys the wreckage of the last decade one wonders at what point and by what kind of knowledge the catastrophe could have been averted. Or was the disease too deeply rooted and of too long duration to yield to any approach of knowledge? Or more fundamental still, is knowledge enough? Is there some ingredient that must be combined with knowledge in a prescription to cure a desperately sick society—some element of passionate faith perhaps, some compelling vision of human dignity and worth, without which knowledge, by itself, is sterile and futile?[36]

For Rockefeller, the missing ingredient was religion. In 1928, at the dedication of the chapel at the University of Chicago, Rockefeller spoke about the place of religion in modern education. The University of Chicago had been the chief recipient of Rockefeller funds for education before Rockefeller arrived at his father's office. The first president, William Rainey Harper, envisioned a university the unity of which derived from God's involvement in all aspects of human life. Affirming this vision, Rockefeller declared in 1928 that for all time "the Chapel centrally located and dominant in its architecture may proclaim that the University in its ideal is dominated by the spirit of religion, all its departments are inspired by religious feeling, and all its work is directed to the highest ends." In strong language Rockefeller argued for the ideal of a religiously based culture:

> There are those who tell us that religion is dying out, that it is no longer in fashion, that there is no place for it in the modern world. While this may be true of many forms of thought and practice that have been called religion, nothing could be further from the truth if one is thinking of the religion of Jesus Christ. The professor in any university—whatever his own religious views may be—who makes light of such vital religion, who belittles it, who undermines his students' faith in it, is unfit to be a leader of youth, is faithless to his trust. The student who thinks it is a mark of independence, of breadth of mind, of freedom, to scoff at such vital religion, to cut himself adrift

36. Fosdick, "Introduction," xii.

> from those abiding principles of truth and character revealed in the spirit of Jesus, is only giving evidence of his own limited vision.

Rockefeller went on to express his confidence that the truths about the physical world taught in the university were in harmony with those taught by religion. Experimental science was indeed the proper yardstick with which to measure religious truth, but one could expect the university and religion to work harmoniously for human betterment.[37]

Dorothy Bass has shown that such celebration of the ideals of the modern university was common at the turn of the century among Protestant modernists. Within twenty-five years, however, universities had slipped their spiritual moorings and usurped a large measure of Protestantism's cultural authority. In 1900, denominational Protestants were confident of the harmony between denominational Protestantism and the "transcendent university"; by the 1920s and 1930s, however, they found themselves on the margins of both the universities and the culture.[38]

Rockefeller worked against the grain of the cultural phenomenon described by Bass. In the twenties and thirties he was not willing to have Protestantism marginalized, and whenever he had the opportunity through the distribution of his vast resources, he tried to keep Protestantism an integral and central part of the university enterprise. For example, twice during the twenties Rockefeller directed his personal Advisory Committee on Benevolence to study the problem of how to carry out religious work properly in the modern university. From 1923 onward, he chose not to give to the denominational chaplaincies and YMCA/YWCA programs, which were stationing themselves at the periphery of universities, but rather to seek programs that reinforced the ideal that religion belonged at the heart of the modern university and the modern world. His support of the University of Iowa School of Religion and the American Association of

37. John D. Rockefeller, Jr., "Dedication of the Chapel at the University of Chicago," 28 October 1928, Archives: Addresses, box 2, folder 143.

38. Bass, "Ministry on the Margin," 48–50.

Religion in Universities and Colleges expressed his pursuit of this ideal.[39]

In Rockefeller's view, religion and education remained partners. The religious person was the one who could see modern scientific progress for what it was—the work of God—and who could offer moral education for the guidance of modernity.

Religion and Medicine

One of the striking features of the Rockefeller philanthropic program was its determination to strategize in grand terms about the world's problems. This characteristic was the product not only of unprecedented availability of resources, but also of the breadth of the Protestant modernist vision. The well-known motto of the Rockefeller Foundation, which was formed in 1909 and chartered in 1913, reflected this vastness: "to promote the well-being of mankind throughout the world." Junior, along with his father and Gates, thought in such large terms from the early days of the foundation. In 1911, Gates philosophized, "Is there not something within us, an instinct which is the harbinger of better things, an instinct of humanity which cannot be fenced in by the boundaries of a merely national patriotism, a sympathy which transcends national boundaries and finds complete expression only when it identifies us with all humanity?"[40] Always eschewing local, personal, or remedial projects, the Rockefeller Foundation sought to identify and treat root causes of the world's ills, to "confine itself to projects of an important character, too large to be undertaken, or otherwise unlikely to be undertaken by other agencies."[41]

39. "Contributions to the field of Student Welfare in Universities and Colleges," Archives: Rockefeller Boards, box 1, folder 1; see also other records of Rockefeller's Personal Advisory Committee on Benevolence, in Archives: Rockefeller Boards, box 1, folders 1, 7, 28. Rockefeller formed this committee in the twenties to assist him in his personal giving. It included Raymond Fosdick and usually four or five others from among Rockefeller's closest associates.

40. Fosdick, *Story*, 15.

41. Fosdick, *Foundation*, 22.

Rockefeller served as president of the Rockefeller Foundation from 1913 to 1917, and as chairperson of the board of trustees from 1917 to 1939. In the early years the bulk of the funds went to medical research. This was due to the fact that Rockefeller embraced Gates's philosophy regarding the religious importance of medical science. For Gates, support for medical research represented the ultimate in universality, the only benefaction that could be directed at once to the whole human race and that was "as universal in its scope as the love of God." Gates opined, "If science and education are the brain and nervous system of civilization, health is its heart. . . . Disease is the supreme ill of human life, and it is the main source of almost all other human ills—poverty, crime, ignorance, inefficiency, hereditary taint, and many other ills."[42] Gates, at the turn of the century, gave himself to a thorough study of the status of medical research. He waded through William Osler's *Principles and Practice of Medicine* in its entirety.[43]

Gates developed a religious devotion to the medical field. Simon Flexner, who served as director of the Rockefeller Institute for Medical Research—the organization that preceded the Rockefeller Foundation—stated that Gates viewed medicine as "a kind of temple of science" in which God was worshipped through the service of all peoples.[44] Gates referred to himself, in his own work at the Rockefeller Institute, as "a sort of hewer of wood and drawer of water in this modern temple of Jehovah."[45] Flexner was a Jew, but this did not dampen Gates's enthusiasm for the "theological" work in which Flexner engaged as a medical scientist. Gates once said that he thought of Flexner's laboratory as a "seminar" and Flexner's work as a kind of prayer.

> To you He is whispering His secrets. To you He is opening up the mysterious depths of His Being. There have been times when,

42. Gates, *Chapters*, 186; Fosdick, *Foundation*, 23–24.

43. William Osler, *The Principles and Practice of Medicine* (New York: Appleton, 1911).

44. Simon Flexner, "Addresses to the Memory of Frederick Taylor Gates: A Meeting at the Rockefeller Institute for Medical Research," 15 May 1929, Archives: Gates Papers, box 3, folder 62.

45. Ibid.

> as I looked through your microscopes, I have been stricken with speechless awe. I felt that I was gazing with unhallowed eyes into the secret places of the Most High. I say if God looks down on this world and has any favorites, it must be the men who are studying Him, who are working every day, with limited intelligence and in darkness—for clouds and darkness are round about Him—and feeling their way into His heart.

Not only was the work of the medical scientist theological, it was also prophetic. Gates thought that traditional ideas about religion were being discarded and the way was being cleared for a future in which religion and ethics were created anew by the ongoing process of scientific discovery. Scientists like Flexner would be the new lawgivers:

> I tell you that as medical research goes on you will find out and promulgate as an unforeseen byproduct of your work new moral laws and new social laws, new definitions of what is right and wrong in our relations with each other. You will educate the human conscience in new directions and new duties. You will make it sensitive to new distinctions. You will teach nobler conceptions of our social relations and of the God who is over us all.[46]

Gates thought that the reconstruction of theology and ethics was the most important task of scientific research.

The Rockefeller Sanitary Commission under the direction of Wickliffe Rose was another predecessor to the Rockefeller Foundation. From 1908 to 1913 it waged an unprecedented campaign against hookworm in the South. In 1913, when the Rockefeller Sanitary Commission became the International Health Board of the Rockefeller Foundation, Rose embarked on a war on the disease, a war that eventually extended to fifty-two countries. Through subsequent campaigns against malaria, tuberculosis, and yellow fever, Rose pioneered principles in the field of public health. During the 1920s, the board devoted twenty-five million dollars to the establishment of institutions devoted to public health around the globe.

Rockefeller and Gates viewed their worldwide extension of medical science much as Protestants of the 1890s had viewed the evange-

46. Frederick T. Gates, "Address on the Tenth Anniversary of the Rockefeller Institute," 1911, Archives: Gates Papers, box 3, folder 62.

lization of the world. For them, medical science carried the grace of God as fully as biblical texts did. Nature remained for them a "book of God" in which "nobler conceptions of our social relations and of the God who is over us all" could be read.[47]

Religion and Social Science

Gates's enthusiasm for medical science and related natural sciences did not extend to the social sciences, but Rockefeller's own education and early career led him to value the contribution of the new sciences. Rockefeller expressed his interests in these fields through the Bureau of Social Hygiene and the Laura Spelman Rockefeller Memorial until the Rockefeller Foundation was reorganized in 1928.

Between 1922 and 1928 the Laura Spelman Rockefeller Memorial, under the leadership of Beardsley Ruml, granted forty-one million dollars to institutions doing pioneer work in fields such as sociology, ethnology, anthropology, psychology, and economics. Ruml did not share transcendent ideas about social science to parallel Gates's regarding medical science. He did, however, share the desire to address the world's ills by investing in the search for scientific remedies rather than by direct expenditure for immediate relief of human suffering. Because of his enthusiasm for science and his belief that Christ's spirit underlay scientific progress, Rockefeller gave Ruml the freedom to spend extensively in fostering the social sciences.

The Bureau of Social Hygiene, which grew out of Rockefeller's grand jury investigation of prostitution, funded research in numerous fields, including venereal disease prevention, drug abuse prevention, police organization, and population control. The bureau allowed Rockefeller to address some of the social concerns voiced by his mentor Elisha Benjamin Andrews. The potential problems accompanying rapid population growth, for example, were made real to Rockefeller by Andrews, and it was not consonant with his piety to leave such matters in the hands of God. Among many projects related to population control, the bureau funded the controversial research of Margaret Sanger.[48]

47. Ibid.

48. Harr and Johnson, *Century*, 49, 190–91.

In 1928, the Rockefeller Foundation was reorganized to encompass the activities of three other Rockefeller boards "relating to the advance of human knowledge."[49] The trustees of the Rockefeller Foundation did not escape the sense of cultural crisis that gripped religious and secular progressives in the twenties. During a time of uncertainty in the wider culture, Raymond Fosdick largely engineered this reorganization and brought the foundation into fields of knowledge that were more directly linked to philosophical questions about human life and progress. Fosdick had become to Rockefeller what Gates had been to his father—a frank and highly trusted counselor on philanthropic matters. As trustee and historian of the foundation, Fosdick recalled that the deliberations of the foundation board during that period took place in an atmosphere of doubt about the easy triumph of knowledge and science as civilizing instruments. It is interesting to note how often during this period the trustees gave—in the words of Fosdick—

> expression to this doubt. What special branches of knowledge should be employed? Is all knowledge equally important? Is anyone wise enough to determine the relative significance of different types of knowledge in a social order struggling for equilibrium?[50]

The responsibility for forming American culture weighed heavily in this uncertain era.

Raymond Fosdick did not share the religious faith of his brother, Harry Emerson Fosdick, who was Rockefeller's pastor. By the age of

49. Fosdick, *Foundation*, 137.

50. Ibid., 135–44. In the twenties, six Rockefeller boards were in operation: the Rockefeller Institute for Medical Research, the General Education Board, the International Education Board, the Laura Spelman Rockefeller Memorial, the Bureau of Social Hygiene, and the Rockefeller Foundation. In 1928, Rockefeller philanthropy was restructured so that the Rockefeller Foundation assumed responsibility for several activities from the following boards: the natural sciences from the General Education Board and the International Education Board; the social sciences from the Laura Spelman Rockefeller Memorial; the humanities and arts from the General Education Board; the medical sciences from the General Education Board; agriculture and forestry from the International Education Board and the General Education Board (see Fosdick, *Foundation*, 143).

fourteen, Fosdick had concluded that the "life of the spirit is not dependent upon obscurantisms of orthodoxy, and that moral ideals do not require an abdication of intelligence and critical judgment." To all of this, his brother Harry would have agreed. From this point, however, Raymond's view of the world moved in a secular liberal direction, while Harry's moved in a religiously liberal one. In 1922, in his late thirties, Raymond confessed that he did not have enough faith "to put on the back of a postage stamp."[51]

Despite Rockefeller's reliance on Raymond Fosdick, his own spiritual journey followed the path of Harry Emerson Fosdick. Throughout the twenties and beyond, Rockefeller continued to view religion as central to culture. The Sunday School lesson referred to at the opening of this chapter contained an analysis of the modern cultural crisis drawn from Raymond Fosdick's "Machine Civilization" and from the day's most popular jeremiad, Winston Churchill's "Shall We Commit Suicide?" Rockefeller and Fosdick agreed on the diagnosis.[52] Rockefeller, however, maintained optimism, based not on the present state of things but on his conviction that Christianity provided an adequate solution if given its proper place in the culture.[53]

Religion and Internationalism

Rockefeller was influenced by Raymond Fosdick in another dimension of his philanthropy: the promotion of international understanding and peace. Fosdick had come by his internationalism as a student of Woodrow Wilson's at Princeton University. Although Fosdick was not able to persuade Rockefeller to support Wilson's League of Nations during its crucial period of public trial, by the late twenties Rockefeller was supporting a number of the activities of the League of Nations, including its library. Fosdick also encouraged Rockefeller to support

51. Raymond B. Fosdick, *Chronicle of a Generation: An Autobiography* (New York: Harper & Brothers, 1958) 19; idem to Rev. Henry Huntington, 25 October 1922, Fosdick Papers, Princeton University, Princeton, NJ, quoted in Daryl L. Revoldt, "Raymond B. Fosdick: Reform, Internationalism, and the Rockefeller Foundation" (Ph.D. diss., University of Akron, 1982) 11.

52. John D. Rockefeller, Jr., "Has Civilization Outgrown Religion?" Archives: Addresses, box 1, folder 120.

53. Ibid., 1; see also Fosdick, *Foundation*, 142–44.

other internationalist groups, including the Foreign Policy Association, the Women's International League for Peace and Freedom, the National Council for the Prevention of War, and the educational campaign for the World Court. Rockefeller's international houses for foreign students, built under the motto "That Brotherhood May Prevail," were another expression of his concern for world harmony.[54]

Rockefeller, in the midst of the war, had proposed that international harmony be built upon interpersonal understanding and application of the Golden Rule. The common effort of the Allies had overcome antagonisms between nations, as well as those between classes, business interests, and denominations; the consequent brotherhood could be preserved and extended through personal relationships. The ideal of brotherhood was not new, Rockefeller reminded his auditors; Jesus of Nazareth had lived it when he encountered the woman taken in adultery, when he associated with publicans and sinners, when he reached out to the physically and spiritually sick. The life of Jesus should be the reference point for solutions to international as well as industrial issues.[55]

When traveling in China in 1921 in connection with the dedication of the Peking Union Medical College (P.U.M.C.), Rockefeller again cited the Golden Rule as the hope for world unity. Pointing to the failure of military force and individualism, he admitted that the West did not possess "the panacea for which the world is looking." Instead of extolling the American scientist as China's savior, he pointed to the "Nazarene Carpenter," saying, "Never has there been so great a need as today for the adoption of this principle: Do as you would be done by."[56] Upon returning home, Rockefeller issued a well-publicized press statement indicating a new appreciation for the ancient civilizations of the East. In it he called for a spirit of "sympathetic understanding, good-will, and fairness" between East and West, which would encourage cultures to learn from one another. The P.U.M.C., however,

54. Revoldt, "Raymond B. Fosdick," 173, 289, 327–37.

55. Rockefeller, *Brotherhood of Men and Nations*, 41.

56. John D. Rockefeller, Jr., address at YMCA in Shanghai, reported in "Father's Example," *The China Press*, 30 September 1921, p. 1, Archives: Rockefeller Boards, box 15, folder 135.

achieved only mixed success in living up to Rockefeller's standards of mutual respect, as the next chapter will show.[57]

Rockefeller seems to have followed his pastor, Harry Emerson Fosdick, in his transformation from hawk to dove between the world wars. In 1939 Rockefeller distributed Fosdick's sermon, "Dare We Break the Vicious Cycle of Fighting Evil with Evil?"[58]

Evaluating Rockefeller Philanthropy

This chapter has argued that Rockefeller carried out his charitable endeavors with the sincere belief that they had transcendent meaning. Not only was his motivation religious, but he also saw the nature of the work as religious and the tools with which it was carried out as gifts of God. This is not to say that such a transcendent vision was inconsistent with acting in one's own best interests.

Questions regarding the social control exercised by Rockefeller philanthropy deserve to be addressed. Did the greedy capitalists of the Gilded Age become philanthropists during the Progressive Era in order to buy off the oppressed classes? In an essay exploring the uniqueness of American economic foundations, Merle Curti hypothesized that foundations "both reflected and helped create" a middle way between a more miserly old-world capitalism and socialism." Curti recalled that, although the first Congressional investigation of foundations (1912) chided them for consolidating an existing status quo, the Reece Committee of the McCarthy era charged them with supporting an un-American collectivism. Beneath these seemingly conflicting charges Curti identified an antirevolutionary function of the foundations: "In relieving class and group tensions and in facilitating the growth of social well-being, philanthropy has in a sense been the American equivalent for socialism."[59]

57. "Rockefeller Sees Rebirth of China," *New York Times*, 4 December 1921, Archives: Rockefeller Boards, box 15, folder 135.

58. Edward H. Todd to John D. Rockefeller, Jr., 26 June 1939, Archives: Rockefeller Boards, box 16, folder 155. See also Miller, *Harry Emerson Fosdick*, 538.

59. Merle Curti, "American Philanthropy and the National Character," *American Quarterly* 10 (1958) 436.

A more complex social control argument has been advanced by recent Marxist scholars who see in the foundations the "sophisticated conservatism" of American capitalists molding the cultures of the world in their own image. Marx and Engels wrote, "The ideas of the ruling class are in every epoch the ruling ideas."[60] Italian Marxist Antonio Gramschi argued that the primary weapon used by a dominant social class was not force of arms, but rather the power to inculcate its world view into the whole of society. The power to define reality for the majority constituted the cultural hegemony of the ruling class.[61] Some scholars have extended this analysis to characterize major foundations as tools of the capitalist class in producing and disseminating the knowledge that constitutes modern Western reality—a reality in which the Caucasian male capitalist reigns supreme. Raymond Williams has written that hegemony "is something more substantial and more flexible than abstract ideology"; it cannot "be understood at the level of mere opinion or mere manipulation." It is

> a whole body of practices and expectations; our assignments of energy, our ordinary understanding of the nature of man and of his world. It is a set of meanings and values which as they are experienced as practices appear reciprocally confirming. It thus constitutes a sense of reality for most people in the society, a sense of absolute, because experienced, reality beyond which it is very difficult for most members of the society to move in most areas of their lives.[62]

60. Edward H. Berman, *The Influence of the Carnegie, Ford, and Rockefeller Foundations on American Foreign Policy: The Ideology of Philanthropy* (Albany: State University of New York Press, 1983) 11–40. Karl Marx and Friedrich Engels, *The German Ideology* (New York: International Publishers, 1947) 39, quoted in Berman, *Influence*, 29.

61. Antonio Gramschi, *Selections from the Prison Notebooks* (ed. and trans. Quintin Hoare and Geoffrey Nowell Smith; New York: International Publishers, 1971).

62. Raymond Williams, "Base and Superstructure in Marxist Cultural Theory," *New Left Review* 82 (1973) 8–9, quoted in Berman, *Influence*, 29–30. See also Arnove, *Philanthropy and Cultural Imperialism*, especially the essays by E. Richard Brown ("Rockefeller Medicine in China: Professionalism and Imperialism," 123–46) on China medicine, James D. Anderson ("Philanthropic Control over Private Black Higher Education," 147–78) on black education, and Donald Fisher ("American Philanthropy and the Social Services: The Reproduction of a Conservative Ideology," 233–68) on social sciences.

That Rockefeller money was a major factor in the formation of a number of important aspects of modern culture can scarcely be questioned. Priorities in the field of public health, directions in black education, and orthodoxies in a host of social and natural sciences were determined, in part, by Rockefeller giving. Barry D. Karl and Stanley N. Katz have warned us, however, that the tensions and disjunctions that exist between research science, private philanthropy, and the political apparatus are too many and too great to trace direct correlations between the will of philanthropists and political realities.[63]

There is, moreover, little evidence that Rockefeller or any of the trustees of Rockefeller philanthropies deliberately sought to mold culture with the perpetuation of the capitalist class in mind. This is not to deny that such motives may have been hidden in either the subconscious minds of the trustees or the trash cans of corporate offices. More to the point of this study, such motives were more often encompassed in what was stated—the conviction that the United States and the world needed the religious ministrations of wealthy Protestants in order to progress toward God's ideals. That such progress would also insure the safety of the present social order might or might not be explicitly stated. That Rockefeller had much to gain by the preservation of this order went without saying.[64]

This discussion raises the question of Rockefeller's role in another exercise of hegemony in American culture—that of Protestantism. In a recent study of the persistence of a "Protestant establishment" in twentieth-century America, William R. Hutchison has pointed out that the term "hegemony" can denote cultural authority that was once enjoyed by natural sanction but has come to depend upon the manipulation of social forces: "Like most other forms of persisting hegemony [Protestantism's] was justified, or at least kept in power, by its patently wide-ranging services to society." Allowing for naive altruism and crediting Protestantism with significant contributions in car-

63. Karl and Katz, "Foundations and Ruling Class Elites," 1–40.

64. Rockefeller's more explicit statements about the role of religion in preserving the American way of life will be discussed in chapter 5, which treats the interdenominational efforts carried on under his direction or with his substantial support.

rying out its leadership in American society, Hutchison nonetheless has charged powerful Protestants with maintaining a status in American culture disproportionate to their numbers.[65]

Rockefeller affirmed that scientific philanthropy was God's will and believed that the maintenance of Protestant moral principles was also God's will. The two propositions were, for Rockefeller, inextricably entwined. For him, modernism served as a vehicle for preserving both a religious sensibility and a set of religious standards. The sensibility escaped many of his contemporaries and the standards were eschewed by many more, but Rockefeller remained a convinced modernist Protestant. Although his vision for society was never fulfilled, Rockefeller's philanthropic endeavors helped perpetuate the waning Protestant guardianship of American culture.

The conflict between technique and ideals is often identified as an aspect of the modern experience. In the classic evocation of Henry Adams, we have moved from the age of the Virgin to the age of the Dynamo, from the age of faith to the the age of technological integration.[66] While assenting to the importance of technique in the making of modern America, John Higham has pointed out that the striking feature of the Progressive Era was not the triumph of technique over ideology, but the "fertile amalgamation of the two." He has written, "For a time it seemed that a modernized Americanism and a social gospel could be the moving spirit of technical society."[67]

Rockefeller epitomized this cultural outlook. For him, liberal Protestantism provided both the perfect framework for an affirmation of modern technical society and the idealism with which to keep the technology working for the benefit of humankind. He hoped that liberal Protestantism might provide the religious component of a modern national ideology. Formed by progressive ideals and insulated by his wealth from their failure, he continued to hold this vision long after

65. William R. Hutchison, "Preface: From Protestant to Pluralist America"; and idem, "Discovering America"; in idem, *Between the Times*, vii–viii, 305–6, respectively.

66. *The Education of Henry Adams: An Autobiography* (Boston: Houghton Mifflin, 1918) 379–90.

67. John Higham, "Hanging Together: Divergent Unities in American History," *Journal of American History* 61 (1974) 24.

most Americans had abandoned it. The difficulties inherent in this unstable mix of religion and science will be explored in the case study that forms the next chapter.

4 The China Medical Board

A Case Study in Religion and Rockefeller Philanthropy

One of the most notable sites of medical service under the Rockefeller Foundation was China. China was one of the first interests of the Rockefeller philanthropic team, and the foundation spent more money there than in any country except the United States. The Rockefeller Foundation's China Medical Board also experienced in full measure the tensions inherent in the mix of modernist faith and secular science that characterized all Rockefeller philanthropy. Its work provides us with an excellent case study of these tensions and Rockefeller's struggle as he worked within them.

Rockefeller interest in China began in 1907, when Gates induced Rockefeller, Sr., to consider an educational institution designed to take Western culture to the East. The Oriental Education Commission, headed by Ernest D. Burton, investigated for the Rockefellers the possibility of founding a university in China which would be similar to the University of Chicago. As this idea developed, Rose's successes in the field of public health and Gates's appreciation for medical science led the foundation trustees to consider the field of medicine as a possible focus of the Rockefeller China program. Over the next four years, Rockefeller and Gates conferred with several advisors who had experience in China, including missionary statesman John R. Mott and President Eliot of Harvard. As had been the case in their survey of American education, the Rockefeller initiative found itself entering a field in which Protestant missionaries were the major players.[1]

The initial Rockefeller assessment of the medical missionary effort in China was not positive. President Eliot's view of medical practice among the mission societies was especially low. In a report to the Carnegie Foundation, Eliot had characterized missionary doctors as overworked and inadequately equipped. Because of these conditions, Eliot believed, the missionaries inevitably allowed their technique to deteriorate and became callous to the real needs of their patients.[2]

The question of the competence of the missionaries, as well as several related religious issues, figured prominently in the conference of China experts convened by Rockefeller in January 1914 to discuss the prospects for medical education in China. Rockefeller headed all the sessions; among the twenty-one who attended were missionary executives, academic specialists, and the full roster of Rockefeller executives from the G.E.B. and the newly formed Rockefeller Foundation.

Mott had recently returned from his fourth trip to China. Its purpose had been a series of regional consultations about uniting the Protestant missionary effort, particularly through regional union Christian schools. He had met with representatives of both one thousand educational missionaries and five hundred medical missionaries from two hundred and thirty-five hospitals. He spoke with urgency about seizing the moment to mold China, which he saw as "literally plastic, in a fluid condition." Japan and Russia had entered the competition over China's future development, thus spurring Mott's enthusiasm for both evangelizing and "civilizing" China. Mott also shared the Rockefeller vision for rationalization of effort along modern scientific lines, and he saw the profusion of missionary endeavors in China as

1. Mary Brown Bullock, *An American Transplant: The Rockefeller Foundation and Peking Union Medical College* (Berkeley: University of California Press, 1980) 31–47.

2. Charles W. Eliot, *Some Roads to Peace*, a report to the Carnegie Endowment for International Peace, 1912, p. 22, quoted in Fosdick, *Foundation*, 83.

an argument for "a body that deals comprehensively and adequately with the situation."[3]

Robert E. Speer, the secretary of the Presbyterian Board of Foreign Missions and a trusted associate, made a case for the proposition that the Rockefeller endeavor should build on and strengthen the widely dispersed Christian institutions in China as a means of meeting the needs of the nation. Speer argued that the missions possessed "in a unique degree the confidence of the Chinese people." Speer believed that education and medicine were tools for winning China to Christ, but he was not an enthusiastic exporter of Western civilization. Education alone would not meet China's needs. Only Christ could free the Chinese from superstitions so that they could develop their natural resources. His missiology focused on "planting the life of Christ" within non-Western cultures and allowing the process of cultural change to take place from within.[4]

Could conversionist aims, even those as nuanced as Speer's, coexist with nonsectarian efforts to extend Western culture to China? James H. Franklin, a missionary executive, assured the group that the missionaries with whom Mott and Speer were working, although quite sincere in their Christian commitments, were moving steadily toward nonsectarian service to the Chinese. The "better schools in China" were conducted without thought of propagating the "distinctive ideas of a sect." Their focus was on putting "the Christ spirit" into their service. Franklin was persuaded that most of them were "willing to sustain the losses in their denomination in order that the greater cause may triumph."

On the afternoon of the second day, the conference began to explore in more detail the idea of cooperating with medical missionaries. Gates asked directly about "the work actually being done by medical missionaries" and whether it might serve as a foundation on

3. The account of these meetings in taken from "China Conference of the Rockefeller Foundation, January 19–20, 1914," Archives: Rockefeller Boards, box 11, folder 91. In the following text, all quotations from the conference correspond to this reference.

4. Robert E. Speer, *Missionary Principles and Practice* (New York: Revell, 1910) 37.

which the Rockefeller effort could build. Randolph T. Shields, another missionary representative, responded that, given the obstacles faced by medical missionaries—such as insufficiently equipped hospitals and as many as a hundred patients a day—"it is remarkable how our medical men have held up under [the] burden and kept practically up to date and done some first class work." Given the pressures, it was simply unrealistic to "expect [the medical missionary] to sit down at night and read the medical journals and do a little research work in his laboratory." Shields conceded that "a great many men have fallen into the rut and have not kept up to date."

The failure of missionary doctors to modernize was one issue; the question of whether those with sectarian aims could work alongside those with purely medical ones was another. Jerome Greene, an original trustee of the foundation, led the way in pressing the issue further. Greene was a product of missionary parents and grandparents, but felt strongly that foundation activities ought by legal right to benefit "mankind" without sectarian aim or distinction of any kind. He asked Mott and Speer to comment on the recruiting policies of groups like the student volunteers and the denominational boards:

> If the recruiting officer should see a chance to make use of a man of good medical training, who combined with that a strong humanitarian impulse, but who had no marked denominational connection and who is not interested or in any way associated with the evangelistic work, would he be taken?

Mott responded that most of those recruited in the student volunteer movement were subject to their own denomination's manuals, which would generally require, "certain qualifications as to a man's views as to Christianity and a desire to propagate those views." Approximately one out of twenty recruited candidates, however, were not placed in jobs under the auspices of the denominational boards, and "a goodly number of those volunteers are animated more by what you speak of as the humanitarian motive and spirit than by a zeal for the propagation of a particular theological expression concerning Christianity." Mott added, "I think that this is true of an increasing number of those who become medical volunteers."

Rockefeller was especially interested in this point and asked Speer, a denominational representative, to discuss this issue. Speer responded that creedal distinctions were of "no interest" to his board. It simply asked that a recruit "belong to our particular body" and "have an especial religious belief." Speer stressed the sacrificial nature of medical missions and expressed his own willingness to recruit anyone who was ready to undertake this difficult calling, even those without any explicitly evangelistic motive. "We meet such men with heartiest sympathy," he assured Rockefeller, "and are seeking for them all the time, and find that as a rule, the difference between them and us is very much less than is imaginable, and if they want to do this thing we have very much more in common than they suppose."

By the end of the conference, Gates was convinced of the desirability of cooperating with the missionary bodies. His thoughts about a comprehensive medical system in China paralleled his proposal for a comprehensive system of higher education in the United States: his philosophy was to use the denominational resources already in place for the nonsectarian purpose at hand. He viewed the medical missionaries as existing resources who could be utilized as part of a comprehensive plan to bring Western medical science to China. They represented five hundred advanced troops, supported by already existing organizations operating under an "humanitarian impulse." Gates argued that the Rockefeller effort should strengthen these five hundred by offering them and others a more thorough medical education. Gates felt that China's need for modern medical science might be met quickly if the Rockefellers acted by "taking up medical schools on the one hand and medical missionaries on the other."

A commission was formed; it was headed by University of Chicago President Harry P. Judson; Dr. Francis W. Peabody of Peter Bent Brigham Hospital; and Roger S. Greene, Jerome Greene's brother, who was serving in Hankow as consul general for the United States. The commission traveled throughout China in order to investigate the possibility of establishing one or more medical schools. Judson, writing about medical missions in a section of the commission's report, was very positive. Judson expressed pleasant surprise to find the degree to which missionaries engaged "not only in a religious propaganda, but as well in large educational and eleemosynary undertakings, hospitals, asylums, schools, colleges, universities." Apart from evangelization, Judson found that

> the missionaries are trying to provide for China in these lines at a large cost of money and men, what Western nations do for themselves, either at public charge or from individual beneficence. . . . Missionary societies generally have assumed frankly the great duties involved in the extensive educational and humane activities which have been going on in China.

The Judson Commission enthusiastically recommended that the foundation support medical education in China by establishing teaching hospitals in Peking and Shanghai, making grants to other hospitals, and giving fellowships to missionaries.[5]

Some members of the Rockefeller team, including Eliot, were not convinced that the foundation should work with the missionaries, despite the findings of the Judson Commission. Writing to Roger Greene, Eliot expressed his disdain for the missionary effort. He claimed that he knew of no one who had seen "any first-class work done in China under the direction of Mission Boards," and questioned whether the commission headed by Judson had actually seen any such work.[6]

On 11 December 1914, the foundation established the China Medical Board (C.M.B.) with Rockefeller as chairperson. Its stated purpose was "the propagation of the true spirit of the Christian religion by promoting the knowledge and practice of scientific and humane medicine in China for the benefit of the Chinese people." The strength of religious feeling in this statement was due only in part to spiritual conviction; the 1903 treaty between the United States and China granted unlimited access to China for "missionary societies," whereas other Americans were restricted in their activities to between fifty and sixty "open" towns and cities. Another stated purpose of the C.M.B.

5. Harry Pratt Judson, "Missionary Medical Schools," in idem, *Report of the China Medical Commission to the Rockefeller Foundation* (New York: privately printed, 1914) 22; see Archives: Rockefeller Boards, box 11a, folder 89a.

6. Charles W. Eliot to Roger S. Greene, 19 December 1914, quoted in Frederick T. Gates, "Shanghai: A View of the Facts," memo, p. 9, Archives: Gates Papers, box 3, folder 65.

was "the gradual and orderly development of a comprehensive and efficient system of medicine in China."[7]

This is not to say that there was not genuine religious intent on the part of those who formed the China Medical Board. Gates closed the first board meeting in December 1914 with a statement of philosophy entitled "Thoughts on Medical Missions and the Spirit of Jesus." Gates declared that the board fully shared "the desire of evangelistic Christians to communicate the spirit of Jesus to the Chinese and to the whole world." Lest one be left with the suspicion that his allusions to the spirit of Jesus were mere pious dilutions of orthodoxy, Gates proceeded with a powerful demonstration of liberal Protestant exegesis of the teachings of Jesus. On the issue of accepting non-Christian co-workers, Gates appealed to the parable of the good Samaritan, in which a "hated heretic" was the hero, and drew from this parable the moral that "a spirit of love may be found even in an alien faith." He demonstrated the primacy of good works over evangelism through an appeal to Jesus's depiction of the Last Judgment, in which those who have ministered to the hungry, thirsty, sick, and imprisoned are rewarded. "No soul have they saved," Gates thundered. In asserting the spiritual value of so mundane a service as care of the physical body, Gates reasoned from the parable of the early and late laborers in the field: "the appraisements of heaven are based not on the magnitude, but on the disinterestedness of the service." Gates concluded with these words:

> And so, acting in the spirit of the Great Teacher, and obedient to his teaching, we may extend our sympathy and, in so far as possible, our aid to all competent physicians and nurses in China who are dedicated to this medical ministration, whether they are working under the auspices of any of the American or European missionary societies, or however diverse the creeds of those societies, or however rigidly those creeds may be interpreted by

7. China Medical Board Articles of Incorporation, Archives: Rockefeller Boards, box 11, folder 92. Robert Lansing to Claudius A. Hand, 24 June 1915, Archives: Rockefeller Boards, box 11, folder 92. Frederick T. Gates and Wallace Buttrick to Roger S. Greene, 13 November 1916, Archives: Rockefeller Boards, box 12, folder 100.

> them, or whether the physicians or nurses are working under boards denominationally independent. Our only requirement need be one which will fully be granted by all, this, namely, that where the Foundation pays for full-time medical service, full-time service shall be rendered within the usual and ordinary meaning of these words.[8]

By Gates's modernist Protestant hermeneutic, "medical service within the usual and ordinary meaning of these words" had become the most sacred of all acts. Religious motivation lay beneath this expression of Rockefeller philanthropy, but the religious aspects of this program went beyond motivation. The liberal religious faith shared by Gates, Rockefeller, and many other members of the Rockefeller team made them aware of the broader religious dimension of the acts themselves. Simply put, Rockefeller saw acceptable service to God where many of his colleagues, whether secular scientists or conservative missionaries, could not see it—namely, in simple service to humanity.

As the plans of the C.M.B. developed, Rockefeller carefully cultivated relationships with the mission boards with which the board hoped to cooperate. To this end, the foundation called upon Dr. Wallace Buttrick, head of the Rockefeller General Education Board, to serve as director of the C.M.B. Buttrick understood missionaries from his days as secretary of the Baptist Home Missionary Society and was able to persuade most of them that the Rockefeller effort would not attempt to control or supersede their own. The two purposes of the C.M.B., as Buttrick presented them, were the contribution of funds to selected mission boards for use in their own medical stations and the establishment of medical colleges with teaching hospitals.

In pursuit of the second of these two purposes, the C.M.B. entered into a harmonious agreement with six mission boards that it would

8. Frederick T. Gates, "Thoughts on Medical Missions and the Spirit and Teaching of Jesus," Archives: Rockefeller Boards, box 11, folder 93. Mary E. Ferguson attributes (*China Medical Board and Peking Union Medical College: A Chronicle of Fruitful Collaboration, 1914–1951* [New York: China Medical Board, 1970] 89) this sermon to Gates, and the style is certainly his. It is signed, "A Member of the Rockefeller Foundation." Corrections written on the text seem to be in Rockefeller's hand. I surmise that Rockefeller edited it for his own use; I know that he used parts of it in his open letter to missionary societies, written on 15 March 1915.

assume financial responsibility for the Union Medical College at Peking.[9] Buttrick assured the mission leaders that the C.M.B. would work in close harmony with them to make the school a "distinctive contribution to the missionary endeavor." He further promised that no teacher unacceptable to the societies would be hired. He assured the London Missionary Society, from whom the property was to be purchased, that "the work of the College would be continued on its present line as a Christian Missionary College." At the same time, Buttrick added, the board felt responsible to create a school "of the highest standard practicable from the standpoint of modern medicine."[10]

In an open letter to all missionary groups in China, Rockefeller pledged to work toward "the most cordial and sympathetic cooperation" with the boards and promised "to select only persons of sound sense and high character, who were sympathetic with the missionary spirit and motive." In summing up his vision of the C.M.B., Rockefeller said, "We desire to supplement the work of the Missionary Boards where it is incomplete, to multiply it where it is inadequate, and always to engraft our additions in an entirely vital way."[11]

In July 1915 the site for Peking Union Medical College was purchased. The board of trustees, along with Mott as chairperson, consisted of representatives of the six mission societies and seven representatives of the C.M.B.; on 14 January 1916, the board met to begin planning the venture. A second commission, consisting of Buttrick, Flexner, William H. Welch, and Gates's son Frederick L. Gates, M.D., was dispatched. This commission's findings contained little to change the attitude of the board toward medical missionaries or a redefinition of its goals. Flexner, in his report to the trustees of the P.U.M.C.,

9. The six boards were the Medical Missionary Association of London, the Society for the Propagation of the Gospel, the London Missionary Society, the Board of Foreign Missions of the Presbyterian Church of the United States of America, the Board of Foreign Missions of the Methodist Episcopal Church, and the American Board of Commissioners for Foreign Missions.

10. Wallace Buttrick, "Memorandum of the Meeting held on January 15, 1915 with Representatives of Four American Missionary Societies," Archives: Rockefeller Boards, box 11, folder 93.

11. John D. Rockefeller, Jr., to twenty-one missionary societies, 15 March 1915, Archives: Rockefeller Boards, box 13, folder 121. See Fosdick, *Foundation*, 80–92.

expressed pride in the work of medical missionaries in China. They had successfully introduced Western medicine into China, and the amount of suffering they had relieved was, in his estimation, "no less than colossal." If their educational efforts were less praiseworthy, it was only because of their lack of qualification as teachers and the lack of proper facilities.[12]

Greene, a member of the original commission, continued to study the mission hospitals and came to a more mature realization, namely, that the chasm between modern medicine and the mission station would not be so easily bridged. Mission hospitals were usually little more than primitive dispensaries. In order to achieve its goals of modernizing China's medical practice, the emphasis would have to be placed on the teaching hospitals which Rockefeller founded.[13]

Although property for a second school was obtained in Shanghai through a merger with the Harvard Medical School in China, a second project never materialized. The major undertaking of the C.M.B. would be the medical school at Peking.

The zeal to take Western science to the Chinese was determinative in decisions regarding the P.U.M.C.'s approach to medical education. Despite China's desperate immediate need for basic health care for the masses, the college offered state-of-the-art Western excellence to the few. The goal of instilling Western science in a generation of Chinese doctors was given priority above the immediate need for basic services. This strategy could be considered consistent with the Rockefeller philosophy that favored building systems and sought to treat causes rather than symptoms. It has also led to the charge that Rockefeller philanthropy was more an exercise in cultural imperialism than in benevolent service.[14]

12. Simon Flexner, "Central and Southern China: Report of the Second China Medical Commission, January 24, 1916," Archives: Rockefeller Boards, box 11, folder 89.

13. Roger S. Greene to Wallace Buttrick, memo regarding "Aid to Mission Hospitals," 17 July 1916; Greene, address entitled "The Medical Work of Christian Missions in China," 19 April 1917; Archives: Rockefeller Boards, box 12, folder 100. For other related materials, see this location.

14. Brown, "Rockefeller Medicine in China," in Arnove, *Philanthropy and Cultural Imperialism*, 123–46.

When the P.U.M.C. was dedicated in September 1921, the invocation by John Leighton Stuart—then president of Peking University and later American ambassador to China—stated the modernist understanding of the harmony of spiritual and scientific aims.

> Creating and Controlling Spirit of the Universe, revealing itself in the beauty and wonder of this visible world, in the heart and conscience of man, and in that One who more than all others has disclosed Thy constant presence, Thy purpose for us, Thy pity for all in need of help and healing, and Thy power, we are gathered here this afternoon to dedicate this institution to the search for Thy truth which relieves human pain and revokes human disease,. . . because we believe that all the finer urgings of the human spirit, all the attainments of science and skill are from Thee, therefore we thank Thee for all these buildings, their equipment, their staff, their program.

The hospital was an expression of God because "all the finer urgings of the human spirit" were expressions of God. The evangelistic task was one of encouraging such urgings to action; the hospital existed, in part, so that its students "may catch the spirit of those who have made this possible—the spirit of service for others, of sacrifice for their fellows, of devotion to the highest ideals of the age, and of loving, devoted activity." The invocation requested that the hospital be "controlled by Thy spirit," and the prayer closed "in the name of Him who more than all others has taught us that knowledge and power lie in concentrated effort for the welfare of our fellow-men." The religion was relatively generic, but remained recognizably Protestant, and its place in the endeavor was unmistakable.[15]

Rockefeller's own dedicatory address stressed the necessity of spiritual training and promised the Chinese the best spiritual influence the West could offer, while welcoming individuals of any religious tradition who could pass "the final test of true religion—the translation of religion into the highest type of life." In an aside to the medical missionary boards Rockefeller assured them that the college existed "to supplement, not to supplant. . . to aid, not to impede them in their

15. John L. Stuart, "Invocation," in *Addresses and Papers, Dedication Ceremonies and Medical Conference, Peking Union College* (Concord, NH: Rumford, 1922) 41.

efforts." On behalf of the C.M.B., Rockefeller promised, "In fullest sympathy with the missionary spirit and purpose, we are desirous of furthering it as completely as may be consistent with the maintenance of the highest scientific standards in the medical school and the best service in the hospital." This was a clear expression of liberal Protestant feelings about the Christian mission. Rockefeller claimed the primacy of Christianity while affirming the value of any religion that produced right conduct. He expressed support for the work of more traditional Christian missionaries, but only insofar as it was consistent with the best that Western civilization could offer.[16]

The Chinese had other ideas about the usefulness of P.U.M.C. A week after its dedication, Rockefeller was honored by a gathering in Shanghai. The address, given by Chichen Nieh, stated the hope that the union of Western medicine and Chinese medicine might be a fruitful one.

> There is, doubtless, much in Chinese medicine that is of real value. This has not been scientifically studied and standardized. When this is done, China will have a real and rich contribution to make to medical science. It is our hope, therefore, that the Peking Union Medical College will help make this contribution possible.[17]

The purpose of the P.U.M.C., however, was not to learn, but to teach both science and religion. Rockefeller's nuanced position—support for the Protestant mission, but only insofar as it affirmed the values of science—was a difficult one to carry out at P.U.M.C. Initially, the commitment of the college to religion dictated the assignment of staff evangelists who worked among the patients. From 1924 to 1932 the director of the Department of Religious and Social Work was Y. Y. Tsu, an Episcopal clergyman who was well respected as a preacher in both Chinese and English. During these same years, Ida Pruitt was on the religious staff of the college, doing pioneer work in religious social work. Despite fears in 1927 that the Chinese nation-

16. John D. Rockefeller, Jr., "Address at the dedication of the Peking Union Medical College Buildings, September 19, 1921," Archives: Rockefeller Boards, box 15, folder 134.

17. Chichen Nieh, "Address in Honor of Rockefeller at Shanghai, September 27, 1921," Archives: Rockefeller Boards, box 15, folder 135.

alists might object to the religious work of the college, the trustees held firm to their commitment to a religious mission. A visit from the London Missionary Society representative in that year confirmed that the religious work being carried out was faithful to the promise to "make a distinct contribution to the missionary endeavor."[18]

A different picture was presented by the college's chief executive officer in China, Henry S. Houghton, in a 1927 letter to the China Christian Educational Association:

> Our college is in a very peculiar situation as far as religious work is concerned, because as it is at present, the Faculty are concerned with the development of the institution as a scientific school and not as a a religious project. Teachers are invited to the school not for their religious interests but for their professional proficiency. Whatever religious work that is done is purely voluntary as far as the student requirements are concerned. As in all professional and especially medical institutions, we are up against the unconscious but pervasive materialistic view of life which negates the religious or spiritual conception. But there is a small number of teachers who are deeply interested in religious work and a small group of students who form the working nucleus among their fellow students.[19]

The continuing strain between secular and religious currents at the college was attested to by a complaint mentioned in 1928 by Dr. Tsu; he felt indifference and occasionally even opposition toward his program from some faculty members. Tsu also referred to some unfortunate cases affecting domestic and social relationships of certain members of the staff, cases about which the Chinese community commented unfavorably.

In 1929 all eleven Western trustees of the P.U.M.C. stepped down in favor of a nationalized board under the leadership of Y. T. Tsur. Roger Greene, who had succeeded Houghton as the highest ranking Rockefeller executive in China, became the focal point of the tensions between religious and secular points of view. Greene, having been recommended by Charles W. Eliot, had joined the venture from the

18. Ferguson, *China Medical Board*, 90–92.

19. Henry S. Houghton, "Religious Life in Christian Universities and Colleges of China, 1927–1928," quoted in Bullock, *An American Transplant*, 116.

outset; he had previously been involved with government service in China. Greene confirmed Tsu's suspicions: some of the strongest members of the faculty were either opposed to the indefinite continuance of the religion department or indifferent to it. Greene reported that many at the college doubted "the propriety of having such a department supported by a scientific institution," and that he, himself, had for some years shared this doubt.[20]

Greene concluded that "our experiment in conducting a religious department in a medical school has not been a success. . . . The main trouble is that the relation actually is not a natural one and that it does not offer adequate field for the exercise of Dr. Tsu's great talents." The ideal situation, Greene continued, would be for Tsu to be settled in a nearby church, where he could continue his ministry to hospital patients and personnel. As the highest ranking Rockefeller executive in China, Greene was encouraged by the New York office to satisfy Tsu's complaint in a manner consistent with Rockefeller's promise to the mission boards.[21]

On 20 June 1929, despite the reorganization and nationalization of the board of trustees of the college, Rockefeller again wrote to the missionaries involved, "I need not assure you that I shall be no less alert in the future than in the past to do what lies within my power to preserve and perpetuate the fine Christian spirit upon which this enterprise was built." Rockefeller specifically affirmed his support for the college's Department of Religious and Social Work, which still held voluntary religious services for the college community.[22]

Greene was now forced to carry out a religious policy for which he lacked both personal conviction and direct organizational author-

20. Until 1929, the board of the college consisted of representatives of the six mission boards, as well as seven representatives of the Rockefeller Foundation's China Medical Board. Roger S. Greene to Margery K. Eggleston, 22 August 1928, Archives: Rockefeller Boards, box 14, folder 130.

21. Ibid.

22. John D. Rockefeller, Jr., to Frank Mason North, Arthur J. Brown, James L. Barton, Thomas Cochrane, Hugh H. Weir, 20–21 June 1929, Archives: Rockefeller Boards, box 12, folder 109. See also the memo prepared for Rockefeller by Margery K. Eggleston, "Religious Work in the Peking Union Medical College—Agreements and Commitments, M.K. Eggleston, 22 April 1930," Archives: Rockefeller Boards, box 14, folder 130.

ity. Greene had always been uncomfortable with the Rockefeller vision for incorporating the missionaries into a scientific medical system, calling the plan "sectarian medicine." While granting that many missionary doctors were broad-minded and free from a preoccupation with conversion, he privately expressed fear that they lacked support from their own mission boards. Greene's father, grandfather, and great-grandfather had all been missionaries. His experience led him to believe that those who supported foreign missions were "not ready for such strong meat as the theory that missionaries are justified in teaching schools and healing the sick without any ulterior motive, however high, but merely because they want to help people in that way." Greene felt that religious ministry and medical service were best carried on independently, and he lacked the resolve to manipulate the Chinese board into keeping Rockefeller's promises to the missionaries.[23]

Rockefeller continued to insist that Greene "earnestly and sincerely [use] his influence to carry out the wishes of those who have organized this enterprise up to date." Throughout the fall of 1930, Greene and Tsu feared for the future of religion in the college, given the increasingly hostile Chinese public opinion about religious work in foreign institutions. Tsu consulted with John Leighton Stuart, who reported to Rockefeller III that "while Greene was fundamentally sympathetic to the religious work, that he hardly dared stand out for it because of the opposition of those with whom he carries on his daily work." Despite the sentiments of the public and the faculty, the Chinese trustees surprised Greene and delighted the American C.M.B. by supporting the continuation of Tsu's post and the religion department, even as the Depression era forced budget cuts in the college.[24]

Greene was caught in the middle; although the Chinese board might yield to Rockefeller pressure out of courtesy, Greene refused to do so.

23. Roger S. Greene to his family, 9 March 1916, papers of Roger Sherman Greene, Houghton Library, Harvard University, Cambridge, MA, quoted in Warren I. Cohen, *The Chinese Connection: Roger S. Greene, Thomas W. Lamont, George E. Sokolsky and American-East Asian Relations* (New York: Columbia University Press, 1978) 33.

24. John D. Rockefeller, Jr., to George E. Vincent, 19 July 1930; Vincent to Rockefeller, 2 October 1930; John D. Rockefeller III to Rockefeller, memorandum, 6 April 1931; Archives: Rockefeller Boards, box 14, folder 130.

When Tsu resigned in the spring of 1933, Greene recommended that the position's funding be halved. F. H. Hawkins of the London Missionary Society protested, winning the support of the New York office. At the initiative of Tsur and a majority of the new P.U.M.C. Board, the full-time salary was maintained and Egbert Hayes of the YMCA took the post. Rockefeller wrote to Greene with thanks and further encouragement,

> You will, of course, understand the peculiar satisfaction I take in what has been done. . . . I realize that radical changes in thought along religious lines have taken place since the founding of the PUMC. and that there is growing up a new school of thought as to how the fundamental and eternal principles underlying Christianity can best be promoted in the world and Christian character developed. On the other hand, so long as the PUMC stands, there can never be a question as to the duty of all those currently responsible for conducting the institutions to carry out with sincerity and wholeheartedness the full spirit of the understanding with the missionary societies upon which it was founded. . . . If [the new trustees] have laid before them from time to time by you, as occasion may require, the substance of the understanding above referred to, they cannot but fall in line under your leadership in carrying it out as a matter of honor, even if not as a matter of conviction.[25]

Rockefeller was soon given additional reason to be concerned regarding Greene's ability to implement Rockefeller's stated policy. Dr. Thomas Cochrane, who until the recent reorganization had been a trustee of the college as a representative of the London Missionary Society, now visited the college in the capacity of a representative of the World Dominion Movement and the Movement for World Evangelism. Cochrane, writing to Rockefeller, expressed profound dissatisfaction with the spiritual state of the college. He believed that the fight over continuation of the religion department might be blinding the board to deeper issues. By not facing these issues, he charged, the C.M.B. was failing to honor its original agreement with the missionary societies. The college, for example, was not choosing its staff with religious principles in mind. The Department of Religious and

25. John D. Rockefeller, Jr., to Roger S. Greene, 16 August 1933, Archives: Rockefeller Boards, box 14, folder 130.

Social Work should have had "much more sympathetic cooperation and a better atmosphere than exists at present." In short, the college was "at a parting of the ways" and "on the down-grade in things which are most essential." The college also lacked "men of character." Cochrane referred to "things which I heard before and after I reached Peking," which he could not repeat in a letter, but which greatly disturbed him. He appealed to Rockefeller to take strong action. At Rockefeller's request, Rockefeller III saw Cochrane in April 1934, at which time Cochrane specified the unmentionable offenses as "considerable drinking and purposeful scheduling of meetings during church hours." Cochrane also thought Greene was "too pro-Chinese; that is, he was trying to put the PUMC in a position to be turned over to the Chinese too fast."[26]

Shortly after Cochrane reported to Rockefeller, the new religious director himself, Egbert M. Hayes, sent Rockefeller his reflections, entitled "Impressions after Six Months in PUMC." Hayes echoed Cochrane's concern that his department alone could not insure that graduates would carry "the spirit of the Great Physician. . . of a Grenfell or a Schweitzer." He reported that doctors and nurses were being sent to the P.U.M.C. "with a fine Christian spirit" and coming back "completely changed." Hayes feared that the decision to maintain the department was "merely a cloak of respectability—a sop thrown to Mr. Rockefeller who insists on the continuance of religious work." In reality, he felt that the college reflected a spirit that was not consonant with either Rockefeller's original agreement with the mission societies or Rockefeller's present desires.[27]

Three days later, Hayes wrote again in a more upbeat mood, ready to launch a "flank attack" on the rampant infidelity by means of evangelistic speakers—including Mott and Sherwood Eddy—on Sunday mornings.[28] Meanwhile, Rockefeller's staff was taking counsel

26. Thomas Cochrane to John D. Rockefeller, Jr., 26 March 1934; John D. Rockefeller III to Rockefeller, 2 April 1934; Archives: Rockefeller Boards, box 14, folder 130.

27. Egbert M. Hayes to John D. Rockefeller, Jr., 11 April 1934, Archives: Rockefeller Boards, box 14, folder 130.

28. Egbert M. Hayes to John D. Rockefeller, Jr., 14 April 1934, Archives: Rockefeller Boards, box 14, folder 130.

regarding Cochrane's letter. "It is a difficult problem to combine an efficient training in modern medicine with evangelical piety," counseled C.M.B. president George E. Vincent.[29]

Rockefeller, however, persisted in the effort. Three months later, at Rockefeller's instigation, the foundation asked Greene to resign from his duties. Although Rockefeller stated to Greene's defenders that Greene's dismissal had been "inevitable and could not have been avoided if there had never been any question of religious work in the college" since Greene had become "increasingly difficult to work with," those close to the affair concluded that religion was the central point of contention. Greene himself was certain that religion was the main issue and believed that Cochrane's interview had marked the turning point in his relations with the board. He wrote to his brother Jerome, a Rockefeller Foundation trustee, portraying himself as a martyr in the cause of academic freedom from "ecclesiastical influence." At the same time, Greene felt he had done nothing to violate Christian ethics. He defended his policy of hiring non-Christian faculty members by reference to the Golden Rule: Americans would insist on the best doctor for themselves, regardless of the doctor's religion; they ought to provide the Chinese with the same choice.[30]

Sinologist Warren I. Cohen has reflected on the firing of Greene and concluded that Greene "had come to believe that the effort to instill Christianity in medical and nursing students was an anachronism in modern China" and that, simply put, "to be right was not sufficient when opposing the Rockefellers." Greene had gotten caught

29. George E. Vincent to John D. Rockefeller III, 21 April 1934, Archives: Rockefeller Boards, box 14, folder 130.

30. John D. Rockefeller, Jr., to F. H. Hawkins, 7 December 1934, Archives: Rockefeller Boards, box 12, folder 102. Mary Brown Bullock cites (*An American Transplant*, 70 n. 68) a letter from Alan Gregg to Roger S. Greene, dated 2 August 1934, in which Gregg states that Greene was fired over the religious issue. See also John D. Rockefeller III's letter to George E. Vincent (4 June 1934, Archives: Rockefeller Boards, box 12, folder 102) in which religious issues top the list of Rockefeller III's concerns for the visit that Henry S. Houghton was to make to P.U.M.C. Roger S. Greene to John B. Grant, 25 October 1934; Roger S. Greene to Jerome Greene, 23 October 1934; papers of Roger Sherman Greene, Houghton Library, Harvard University, Cambridge, MA, box 13, folder 316.

between the policy of Chinese self-determination and a promise made by Rockefeller himself. Raymond Fosdick confided to the college's historian that Rockefeller's conduct had been the product of a "bad commitment." The underlying issue was one of authority. Was the P.U.M.C. board of trustees to be genuinely self-determining, or would the wishes of the donor always hold sway? The new board seemed to be willing to yield to the pressure of personal respect for the donor, just as Rockefeller's American boards had always done. Greene, however, was not a skillful politician when forced to play middleman in this arrangement.[31]

The incident brought into focus the way in which Rockefeller influenced the boards that distributed family money. In November 1934 Jerome Greene met with Rockefeller and Thomas M. Debevoise, Rockefeller attorney, ostensibly to discuss a letter that he had written on 29 June 1934 to Fosdick; this letter contained suggestions about improving the process by which foundation decisions were made. In that letter Greene stated his feeling that the trustees of the foundation were dealing with its business in too perfunctory a manner, leaving to the staff and a few of the trustees the real direction of the foundation. In words reminiscent of Gates's apocalyptic thunderings about the importance of the foundation, Greene suggested that every trustee ought to make the foundation "second only to his principal occupation" and that quarterly meetings ought to be held.[32]

In the November interview Greene stated that the neglect of the trustees in general had created a situation in which "vital matters tended to gravitate to a small group accessible to the office of the Foundation, chiefly Mr. Rockefeller, Mr. Fosdick, Mr. Debevoise and perhaps the president of the Foundation [Vincent]." Greene recorded in his personal account of the meeting that Mr. Rockefeller "bridled at this and interrupted to ask what evidence I had to support this contention." After stating his belief that he might be able to present such evidence, Greene confided in Rockefeller the depth of his concern over the matter as one who had been involved in the process of

31. Cohen, *Chinese Connection*, 195–96. Raymond B. Fosdick to Mary B. Bullock, 27 July 1970, quoted in Bullock, *An American Transplant*, 69.

32. Jerome Greene to Raymond B. Fosdick, 29 June 1934, Archives: Rockefeller Boards, box 12, folder 102.

securing the foundation charter. The Rockefellers had argued for the desirability of charitable trusts on the premise that it was in the public interest to have the fortunes on which they were based in public rather than private control. Greene recounted a debate held at the editorial office of the *New Republic* with Justice Brandeis, before his appointment to the Supreme Court, in which Greene had used this line of argument in representing the Rockefellers. Now Greene feared that Rockefeller had not really divested himself of control over the funds given to the foundation.

With regard to evidence of Rockefeller interference, Greene presented the matter of his brother's dismissal. Although his letter of 29 June had raised in a general way the issues that now troubled Greene, the way in which his brother had been treated was clearly the animus of his meeting with Rockefeller. Greene, as a foundation trustee, had been told on 6 July that the China Medical Board had unanimously and irrevocably recommended Roger's dismissal. Jerome questioned the meaning of "unanimous." Two trustees, Alan Gregg and Henry S. Houghton, had not been consulted (both were out of the country); moreover, "two of the members [Willard Richardson and Robert Gumbel]. . . were admittedly dummies, filling places for which competent members were shortly to be appointed." The remaining members of the board were Vincent, Fosdick, and Rockefeller III, "one of them personally retained by Mr. Rockefeller as his counsel, one a pensioner of the Foundation, and one a son of Mr. Rockefeller." Greene focused his comments on Rockefeller III, expressing the opinion that his appointment to the board had been premature and raising questions about family control of the foundation.[33]

Greene recorded that "except for the brief and quite proper interruption at the beginning of our conversation, Mr. Rockefeller listened to the above recital with great patience and good nature." Rockefeller thanked Greene for his frankness and expressed his assurance that his aims were the same as Greene's and that if there was basis to Greene's concerns, Rockefeller himself was also concerned. Debevoise offered in conclusion the thought that Mr. Rockefeller had perhaps too little

33. Jerome Greene, notes on his appointment with John D. Rockefeller, Jr., 16 November 1934, enclosed in Jerome Greene to Thomas M. Debevoise, 17 November 1934, Archives: Rockefeller Boards, box 12, folder 102.

contact with the officers of the foundation and that it was often remarked in the office that Rockefeller had less weight in proposing projects to the board than any other trustee. Rockefeller agreed, stating that Greene's own suggestions were more likely to carry weight with the board than his own. Greene agreed that open and frank participation by Rockefeller was too infrequent. Greene thought that although his many occupations made this inevitable, Rockefeller's reticence only served to support the power and mystique of his entourage in carrying out his wishes.[34]

In a lengthy letter to Fosdick, Greene labeled the incident concerning his brother "a flagrant use of money power." He charged, "The decision was made by a group so entirely identified with Mr. Rockefeller that it was in effect a Rockefeller edict. . . autocratic, ruthless and even disingenuous." He recommended that "the question of principle involved in Mr. Rockefeller's relation and that of his entourage to the foundation" be brought before the trustees. "I feel sure there is a question that ought to be faced and that not to face it has elements of grave danger both to the Foundation and to Mr. Rockefeller."[35]

In a letter to Debevoise, Greene was more respectful toward Rockefeller, but no less emphatic. He expressed the opinion that Rockefeller's characteristic "modesty and unselfishness" made it impossible for him to comprehend the "awe and deference" paid to his wishes. Greene vividly described the problem as he perceived it,

> The somewhat Olympian aloofness which his preoccupations make inevitable tends to create the impression of an unseen power working through a few persons possessing his confidence. And those persons do, as a matter of fact, wield an influence justly or unjustly attributable to their relationship with him.[36]

Allowance must be made for Greene's personal animus. His comments, nevertheless, reflect the situation that existed to some degree on every Rockefeller board. Rockefeller genuinely wanted the counsel of experts and readily deferred to it on matters of substance. On a

34. Ibid.

35. Jerome Greene to Raymond B. Fosdick, 30 November 1934, Archives: Rockefeller Boards, box 12, folder 102.

36. Jerome Greene to Thomas M. Debevoise, 17 November 1934, Archives: Rockefeller Boards, box 12, folder 102.

matter of administration or policy, however, he held the reins until his retirement in 1940, and the fact that the issue of authority was not raised many more times during his career attests to the benevolent nature of his patriarchy.[37]

Although the deeper issue was an administrative one, the differences with regard to religious policy were real. Rockefeller insisted that the modernist Protestant view of the religious mission of medical science be maintained in the P.U.M.C. Roger Greene was willing to abandon this vision; it was, in fact, a vision foreign to him. Nor was Greene alone in doubting the practicability of Rockefeller's sensibilities about the relationship between religion and science. Administrators like George Vincent and religious leaders like Thomas Cochrane were equally pessimistic about Rockefeller's project.[38]

A year after Greene's dismissal, acting director Houghton proposed scrapping the religion department, saying,

> The contrast of ends sought in education and science—practical, clear-cut, quantitative—with aims as elusive and imponderable as they appear to be in this sort of religious enterprise, is very great. The cultivation of social and spiritual values seems difficult, somehow, to integrate convincingly with medical research and teaching, or even with the practical technics of social service. . . . The Department in its present form is likely to continue indefinitely to be what it is today—extraneous, alien, peripheral.[39]

Houghton did not propose that spiritual values be ignored, but rather that moral idealism be fostered as a natural function of medical training. As for explicitly religious activities, these were to be left to the personal initiative of students, many of whom were from Christian homes and naturally would continue the student Christian fellowship.

37. For the reactions of members of Rockefeller's staff to Jerome Greene's interview, see Archives: Rockefeller Boards, box 12, folder 102.

38. George E. Vincent to John D. Rockefeller III, 21 April 1934, quoted in Bullock, *An American Transplant*, 68.

39. Henry S. Houghton, "Memorandum: Social and Religious Work," sent to John D. Rockefeller, Jr., by Raymond B. Fosdick, 16 May 1935, Archives: Rockefeller Boards, box 14, folder 130.

A weary Egbert Hayes supported this change in policy in his final report and correspondence to Rockefeller.[40]

The department was rescued, however, by the recommendation of a committee, and it continued to function during the troubled times of the Japanese War. In 1939, its director, C. F. Li, was placed under house arrest for several months, but by fall of the next year, normalcy had been restored. The Department of Religious and Social Work discussed whether religious figures such as William Ernest Hocking should be sent in order to bolster the spiritual atmosphere of the college.[41]

In December 1941, Japanese occupied the hospital, and the trappings of Protestant religion took on an ironic meaning:

> I had to entertain almost every other day the soldiers on the pipe organ. They kept on asking me to play "Nearer My God to Thee." I did not know the meaning at the beginning and asked why they liked that song so much. I was told that they were told that when an American ship sank they always played or sang this hymn. They liked to hear it because they believed all the American warships were being sunk.[42]

After the reopening of the college in the fall of 1945, Cochrane again wrote to Rockefeller, reminding him of the "gentlemen's agreement" to maintain the religious nature of the college. Rockefeller responded with characteristic consistency,

> The PUMC represented the union of the religious spirit and the scientific spirit. The importance of both was recognized from the outset and has continued to be recognized throughout the years. Those who follow in the leadership of this great undertaking would be untrue to the hopes, aspirations and obligations of

40. Egbert Hayes, "Department of Religious and Social Work: Report for the Year 1934–1935," in idem to John D. Rockefeller, Jr., 8 April 1935, Archives: Rockefeller Boards, box 14, folder 130.

41. Richard H. P. Sia, "Report of the Sub-committee on The Department of Religious and Social Work," 2 June 1936; Agnes M. Pearce, "Evidences of Continuation of Religious Work in the Peking Union Medical College," 16 December 1946, p. 4; Archives: Rockefeller Boards, box 14, folder 130.

42. Dr. Stephen Chang to Claude E. Forkner, July 1943, Archives: Rockefeller Boards, box 13, folder 111.

> its founders should they ever cease to carry out the spirit as well as the letter of these obligations and beliefs. Such an outcome is unthinkable.[43]

Despite Rockefeller's commitment, there seems to have been no improvement in the religious climate of the reorganized college in the five years before it was nationalized by the Communists. The religious spirit and the scientific spirit were never successfully united. The major obstacle to uniting the two was not, as Rockefeller had initially feared, the proselytizing commitment of the sects. It was instead the secularizing power of medical science. Rockefeller's religious sentiment enabled him to affirm the activity of God in science, but this sentiment proved as elusive to Chinese students as it was to many of Rockefeller's American colleagues.[44]

43. Thomas Cochrane to John D. Rockefeller, Jr., 1 November 1946; Rockefeller to Cochrane, 7 January 1947; Archives: Rockefeller Boards, box 14, folder 130.

44. Mary Ferguson, "Report to the Trustees of the PUMC," 13 March 1946, Archives: Rockefeller Boards, box 13, folder 112.

"In a hundred years...it is hoped and expected that the people of our country will be wiser and better and happier than now," wrote the morally earnest Rockefeller at age eleven.

"One sees all sorts of men were viewing life, duty, pleasure and the hereafter so differently," wrote Rockefeller from Brown University in 1896.

Frederick Taylor Gates, a liberal Baptist visionary, became Rockefeller's mentor when the young man entered his father's office in 1897.

William Lyon Mackenzie King (far left) introduced Rockefeller to the realities of life at the Colorado Fuel and Iron mines in the fall of 1915.

In his 1917 speech, "The Christian Church—What of Its Future?" Rockefeller called for the promotion of "applied religion" that would address "all the great problems of human life."

The Rockefeller philanthropic tradition was passed down through the generations in settings such as this World War I Red Cross meeting, where John D. III (cap with cross) and Abby (no cap) appeared with their parents and their grandfather.

Rockefeller, an executive committee member for Billy Sunday's 1917 New York Crusade, is shown here at the dedication of the Crusade Tabernacle. A few months later Rockefeller would alienate his fundamentalist friend by becoming a leading spokesperson for Protestant modernism.

Rockefeller joined a delegation of the Interchurch World Movement on a fund-raising tour in the spring of 1920 in a grand post-war attempt to marshall the forces of Protestantism to establish the kingdom of God in America.

Rockefeller joined Starr Earl Taylor, General Secretary of the Interchurch World Movement on the 1920 fundraising tour.

Rockefeller poses with Western dignitaries at the dedication of the Peking Union Medical College, September 1921. Front row, left to right: Henry S. Houghton, Paul Monroe, William H. Welch, Rockefeller, F. H. Hawkins, James Christie Reid. Second row, left to right: Francis W. Peabody, Margery K. Eggleston, Edwin R. Embree, James L. Barton, Richard M. Pearce, George E. Vincent, Roger S. Greene, Martin Ryerson.

The business of the Protestant Establishment was often conducted in venues like this exclusive New York social club, where Rockefeller's money afforded him a unique place of influence.

Rockefeller's charitable concerns regularly enabled him to cross lines of race and denomination. Rockefeller and his wife, Martha Baird Rockefeller, are pictured here with Benjamin E. Mays, President of Morehouse College, and Francis Cardinal Spelman of New York.

5

The Religion of the Inarticulate

The Protestant Establishment and Common Religion

In December 1917 Rockefeller stood before the Baptist Social Union of New York to deliver an address which later became his best-known statement on religion. He had recently returned from visiting Europe and was deeply impressed by the simple devotion to humanity he had witnessed amid the ravages of war. These self-sacrificing individuals perfectly expressed Christian values without any formal connection to religion. Theirs was "the Religion of the Inarticulate: expressed in life, not in words."[1]

Rockefeller borrowed the phrase "the Religion of the Inarticulate" from Donald Hankey, an Anglican missionary to working men and later to soldiers. In a popular book of devotional reflections, published after he was killed in action, Hankey had used the phrase to describe the vital religion of the broad group of people who "believed absolutely in the Christian virtues of unselfishness, generosity, charity, and humility," but who rejected Christianity as smug and formalistic.[2]

1. Rockefeller, "The Christian Church."
2. Donald Hankey, *A Student in Arms* (New York: Dutton, 1917) 108–9.

Given the religious sensibilities of this great multitude, Rockefeller suggested that one of three things would happen in American religion:

> Either the church must have a new birth and be reorganized to meet this great opportunity and the deepest need of the people, or. . . the Religion of the Inarticulate will develop its own church, finding its leaders among the laity, and that church will be the church of the future, and if that happens it will be conclusive proof that the church of today has failed. . . . The third possibility is that this unorganized spiritual force which is silently dominating millions will not be conserved, but will die.

The second alternative, that the followers of "the Religion of the Inarticulate" would create their own church, was possible, Rockefeller thought. He believed, however, that "the first alternative, that the church of the present day be re-born and reorganized," was the logical and the natural solution of the problem. In his speech, Rockefeller discussed the features of such a "re-born church,"[3] and in his subsequent career, he frequently attempted to realize this goal.

Rockefeller also carried on much religious philanthropy that seemed to many contemporaries and historians to be in pursuit of the other possible alternative, a new ecclesiastical structure that could embody the modern spirituality of good works expressed by the "inarticulate." This chapter will focus on this part of Rockefeller's religious work—his sponsorship of a series of organizations that, although they stood outside traditional denominational forms, still pursued the goal of a modern religious expression built from the materials of Protestantism. The following chapter will treat Rockefeller's contributions to more traditional and enduring denominational and interdenominational institutions. Rockefeller was involved in works of both types, because the third alternative suggested in his 1917 speech—the death of the modern religious impulse—was unthinkable to him. He remained firmly convinced that modern social life needed strong religious institutions.

The vision of "a united church uniting a divided world" was not new to American Protestants. Robert Handy and a host of others have shown how Protestants marched to variations on this theme from the time of legal disestablishment in the early nineteenth century until a

3. Rockefeller, "The Christian Church."

"second disestablishment" in the early twentieth century.[4] Even after Protestantism was no longer numerically dominant or secure in its place in the culture, many Protestants continued to work as a kind of religious establishment centered in cooperative Protestantism. Rockefeller took a leading role in a series of interdenominational efforts designed to enable Protestantism to continue to function as America's common religion.

Rockefeller Interdenominational Work before the War

During Rockefeller's early days in his father's office, Senior was continually inundated with requests for money from religious groups. Gates had begun the process of rationalizing the family's charitable giving. Gates's interdenominational convictions, quickly assimilated by Rockefeller, were especially important in this process.

Senior also continued giving to dozens of Baptist groups. These included the national groups—such as the Foreign and Home Mission Societies, the Education Society, the Publication Society, and the Ministers' Home Society for Aged and Infirmed Ministers—as well as state and local mission societies near his homes. Increasingly, however, Senior directed his giving toward interdenominational endeavors. These included revivalist organizations such as the Evangelistic Committee of New York City, which from 1905 until 1917 held tent campaigns throughout the city featuring Billy Sunday and others. There were also ventures in social outreach, such as YMCA projects under the leadership of John R. Mott.[5]

A major episode in Rockefeller's development as a religious philanthropist occurred in 1911 and involved Mott. Mott, representing the Continuation Committee of the World Missionary Conference, Edinburgh, approached Rockefeller, Sr., with a request for a one million

4. Robert T. Handy, *A Christian America: Protestant Hopes and Historical Realities* (New York: Oxford University Press, 1971) 184.

5. After the war, Rockefeller, Sr., gave minor support to revival meetings in New York City; he lunched with Gypsy Smith in January 1920, expressing his willingness to support a campaign later that year. See John D. Rockefeller, Jr., memo, 29 January 1920; Archives: Religious Interests, box 46, folder 364; also see other materials in the same location.

dollar endowment for a center to promote and unify the missionary forces of the West. In China and elsewhere, Mott saw interdenominational cooperation as the most important issue facing the world missionary enterprise. In an extended interview with Gates, Mott described the hindrances to Protestant unity that he had encountered in his twenty-three years as an international leader of interdenominational causes. He stated that he wished to spend the rest of his life working for the unification of the Protestant mission. Mott was seeking funds for a multifaceted program, including research, education, and the development of a world mission archive, but his aim was "to bring together in confidence for future cooperative effort on a larger scale the leaders of the aggressive forces of Christianity."[6]

Gates ended the interview by explaining Senior's policy of not endowing organizations and suggested that Mott might expect, at most, an initial contribution of fifty thousand dollars, with annual contributions that would by five thousand dollars each year. Upon reading the pertinent materials, including a transcript of Mott's interview with Gates, the younger Rockefeller was very enthusiastic. He suggested that the family accept Mott's counterproposal—a total pledge of five hundred thousand dollars over ten years, beginning with seventy thousand dollars the first year. "I feel that we should uphold Mr. Mott's hands. He is unquestionably the man for this work. I do not believe there is any living man who could accomplish what he is in a position to accomplish. I feel, therefore, that we should help him financially to as great an extent as we can without injuring his work." The report that eventually reached Senior from Rockefeller, Gates, and Starr Murphy spoke of the danger of moving beyond the consensus of the missionaries themselves with regard to interdenominationalism, and Senior did not see fit to fund the venture in 1911.[7]

The episode was an important one, nonetheless, because Mott's request came at the time when Rockefeller was considering the work

6. Frederick T. Gates interview with John R. Mott, 23 June 1911, Archives: Religious Interests, box 46, folder 365.

7. John D. Rockefeller, Jr., to Frederick T. Gates, 4 July 1911; Starr J. Murphy to Rockefeller, 18 July 1911; Archives: Religious Interests, box 46, folder 365.

of the Baptist Board of Foreign Missions, to which his father had been the major contributor, and developing what would be lasting convictions about interdenominational effort. During the summer of 1911, Rockefeller was evaluating criticisms about inefficiency which a member of the Baptist board had made. Rockefeller turned to Gates for counsel, and Gates responded with a handwritten note giving a sweeping statement of his vision for Christian mission. According to Gates, there was one central problem with the Baptist endeavor—sectarianism: "*because of Bigoted Sectarianism* which puts four or five evangelical churches all over the United States in communities which should *unite* on *one* & thus get. . . an able pastor and leader. There are five times *too many ministers to be supported at home.*" The following was crossed out of the letter preserved in the Rockefeller files, but remained legible: "Conclusion. Sight lies with Mott & *his* plans. No small changes or inquiries in Boston will touch the root of the matter."[8] A week later, Gates wrote with further thoughts on the subject and concluded that "the faults are faults of *policy*, and that these faults lie in the *nature* of the home situation, the ministry and the churches and their current beliefs, that these are *slowly* to be changed and by the operation of forces that are *cosmic* and that we can do something to help the matter, but only indirectly."[9]

Throughout the fall of 1911, Gates continued to share his thoughts on the subject with Rockefeller. In an October memo Gates described what he saw as the state of Protestantism in America. It consisted, he thought, mostly of rural churches, small, struggling, impoverished, yet continuing to compete. Gates favored the union of evangelical churches in each locality—both in America and on the mission field. He was convinced that union was the rational way to insure adequate resources for worship centers and mission programs. Sectarianism was an offense to his progressive sensibilities. It was "the curse of religion at home and abroad; a blight upon religion, whether viewed from an economic, intellectual or spiritual standpoint." As Gates saw

8. Frederick T. Gates to John D. Rockefeller, Jr., 23 July 1911, Archives: Religious Interests, box 46, folder 365.

9. Frederick T. Gates to John D. Rockefeller, Jr., 30 July 1911, Archives: Religious Interests, box 2, folder 5.

it, the unification of evangelistic denominations would "solve more problems of human progress than any other single reform."[10]

When Mott renewed his request in 1913, it was referred to the newly formed Rockefeller Foundation. The foundation's officers, including executive secretary Jerome Greene, were in the process of defining what kinds of projects it would sponsor. Greene's family had deep roots in the missionary tradition. He found himself favorably disposed toward Mott's plan, although he had two reservations. The first regarded suspicions about Mott's sincerity based on Mott's practice of cultivating support from conservatives as well as liberals. The second, which would also be an issue in Greene's thinking about the China Medical Board, was his concern for the proper use of foundation funds. He felt that "the well-being of mankind" precluded "any proposal to advance the purely sectarian or denominational interests of any religious bodies."[11]

Greene drafted a response to Mott stating that any religious programs funded by the foundation must not present Christianity as the only true religion, nor should it try to displace other religious traditions. In contrast, such a religious program must express "the hunger and thirst of the human soul after righteousness"; it must make "an ethical and spiritual contribution to the life of non-Christian peoples" and be open to receive from those to whom it came "much that is valuable in their own religious traditions or instincts."[12]

Although Rockefeller agreed with Greene's sentiments, he expressed reservations about Greene's proposed reply to Mott. It set a requirement that Rockefeller thought would "prove an insurmountable barrier" to Mott, given the general state of mind found among the churches. Rockefeller agreed that Greene's response articulated ideals toward which the foundation should strive, but he also thought that the foundation would find no mission organization that presently embodied them. Mott's plan would "be the most potent factor imagin-

10. Frederick T. Gates to John D. Rockefeller, Jr., 19 October 1911, Archives: Gates Papers, box 3, folder 58.

11. Jerome Greene to John D. Rockefeller, Jr., 23 July 1913, Archives: Religious Interests, box 46, folder 365.

12. Jerome Greene, draft of letter to John R. Mott, 21 July 1913, Archives: Religious Interests, box 46, folder 365.

able" in bringing American Protestants one step in the desired direction. Mott not only shared the ideals that Greene had expressed, but also had a stature within Protestant circles that enabled these ideals to be heard. Rockefeller suggested that the board view Greene's principles as guidelines rather than requirements and recommended that the foundation fund Mott's proposal.[13]

The board referred the matter to its executive committee, which consisted of Murphy, Gates, Greene, and Rockefeller. The executive committee decided that insofar as Mott's plan would "help to present the Christian religion to the non-Christian world not only more efficiently and economically, but also in a broadly humanitarian, as distinguished from a sectarian spirit, the project was one that might legitimately command the sympathy and aid of the Rockefeller Foundation." The committee, however, also commissioned Greene to contact the executives of several of the denominational mission boards that Mott hoped to unite, including members of the Baptist Missionary Board, Robert E. Speer of the Presbyterian Board of Foreign Mission, Arthur S. Lloyd of the Missionary Society of the Protestant Episcopal Church, and James L. Barton of the American Board of Commissioners for Foreign Missions. All praised Mott's abilities and goals, but felt that such an effort should be undertaken by the cooperating denominational agencies themselves, not by a free agent like Mott. According to Greene, Speer spoke strongly, stressing that Mott thought of himself as "a champion of Christianity rather than as a champion of the Christian Church." Speer thought that Mott's interdenominational involvements had led him to forget the importance of the "Church as an historic institution." Speer, Greene reported, attached great importance to the "Church in its various denominational forms" and felt "bound to jealously guard its prerogative as God's agent on earth for the accomplishment of His Divine purposes." Greene decided to recommend against Mott's plan.[14]

Based on Greene's recommendation, the foundation rejected Mott's request, having "come to the conclusion that the success, and indeed

13. John D. Rockefeller, Jr., to Jerome Greene, attached to Greene's draft letter of 21 July 1913, Archives: Religious Interests, box 46, folder 365.

14. Jerome Greene, memos, 8 September and 21 October 1913, Archives: Religious Interests, box 46, folder 365.

the justification, of the whole enterprise properly depends upon its being both initiated and controlled by the boards and agencies themselves." In his letter to Mott, Greene explained that the foundation wished to avoid any appearance of pressuring Protestant missionary agencies "to go further in the direction of cooperation and unity than their own independent desire or a due consideration for the sentiment of their respective constituents would permit." If, however, the agencies themselves were to formulate a plan along the lines of Mott's, the foundation would entertain a request for up to one-half of its cost.[15]

Never one to look a gift horse in the mouth, Mott proceeded to use his political skills to obtain the cooperation demanded. By March 1914 Mott had secured the necessary support; in April, the Foundation approved a four hundred and fifty thousand dollar grant over ten years. The resulting Committee of Reference and Counsel, Foreign Missions Conference of North America worked together with the Student Volunteer Movement, the World's Student Christian Federation, and the Edinburgh Continuation Committee on research, strategy, and training. The achievement and steadily growing support of the denominations for this enterprise pleased Rockefeller so much that he personally contributed more than one hundred and sixty thousand dollars to its programs, including the Missionary Research Library, which was housed at Union Seminary in New York.[16]

Historian Charles Harvey has written two illuminating articles about both the relationship between Mott and Rockefeller and the differences between Mott and Speer regarding the importance of the church.[17] Harvey rightly traces the reticence of Speer and other denominational representatives regarding some Mott and Rockefeller initiatives to their doubts as to whether lay leaders like Mott and

15. Jerome Greene to John R. Mott, 3 October 1913, Archives: Religious Interests, box 46, folder 365.

16. Correspondence between John D. Rockefeller, Jr., and the Committee of Reference and Counsel, 1914–29, Archives: Religious Interests, box 46, folder 365; memo entitled "Missionary Research Library," 21 December 1933, Archives: Religious Interests, box 47, folder 367.

17. Charles E. Harvey, "John D. Rockefeller, Jr., and the Interchurch World Movement of 1919–1920: A Different Angle on the Ecumenical Movement," *CH* 51 (1982) 198–209; and idem, "Speer Versus Rockefeller and Mott, 1910–1935," *Journal of Presbyterian History* 60 (1982) 283–99.

Rockefeller ought to be allowed to modernize the Protestant mission at a pace opposed by denominational constituencies. Although Harvey suggests that Rockefeller agreed more with Mott than with Speer on this matter, there is much evidence to suggest that Rockefeller was sympathetic to both. Rockefeller found in Mott a dynamic spokesperson who shared his ideals, but found in Speer a deliberate style more resonant with his own. As the next chapter will show, Rockefeller lent support not only to a series of ventures urged by Mott, but also to denominational and federal expressions of Protestantism.

Before the war, moreover, the tensions between Mott's vision and Speer's were not yet apparent to most Protestants. Idealism and enthusiasm for the common cause of Protestant conquest more than compensated for disagreements over style and method. Every Protestant leader—Speer included—was in a hurry, and the taint of Rockefeller money was not sufficient cause for qualms. In 1914 Mott was able to gain for his initiative the denominational support that Rockefeller required, and thus—somewhat ironically—he was able to free the endeavor from the appearance of control by those outside denominational circles. Greene wrote to Ivy L. Lee, "There could not be a clearer case of the unwillingness of the Rockefeller Foundation to assume an initiatory or controlling function."[18]

In the immediate postwar period, enthusiasm for a unified Protestant crusade seemed to return to its prewar level. The last gasp of such enthusiasm, however, would be the ill-fated Interchurch World Movement of 1919–1920. After the demise of this movement, promotion of the two expressions of Protestant ideals—the denominational and the national—could not be held together effectively. Denominational Protestantism would become a major institutional force in American life; its interests, however, were not primarily centered in rhetoric about a Christian America. The "Religion of the Inarticulate"—a common religion for American culture—would remain the dream of a few. Rockefeller would be a patron of both.[19]

18. Jerome Greene to Ivy Lee, 30 April 1914, Archives: Religious Interests, box 46, folder 365.

19. John D. Rockefeller, Jr., to James M. Speers, 5 May 1919; Speers to Rockefeller, 9 July 1919; Archives: Religious Interests, box 38, folder 315.

The Interchurch World Movement: The Inarticulate Say "No"

The Interchurch World Movement (I.W.M.) was an unsuccessful attempt to unify all the missionary and benevolent endeavors of the major Protestant denominations and parachurch groups into a single coordinated effort. It was constructed on the assumption that the United States would support Protestantism's peacetime crusade as it had supported the war. The idea of the I.W.M. was launched on 17 December 1918 at a meeting of one hundred and thirty-five representatives of American Protestant mission boards and related agencies. As Presbyterian representative William Adams Brown remembered four years later, veteran leaders of the Protestant mission—secretaries of church boards, professors in theological seminaries, home and foreign missionaries—fell "under the spell" induced by "the vision of a united church uniting a divided world." They agreed to launch a major Protestant offensive to win America and the world; "difficulties were waved aside, doubters were silenced."[20]

A committee of twenty, including both Mott and Speer, carried forward the vision of this group. It announced the formation of the I.W.M. on 6 February 1919. Ignoring the existence of the Federal Council of Churches and other interdenominational groups, the I.W.M. proposed to make itself the organizing agency for the forces of American mainline Protestantism.[21]

Not everyone was as impressed as William Adams Brown. Cornelius Woelfkin, pastor of Fifth Avenue Baptist, wrote to Rockefeller a few days after the I.W.M. was formed, expressing bewilderment over the momentum of the movement. Although he supported "closer cooperation in our united service," Woelfkin remarked at the lack of specificity of program in an organization making such large claims. Perhaps, he concluded, like "the proposition of the League of Nations," the undertaking contained merit, but would need "frank discussion" before it found its final form.[22]

20. William A. Brown, *The Church in America: A Study of the Present Condition and Future Prospects of American Protestantism* (New York: Macmillan, 1922) 119, quoted in Sydney E. Ahlstrom, *A Religious History of the American People* (New Haven: Yale University Press, 1972) 897.

21. See Hopkins, *Mott*, 569–74.

22. Cornelius Woelfkin to John D. Rockefeller, Jr., 14 February 1919,

Rockefeller took no role in the I.W.M. during 1919, despite various attempts to recruit his participation. At the World Survey Conference in Atlantic City in January 1920—the first major public event of the I.W.M.—Rockefeller first associated himself with the movement. In this meeting, seventeen hundred of Protestantism's religious, educational, and social-scientific leaders gathered to hear reports based on nine months of surveying the resources and field work of Protestantism's major enterprises. It was reported that "140 different boards representing thirty-four Protestant denominations, covering the entire range of Christian activity"—between eighty and ninety percent of all American Protestant missions—had affiliated with the movement, and twenty of Protestantism's major parachurch organizations had joined them.[23]

Rockefeller gave a major address at the conference, praising the movement in extravagant terms. He stated his belief that the I.W.M. would "become the greatest force for righteousness in the whole world." Rockefeller presented a list of "advantages accruing to the churches" from the movement. At the top of his list were efficiency, economy, and scientific grounding. Modernity demanded of the church a new degree of scientific sophistication in carrying out its ministry. As Rockefeller put it,

> For too long a time has the church felt that the rule-of-thumb was sufficiently accurate as a guide and measure in its work. This great survey is prophetic of a new era in Christian work. It is just such a survey as the conservative business man makes of any field which he is proposing to enter.

Only a modernized Protestantism was fit for guardianship of America and the world, and the I.W.M. epitomized modern ideals.[24]

In Rockefeller's view, efficiency and economy would obviously be achieved by cooperation. If the traditional ideal of Protestant benevolence was the long-range context for the interdenominational efforts

---

Archives: Religious Interests, box 38, folder 315.

23. William B. Millar to John D. Rockefeller, Jr., 24 February 1919; John R. Mott to Rockefeller, 13 November 1919; Archives: Religious Interests, box 38, folder 315.

24. John D. Rockefeller, Jr., "All Paths Meet at the Mountain Top" (New York: I.W.M., 1920) pp. 1–7, Archives: Religious Interests, box 39, folder 321.

supported by Rockefeller between 1919 and 1934, the war effort was the more recent context. For Rockefeller and the enthusiasts of the I.W.M., the lesson of the war was that cooperation under centralized leadership was essential to victory. Rockefeller reasoned that the war industries had brought the nation victory because they had been willing to cooperate under a general committee of management. If the cooperative principle were applied during times of peace, "the Christian people of the land would stand effectively against the foes of righteousness and overthrow the cohorts of evil."[25] The churches themselves had cooperated extremely effectively during the war, concluding their war-related efforts by participating in the "largest voluntary offering in the history of the world," the one hundred and seventy-five million dollar United War Work Campaign.

Of course, modern businessmen had already known the advantages of combination of effort, and big business also provided models for the I.W.M. The movement's promotional literature announced, "Christ needs big men for big business. . . the biggest business of the biggest man in the world. Christ was big, was He not? None ever bigger. Christ was busy, was he not? None ever busier. He was always about His Father's business."[26]

Businesslike efficiency was one of the chief selling points during the movement's fund-raising effort. On an I.W.M. promotional tour, Rockefeller himself assured crowds in at least two cities that there was no waste in the massive operations of the movement. A fund-raising pamphlet published by the I.W.M. was entitled, "The Church Takes a Leaf From Successful Business." It read, "Do you know why nine out of every ten business ventures fail? *They lacked the facts! . . . The church today has the facts.*"[27]

25. Ibid., 2–3.

26. Eldon Ernst, *Moment of Truth for Protestant America: Interchurch Campaigns Following World War One* (Missoula, MT: Scholars Press, 1972) 89. For background, see Alan Trachtenberg, *The Incorporation of American Culture: Culture and Society in the Gilded Age* (New York: Hill & Wang, 1982); and Rolf Lunden, *Business and Religion in the American 1920s* (New York: Greenwood, 1988) 1–88. Compare Bruce Barton's concept of Jesus in *The Man Nobody Knows.*

27. I.W.M., "The Church Takes a Leaf from Successful Business," March 1920, p. 2, Archives: Religious Interests, box 39, folder 325.

In another statement written for the I.W.M., Rockefeller focused on the need for modernizing one of the churches' central ministries—education. Rockefeller pronounced the Sunday School in need of reorganization. Despite its dedicated and earnest teachers, the typical Sunday School offered "a grade of teaching we would not tolerate in our day schools," he lamented. Unless the churches provided "special training" for their teachers, they could not expect "efficiency and a higher grade of instruction." For Rockefeller, the issue was simple—Protestantism could no longer succeed with nineteenth-century methods. It needed to embrace the same progressive values on which Rockefeller was building his secular philanthropy.[28]

At the Atlantic City meeting, Rockefeller was elected to the Executive Committee of the movement and asked to serve as vice-chairperson, although he declined the latter position.[29] One thing that attracted Rockefeller as well as Mott, who chaired the Executive Committee, was their desire that the I.W.M. was leading denominational leaders in the interdenominational path. Perhaps, they hoped, American Protestants were ready for rapid movement toward interdenominational principles. Mott seemed to speak for the movement as a whole when he said,

> Without sacrificing our distinctiveness, we want to realize our unity and solidarity as we gather around the figure of our Lord with open minds, responsive hearts, and, I would say, hair-trigger wills—by that I mean wills that are eager to leap into action when we see a clear path.[30]

A second point of attraction for Rockefeller was the movement's importance to the nation. In an article that Rockefeller wrote for the movement but which was never used, Rockefeller expressed the hope that denominational Protestantism might be ready to modernize itself for the ongoing function of providing a common religion for American culture. Rockefeller stated that he was a church member, in part, because he believed that "the state, the nation, business and social life"

28. Rockefeller, "Why I Am A Church Member."

29. William H. Foulkes to John D. Rockefeller, Jr., 10 January 1920; Rockefeller to Foulkes, 29 January 1920; Archives: Religious Interests, box 38, folder 317.

30. Quoted in Hopkins, *Mott*, 571.

were all "built upon the Christian church." According to Rockefeller, most Americans realized that social order was built on the principles of "right, justice and fair dealing which the church more than any other institution stands for and maintains in the community." The church undergirded the financial system, public morality, marriage, temperance, and Sabbath observance. Although the church might be justly charged with narrowness, Rockefeller wrote that nevertheless it had "stood for that which was highest" and that "we must ever look for leadership and moral support in maintaining these standards."[31]

One would have expected in this piece, which is the closest thing to a "personal testimony" that we have from Rockefeller, that he would have spoken primarily of religion in its social function. The center of Rockefeller's religious concern was not in spiritual experience or theology, but in a social gospel—not the social gospel of a reformer, but that of a philanthropic builder interested in social stability.

This is not to say that Rockefeller did not sound notes of prophetic reform in describing his vision for an America imbued with religious principles. He denounced any church member "who sanctions, much less promotes, principles in his business that are contrary to the teachings of Christ." The church, Rockefeller wrote, had to recognize its responsibility for social problems, such as "the employment of children in industry, the sweat shop, unsanitary working conditions, the crowded and unwholesome living conditions too often found in crowded cities, the lack of wholesome amusement and recreation, inadequate health and safety precautions."

Nor does the characterization of Rockefeller as a philanthropist interested in social stability suggest that Rockefeller's social gospel required no personal commitment. Rockefeller professed to live in accordance with a "profound conviction" about the church's importance and a "profound belief" in "God's love as manifested in Christ's life." In language made popular by social gospel novelist Charles Sheldon, Rockefeller stated, "Although a very imperfect follower of that God to whose service my life is dedicated, although constantly

31. Rockefeller, "Why I Am a Church Member."

making mistakes, the purpose of my life is to follow in His footsteps."[32]

Rockefeller was willing to accept the narrowness of denominational particularity to insure the greater good of social stability. The I.W.M. seemed to represent a united religious front against the forces of evil in America. There were, however, substantial flaws in the seamless garment. Although the I.W.M. was called into being by denominational and parachurch executives, these executives had no clear mandate from their constituencies. The rhetoric of the group bespoke unity for Protestant Christendom, but its structure lacked the philosophical clarity of the Federal Council of Churches. The question of duplication of the council's efforts initially troubled Rockefeller. Starr Earl Taylor, the movement's general secretary, assured Rockefeller that the best minds felt that despite the dangers of duplication, the I.W.M. ought to proceed. He also acknowledged that "when things are sufficiently settled as to permanent policy," the I.W.M. would have to attend to "the whole big question of relationships on a national and international scale."[33]

Rockefeller, like many others, laid his doubts aside and began to perform various tasks for the movement. In February he solicited a public statement of support from his father. The statement called for an application of the spiritual forces that had won World War I to the task of establishing the kingdom of God and recommended the I.W.M. as having the potential to "contribute largely to this end." During the months of March and April 1920, he devoted a great deal of his time to promoting the movement in preparation for its unprecedented united fund-raising drive to be held from 25 April until 2 May.[34]

Little did he suspect that the organization would be in total disarray by the end of the fund-raising drive. As historian Eldon Ernst has

32. Ibid.; see also Sheldon, *In His Steps*.

33. John D. Rockefeller, Jr., to Starr E. Taylor, 10 February 1920; Taylor to Rockefeller, 27 February 1920; Archives: Religious Interests, box 38, folder 317. The Federal Council was to do its part for the I.W.M., devoting *Federal Council Bulletin* 9 (1920) entirely to the work; see Archives: Religious Interests, box 39, folder 324.

34. John D. Rockefeller, Sr. to Starr E. Taylor, 1 March 1920, Archives: Religious Interests, box 38, folder 317.

pointed out, the movement was structured in such a way that it depended on the nonsectarian Protestant public for its success. Although several denominations underwrote loans for the quickly burgeoning administrative tasks of the movement, no denominational money was given or budgeted for that purpose. The loans underwritten by denominations were to be repaid after the United Simultaneous Financial Campaign, during which the I.W.M. was to appeal to the "friendly citizens" of Protestantism in America for forty million dollars for its administrative expenses, while the denominations were to raise an additional three hundred million dollars from their specific constituencies.[35]

This nonsectarian "friendly citizens campaign" especially attracted the attention of Rockefeller. He saw the movement as an opportunity to appeal to the "inarticulate" masses as a part of a nationwide religious crusade. For this reason, during the month of March, Rockefeller threw himself wholeheartedly into the fund-raising campaign. He wrote a magazine article, quoted above, entitled "Why I Am a Church Member." He underwrote a loan of one million dollars to insure the movement's survival until after the campaign. He spoke on behalf of the movement in New York, Rochester, and Chicago and recruited participants for a promotional tour of fourteen cities, scheduled for mid-April, which would begin in the nation's capital and would culminate in a rally in his home city, New York. His correspondence in recruiting participants for this tour provides a colorful chronicle of the failure of Protestantism's "friendly citizens" to answer the call to battle.[36]

Rockefeller called on the full range of his business, educational, and political contacts for the campaign tour. In no other file of Rockefeller correspondence does one find so many letters of rejection.

35. Eldon Ernst's fine study of the I.W.M., *Moment of Truth for Protestant America: Interchurch Campaigns Following World War One*, was written without benefit of the Rockefeller files and does not treat Rockefeller's role in the movement extensively.

36. Lyman L. Pierce to John D. Rockefeller, Jr., 6 February 1920; Rockefeller to Abram E. Cory, 7 March 1920; Archives: Religious Interests, box 38, folder 321. Rockefeller to W. P. Belknap, 30 April 1920, Archives: Religious Interests, box 38, folder 318.

Secretary of State Robert Lansing was too busy; Secretary of Labor William B. Wilson was ill; Interior Secretary Franklin K. Lane had a daughter's wedding to plan; financier George W. Perkins was not well; wartime food administrator Herbert Hoover had duties to attend to as president of the Engineer's Society. Governors William G. Sproul of Pennsylvania, Henry J. Allen of Kansas, and former Governor Myron T. Herrick of Ohio sent regrets, as did Senators Carter Glass of Virginia and Selden P. Spencer of Missouri. Congressman James W. Good of Iowa sent regrets because of the press of business in Washington. AFL Secretary Frank Morrison found it impossible to consider the invitation because of federation business. Economist Roger W. Babson would try to make three meetings, but the entire trip would be impossible. Businessman James C. Colgate, a member of Fifth Avenue Baptist Church, was not able to travel on such short notice.[37]

Both Rockefeller and Taylor asked Billy Sunday to endorse the drive. The evangelist offered only halfhearted support because of the involvement of liberals, because religious promoters rather than spiritual leaders were at the helm, and because he discerned an antirevivalistic spirit in the outlook of the group.[38]

Real estate tycoon Alfred Marling, a Presbyterian, along with philanthropist Cleveland Dodge and former Justice Charles Evans Hughes, a member of Fifth Avenue Baptist Church, agreed to serve with Rockefeller on the committee for the New York meeting. Arthur E. Bestor, president of the Chautauqua Institution and also a Fifth Avenue Baptist member, agreed to take the responsibility of executive chairperson of the financial campaign, but only after making clear that he had little time for administrative details. Even Mott, anxious to turn his attention to international responsibilities, planned to resign

37. Robert Lansing to John D. Rockefeller, Jr., 12 March 1920; Edward S. McGraw to Rockefeller, 13 March 1920; Franklin K. Lane to Rockefeller, 14 March 1920; Rockefeller to George W. Perkins, 17 March 1920; Herbert Hoover to Rockefeller, 18 March 1920; Rockefeller to William H. Foulkes, 25 March 1920; memo entitled, "Re. Interchurch World Movement: Telegrams, Letters"; Rockefeller to Lyman L. Pierce, 29 March 1920; Archives: Religious Interests, box 38, folder 317.

38. John D. Rockefeller, Jr., to William A. Sunday, 29 April 1920; Sunday to Starr E. Taylor, 5 May 1920; Rockefeller to John R. Mott, 26 March 1920; Archives: Religious Interests, box 38, folder 318.

from the Executive Committee in late March until Rockefeller and others persuaded him otherwise.[39]

By 31 March 1920, Rockefeller was beginning to foresee a dismal financial picture. He wrote to James Speers, treasurer of the movement, making a formal offer to underwrite one million dollars of the I.W.M.'s expenses and suggesting "further reductions from the budget."[40] At the same time Rockefeller solicited a one million dollar contribution from his father. Senior responded cautiously, not only because he had already given nine million dollars to Baptist causes in the past year, but out of fear of the financial projections of the movement:

> It occurs to me that in this large movement we must be careful to observe our limitations so that we shall not be expected to give unless the amounts desired are secured; in other words, that we do not give at the inception of the undertaking and then find ourselves, because of our prominent relation to the movement, obliged to stand in the gap and give for others, who might conclude that we should see it through. I think we should be very careful on this point.[41]

Junior responded with the suggestion that Senior stop giving directly to the Baptists, and give between fifty and one hundred million dollars to the Spelman Memorial for transfer to the I.W.M. when it proved sufficiently stable to handle the donation. In still another appeal to his father for support, Rockefeller stated that the importance of the I.W.M. could not, in his opinion, be overestimated: "As I see it, it is capable of having a much more far-reaching influence than the League of Nations in bringing about peace, contentment, good-will and prosperity among the people of the earth."[42]

As the days passed and the situation grew more desperate, Senior at last responded to Junior's request. He agreed to announce an un-

39. Arthur Bestor to John D. Rockefeller, Jr., 25 March 1920, Archives: Religious Interests, box 38, folder 318.

40. John D. Rockefeller, Jr., to James M. Speers, 31 March 1920, Archives: Religious Interests, box 38, folder 317.

41. John D. Rockefeller, Jr., to John D. Rockefeller, Sr., 1 April 1920; Rockefeller, Sr., to Rockefeller, 7 April 1920; Archives: Religious Interests, box 38, folder 317.

42. John D. Rockefeller, Jr., to John D. Rockefeller, Sr., 16 April 1920; Rockefeller, Jr., to Rockefeller, Sr., 21 April 1920; Rockefeller, Jr., to Rockefeller, Sr., 3 May 1920; Archives: Religious Interests, box 38, folder 318.

conditional pledge of five hundred thousand dollars. He also said he was willing to give one hundred and twenty-five thousand dollars when the I.W.M.'s receipts reached five, six, seven, and eight million dollars—in total, an additional five hundred thousand dollars, but he wondered whether it might not be wiser to "delay and see what others do" before announcing this additional series of gifts.[43]

The promotional tour was a mixed success. Governor Milliken of Maine was one of the few celebrities to join Rockefeller and executives Starr Taylor, James Speers, Wilton Merle Smith, and William Foulkes. Business manager Abram E. Cory reported that meetings were well attended, with the largest crowd—eight to ten thousand—gathered in Kansas City. The substance of Rockefeller's remarks at each stop on the tour was the same as his Atlantic City address; he proclaimed that the I.W.M. would give America the modern church it needed.[44] While on the tour, Rockefeller sent wires to thirty-three of New York's leading families, including the Morgans, the Astors, the Du Ponts, the Pratts, and the Sloanes, encouraging them to support the New York meeting.

At home, Arthur Bestor drew on his experience in marketing Chautauqua's offerings of adult education and popular entertainment to hawk the New York gathering as "a remarkable meeting at the Hippodrome. . . with panoramic views, a series of striking pictures, [and] a large chorus."[45] Rejections, however, continued to pour in. The most painful of all came from Rockefeller's Sunday School mentor, Charles Evans Hughes, who at the last minute was forced to withdraw as master of ceremonies because of the severe illness of his daughter. The New York City meeting went on without him and without many others.[46]

43. John D. Rockefeller, Sr., to John D. Rockefeller, Jr., 27 April 1920; Archives: Religious Interests, box 38, folder 318.

44. "Substance of Remarks of John D. Rockefeller, Jr., at Interchurch World Movement Meetings," Archives: Religious Interests, box 39, folder 321.

45. Arthur Bestor to a long list of potential supporters, 14 April 1920, Archives: Religious Interests, box 38, folder 317.

46. Charles E. Hughes to John D. Rockefeller, Jr., 15 April 1920; Archives: Religious Interests, box 38, folder 317. See also James M. Speers, Abram E. Cory, Raymond B. Fosdick, and Carl Van Winkle, "History of the Interchurch World Movement," unpublished official documents bound in 2

After the tour Rockefeller retreated to Hot Springs, Virginia, but continued to send telegrams for the financial campaign, which lasted from 25 April until 2 May, while at the same time hosting meetings of the General Education and China Medical Boards. Seventy of America's wealthiest persons and families were assiduously solicited, including those listed above, as well as the Frick, Macy, Carnegie, Pinchot, Sage, and Vanderbilt families. Only Arthur Curtiss James (a New York merchant), and Mrs. Willard D. Straight (wife of the prominent ex-consul general to China) responded with significant contributions. Cyrus McCormick could usually be counted on to contribute to Protestant crusades, but even substantial correspondence with Rockefeller failed to convince McCormick of the wisdom of the united movement.[47]

Despite the efforts of Rockefeller and others, the I.W.M. campaign to "friendly citizens" was an utter failure. It raised only three million dollars, one third of which came from the elder Rockefeller. The United Drive as a whole raised one hundred and seventy-six million dollars; although this was the largest single offering ever received for religious work, it was only half the desired amount. Only Rockefeller's intervention—which included contributions of more than one and a half million dollars and the assignment of family lawyer Raymond Fosdick to the task of sorting out the financial records—saved the movement from more serious scandal.

Fosdick entered the office in mid-May at the request of Rockefeller and Taylor and kept Rockefeller informed as he unraveled the tangle of the I.W.M. office. Ironically, given the movement's rhetoric about the application of scientific principles to religious endeavor, the organization had been an administrative disaster.[48] An auditor reported to

---

volumes for office use, vol. 2, chap. 5, p. 128, Archives: Religious Interests, box 40, folder 327.

47. John D. Rockefeller, Jr., to John D. Rockefeller, Sr., 3 May 1920, Archives: Religious Interests, box 38, folder 318. Rockefeller to list of seventy, Archives: Religious Interests, box 39, folder 323; in this location, see especially Rockefeller to Cyrus H. McCormick, 4 and 26 May 1920; McCormick to Rockefeller, 21 June 1920.

48. John D. Rockefeller to Starr E. Taylor, 17 May 1920; Rockefeller to Raymond B. Fosdick, 19 May 1920; Archives: Religious Interests, box 38, folder 318. See Fosdick to Rockefeller, 7 June 1920, Archives: Fosdick Pa-

Fosdick that the handling of the affairs of the movement bespoke "criminal carelessness." Years later, when Fosdick was preparing his biography of Rockefeller, an office associate commented on the irony of the fact that the meticulous Rockefeller had defended the operations of the movement on the assurances of its officers: "The way poor Mr. Rockefeller was 'worked' by these ecclesiastical politicians was truly astounding. Think of 'using' him to refute charges of extravagance."[49]

On 28 June the movement discontinued activities. On 2 July Fosdick suggested to Rockefeller that he consider paying the debt of between five and six hundred thousand dollars. A week later, things looked somewhat better to Fosdick. The movement had been placed under the direction of a subcommittee consisting of Fosdick and James Speers. Fosdick urged Rockefeller to lend some of the needed money against denominational underwriting, but not to supply it all. In August the movement was placed in the hands of a committee on reorganization under the direction of Methodist bishop Thomas Nicholson. In October Rockefeller joined the denominations that had underwritten the movement in clearing its bank indebtedness. He wrote a check for one million dollars. Although he formally resigned from the Executive Committee of the I.W.M. on 17 January 1921, Rockefeller continued to shoulder financial responsibility for the movement. On 19 January 1921, Rockefeller fully secured a loan so that the I.W.M. could pay three-quarters of a million dollars in back rent, and he pledged to pick up all other outstanding expenses. In the spring of 1922 he agreed to pay for the writing of the history of the I.W.M. On 13 November 1922, he surrendered four hundred thousand dollars of the seven hundred thousand dollars that he had underwritten. An

pers, box 1 folder 2, for an example of Fosdick's reports to Rockefeller. See Rockefeller to James M. Speers, 11 August 1920, Archives: Religious Interests, box 39, folder 319, regarding the extent of Rockefeller's knowledge of the situation.

49. D. B. Victor to Raymond B. Fosdick, 26 July 1920, Archives: Religious Interests, box 39, folder 319; Tyler Dennett to John D. Rockefeller, Jr., 17 April 1920, Archives: Religious Interests, box 38, folder 318. Alexander W. Armour to Fosdick, 20 April 1951, Archives: Fosdick Papers, box 1, folder 2.

additional thirty thousand dollars cleared the movement's debts in June 1923. Rockefeller's personal contributions by that time totaled a million and a half dollars.[50]

The extent of Rockefeller's involvement in the I.W.M. bailout was generally unknown, and Rockefeller steadfastly kept this knowledge from the public. When, for example, a Baptist from Watertown, Massachusetts, prompted by a newspaper report of Rockefeller's purchase of the fifteenth-century tapestries, "Hunting for the Unicorn," at between one and one and a half million dollars, wrote to ask why he did not contribute to the Baptist denomination the million dollars it had lost as a result of its underwriting of the I.W.M., the response of Rockefeller's staff did not betray the extent of his own financial involvement in the endeavor.[51]

Eldon Ernst has understood the I.W.M. episode as a "moment of truth" for American Protestantism, a failure that "helped open Protestants' eyes to the fact that they and their churches no longer commanded the authority, power, influence, or even respect which they had long enjoyed in America."[52] Modern America was too diverse, and its problems were too complex for an increasingly divided Protestantism to master.

One example of the I.W.M.'s inability to represent a united American Protestantism was the controversy that surrounded the Industrial Relations Department, which was under the direction of Fred B. Fisher. The Bolshevik Revolution of 1917 had left the American Protestant psyche raw and uncertain about its commitment to progressive eco-

50. Raymond B. Fosdick to Starr J. Murphy, 29 June 1921; Fosdick to John D. Rockefeller, Jr., 2 July 1921; Fosdick to Rockefeller, 9 July 1921; Rockefeller to Fosdick, 12 July 1921; Thomas Nicholson to Rockefeller, 19 August 1921; James M. Speers to Rockefeller, 18 January 1921; Archives: Religious Interests, box 39, folder 319. Rockefeller to Fosdick, 19 January 1921; Rockefeller to Fosdick, 11 March 1922; Al Boulware to Fosdick, 13 November 1922; Willard S. Richardson to Fosdick, 28 June and 12 July 1923; Archives: Religious Interests, box 39, folder 320.

51. N. F. MacKean to John D. Rockefeller, Jr., 27 March 1923; Willard S. Richardson to MacKean, 29 March 1923; Archives: Religious Interests, box 39, folder 320.

52. Ernst, *Moment of Truth*, 171.

nomic reform; nonetheless, the I.W.M. continued to conduct its research in the prewar social gospel tradition.

On 10 May the Special Commission of the Industrial Relations Department—which was appointed to investigate industrial unrest, and particularly the national steel strike of 1919—presented its report to the Executive Committee. The report, authored by Bishop Francis J. McConnell, upheld the right of collective bargaining and confirmed with hard evidence the plaints of labor about wages, hours, and working conditions. Rockefeller was a member of the committee to which the report was referred for review, but resigned on 20 May without having studied the report because he was spending several months in California. He also expressed the opinion that "it is better that I should not be a member of the committee," although he did not give reasons for the opinion.[53]

A firestorm of capitalist protest resulted when the Executive Committee made the report public five weeks later. Despite the fact that he had apparently tried to avoid the issue, Rockefeller was drawn into the controversy. The doom of the I.W.M. financial campaign, with which he had publicly cast his lot, had been sealed before the report was released, but many linked the two incidents. One New York newspaper ran a front page headline declaring, "Interchurch Drive Halted Largely Due to Steel Survey: Capital Practically Served Notice on Combine to Keep Hands Off Industrial Relations: Report on Big Strike Upholds Men's Claims: Pittsburgh Millionaires Restricted Gifts to Work—Then Presbyterians Withdrew."[54] Another newspaper reported that Rockefeller had severed his relationship to the I.W.M. because of the report, an error that Rockefeller took pains to correct.[55]

53. William H. Foulkes to John D. Rockefeller, Jr., 29 April 1920; Starr J. Murphy to Rockefeller, 20 May 1920; Rockefeller to Foulkes, 20 May 1920; Archives: Religious Interests, box 38, folder 317.

54. *New York World*, 2 July 1920, Archives: Religious Interests, box 39, folder 324.

55. "The Church and Mammon," editorial, *Yakima Leader*, 29 October 1920; John D. Rockefeller to Raymond B. Fosdick, 19 November 1920; Fosdick to Rockefeller, 29 November 1920; Rockefeller to editor, 7 December 1920; Archives: Religious Interests, box 39, folder 324.

Rockefeller publicly affirmed his support for the work of the I.W.M.'s Industrial Relations Department and served on a subcommittee that refuted a charge from the Ohio Manufacturer's Association that "Anarchists" and "I.W.W.'s" (Industrial Workers of the World)—the radical wing of the labor movement—were involved in the Industrial Relations work of the movement. At issue in this particular aspect of the affair was Roger N. Baldwin's alleged involvement with the department; he had worked with the American Civil Liberties Union, of which Union Seminary professor Henry F. Ward was president. It seems that Baldwin was a card-carrying I.W.W. member and had worked with labor organizer William Z. Foster during the steel strike. There was no evidence that Baldwin worked with the I.W.M., and Ward, who did work with the department and whose liberalism was itself objectionable to many, managed to avoid any of the direct radical affiliations on which accusations thrived.

Rockefeller also became involved in a related "Red scare" episode in November 1920. John B. Trevor, a former I.W.M. executive, was contacted by an assistant attorney general concerning a report authored by an executive of the Federal Council of Churches. This report, based on information gathered by the I.W.M., dealt with two hundred deportation cases involving alleged political radicals. The cases were from the winter of 1919–1920, but the assistant attorney general believed that the report was an attempt to damage federal cases that were pending at that time. Trevor told Rockefeller that the F.C.C. report was based on hearsay and was "infinitely worse than the Interchurch Report regarding the Steel Trust."[56]

At Trevor's request, Rockefeller sought information from Robert Speer, then president of the F.C.C. Speer told Rockefeller that the report was "a very temperate statement, based not on hearsay at all but on the actual testimony taken in various cases." Speer subsequently assured Trevor that the report would not be published in time to influence any related cases. To Trevor's dismay, however, the National Popular Government League, which he characterized as "the radical members of the Harvard Law faculty et al.," issued a report

56. John B. Trevor to John D. Rockefeller, Jr., 23 November 1920, Archives: Religious Interests, box 31, folder 246.

that Trevor thought was based on the unpublished research of the F.C.C. Trevor suspected conspiracy and again contacted Rockefeller. Raymond Fosdick read the report for Rockefeller and produced a six-page letter clearing the F.C.C. from Trevor's charges of radicalism and conspiracy. Rockefeller communicated his support to Speer, sending along a copy of Fosdick's letter. Such controversy within Protestant ranks weakened the Protestant voice on social issues in the twenties.[57]

Controversy over the steel strike report was kept alive by the publication of *Public Opinion and the Steel Strike of 1919: Supplementary Reports to the Commission of Inquiry, Interchurch World Movement* (1921), a volume supporting the report, as well as Marshall Olds's *Analysis of the Interchurch World Movement Report on the Steel Strike* (1922), which raised the old charges of radical involvement. Throughout the twenties, the I.W.M. report was used as evidence by those seeking to induce "Red scare."[58]

During the controversy over the steel report, the Protestant press praised Rockefeller's industrial relations plan, contrasting it with the intransigence of steel industry management. Rockefeller's moderate program of nonunion representation was considered noteworthy during the reactionary twenties. In an article entitled, "Mr. Rockefeller Versus Judge Gary," which Ivy Lee found especially interesting, Alva W. Taylor touted Rockefeller's representation plan for *Christian Century* readers.[59] Lee wrote to Rockefeller, remarking with pleasure that

57. John D. Rockefeller, Jr., to John B. Trevor, 1 December 1920; Rockefeller to Robert E. Speer, 4 December 1920; Speer to Rockefeller, 11 December 1920; Trevor to Rockefeller, 21 December 1920; Archives: Religious Interests, box 31, folder 246. Raymond B. Fosdick to Rockefeller, 10 February 1921; Rockefeller to Speer, 22 February 1921; Archives: Religious Interests, box 31, folder 247.

58. Heber Blankenhorn, ed., *Public Opinion and the Steel Strike of 1919: Supplementary Reports to the Commission of Inquiry, Interchurch World Movement* (New York: Harcourt, Brace, 1921; Marshall Olds, *Analysis of the Interchurch World Movement Report on the Steel Strike* (New York: Putnam's, 1922).

59. Alva W. Taylor, "Mr. Rockefeller Versus Judge Gary," *Christian Century* 37 (1920) 18–19.

Rockefeller was getting favorable press, even from one whom Lee considered "a radical almost approaching the socialistic in his views."[60]

The Rockefeller staff, however, still showed sensitivity to the steel report issue years later. When a Yale Divinity School student inquired about the report in a letter to Rockefeller, Arthur Packard counseled Fosdick to give a response that "guards against any possible adverse interpretation." Fosdick responded simply that the controversy over the report was not a factor in the movement's failure.[61]

Fosdick's opinion that the controversy over the I.W.M.'s steel report was not a major cause of its demise has been upheld by contemporaries and later scholars. Arthur Bestor cited several major factors: weariness from war drives on the part of those who might have been expected to give, lack of clarity about relations with the denominations, and the fact that those who did give and work on the campaign did so through their denominations, leaving the interdenominational fund bare.[62] Others thought that Protestant leaders should never have attempted a unification of effort. *The Nation* announced the failure of I.W.M. as "The Collapse of the Christian Soviet." It argued that the lesson to be learned was that "a soviet cannot be imposed by a tiny minority at the top. Neither Lenin nor John D. Rockefeller, Jr., can as yet create a new economic instrument of government in these United States; not even a Christian soviet in ecclesiastical government." The editorial went on to make the favorable analogy between democracy and the Federal Council of Churches.[63]

Starr Earl Taylor and James Speers blamed the failure of the I.W.M. on the unwillingness of the denominations to approve "the original plan," which proposed that the movement's expenses be covered by

60. Ivy Lee to John D. Rockefeller, Jr., 16 September 1920; Archives: Religious Interests, box 39, folder 322.

61. Arthur W. Packard to Raymond B. Fosdick, 6 August 1946; Fosdick to L. H. Wigren, 20 August 1946; Archives: Religious Interests, box 39, folder 320. For a list of opinions concerning why the movement failed, see H. F. Laflamme, "The Interchurch World Movement," and other undated materials, Archives: Religious Interests, box 38, folder 317.

62. Arthur Bestor to John D. Rockefeller, Jr., 30 April 1920, Archives: Religious Interests, box 38, folder 318.

63. *The Nation*, 10 July 1920, Archives: Religious Interests, box 39, folder 324.

taking five percent from the total of the united campaign.[64] A *Christian Century* editorial cited "sectarian selfishness, suspicion and arrogance."[65] The subsequent denominational growth, compared to the decline of voluntary societies, tends to confirm the view that the I.W.M. debacle did very little damage to the denominations, while it represented a watershed for those groups that depended on the support of a supposedly Protestant public.

Further opinions regarding the movement's demise were expressed by Alexander W. Armour and Rockefeller himself. In an interoffice memo entitled "Much That Might Be Told," Armour, who acted as treasurer during the dissolution process, summarized the failed strategy of the movement in an avalanche of biblical images:

> It would seem that the devil took this group up to the top of an exceeding high mountain and showed them the Friendly Citizens of the world and said: "These will put organized Christianity on the map if you'll only recognize them and make your appeal in that quarter." And they fell down and worshipped the idea. As a result we find ourselves groping in the ruins of an ecclesiastical collapse such as the world has not known since the time when the Tower of Babel crashed to the ground in the land of Shinar.[66]

Rockefeller's own reflections on the failure found two chief causes: "the unprecedented rapidity of its growth and development" and "the large scale on which it was planned." Rockefeller's own counsel had been in the direction of a slower beginning, as he reminded one officer. Rockefeller now elaborated on this idea; if foreign missions organizations had first been united, then home mission organizations, and so on until all lines of activity had been included, the endeavor might well have succeeded. "Perhaps I held this view," Rockefeller concluded, "because the development of new things which originate in our own office has always been along these slower and more con-

64. Starr E. Taylor, "What Happened to the Interchurch World Movement," 8 July 1920; James M. Speers to John D. Rockefeller, Jr., 17 August 1920, Archives: Religious Interests, box 39, folder 319.

65. "Who Killed Cock Robbin," *Christian Century* 37 (1920) 6.

66. Alexander W. Armour to Raymond B. Fosdick, Archives: Fosdick Papers, box 5, folder 2.

servative lines."[67] In discussions with Speers about future plans for interdenominational work, Rockefeller commented on the desirability of more conservative leadership. The Federal Council of Churches, overlooked during the I.W.M. enthusiasm, gained Rockefeller's appreciation for its more cautious approach to Protestant unity and cultural influence, especially when Robert E. Speer was chosen as president in 1920.[68]

The Institute for Social and Religious Research

The I.W.M.'s collapse, which occurred less than two years after it was born amid high hopes, seems to lend credence to Robert Handy's notion of a "second disestablishment" in which Protestantism lost its privileged place in American public life. In the 1920s, prewar crusades such as the Student Volunteer Movement for Foreign Missions, the Sunday School movement, and the Men and Religion Forward Movement seemed to be mired in "drift and indecision," to use Winthrop Hudson's phrase.[69]

During this time, Rockefeller continued to hope and work for a Protestant expression broad and modern enough to serve as America's religious guardian. Despite the fact that the realities of the I.W.M. did not match its rhetoric, Rockefeller maintained his conviction that the principles of businesslike efficiency, scientific research, and cooperative action—the same principles employed in all Rockefeller philanthropies—could refurbish the Protestant crusade.

Rockefeller established the Institute for Social and Religious Research as a tool for modernizing and promoting Protestantism. The institute had its origin in a conversation between Rockefeller and Starr Taylor during their I.W.M. speaking tour. Taylor suggested that Rockefeller found an interchurch foundation to support the work of bringing about a united Protestantism. Throughout the summer of 1920,

67. John D. Rockefeller, Jr., to James Speers, 21 August 1920, Archives: Religious Interests, box 39, folder 319.

68. Ibid.

69. Robert Handy, "The American Religious Depression," *CH* 29 (1960) 2–16; and idem, *A Christian America*, 159–84. Winthrop S. Hudson, *Religion in America* (New York: Macmillan, 1981) 359–78.

as the movement collapsed, three I.W.M. executives, Daniel Poling, Ralph Diffendorfer, and Abram E. Cory, continued to encourage Rockefeller to perpetuate the movement's work through an endowed organization. By the fall, Rockefeller was consulting with Fosdick, Murphy, and others about this possibility.[70]

Rockefeller especially valued Speer's counsel on this issue and invited him to North East Harbor, in Maine, to discuss the idea. Speer responded at length in a subsequent letter. While he agreed with Rockefeller that Protestant denominations needed greater efficiency and cooperation, Speer was not sure that an "independent self-contained endowment" was a good idea. If one were founded at all, Speer counseled, it should be an "unpretentious agency" directed by "trusted men." Such an agency should not conduct any programs, but could engage in research and could assist in carrying out denominational initiatives. Any organization that attempted more than this, Speer warned, would become "but only another denomination advocating the reduction of the number of denominations at the same time that it has added to them."[71]

In October, Poling, Diffendorfer, and Cory made a formal proposal to Rockefeller for an organization under Rockefeller's personal direction, funded annually by him. This organization would finish the I.W.M. surveys and, with a special focus on hinderances to cooperation, would study the problems facing Protestant churches. The group would be "free of ecclesiastical limitation and supervision." It would "begin modestly" and be supervised by a "small, carefully selected, thoroughly competent, and sympathetic committee."[72]

70. Starr E. Taylor to John D. Rockefeller, Jr., 10 May 1920; Abram E. Cory to Rockefeller, 19 August 1920; memo from Daniel Poling, Ralph Diffendorfer, and Cory to Rockefeller, 19 August 1920; Rockefeller to Cory, 24 August 1920; Cory to Rockefeller, 31 August 1920; Rockefeller to Starr J. Murphy, 13 September 1920; Archives: Religious Interests, box 41, folder 331.

71. John D. Rockefeller, Jr., to Robert E. Speer, 14 September 1920; Rockefeller to John R. Mott, 26 October 1920; Speer to Rockefeller, 5 October 1920; Archives: Religious Interests, box 41, folder 331.

72. Memo from Daniel Poling, Ralph Diffendorfer, and Abram E. Cory, 5 October 1920, Archives: Religious Interests, box 41, folder 331.

A month later, Rockefeller hosted a small group, including Speer and Mott, which discussed the possibility of such a "foundation for the advancement of cooperative Protestantism." The group asked Charles R. Watson to construct an organizational plan along the lines of that proposed by Poling, Diffendorfer, and Cory. Rockefeller invited Ernest D. Burton, president of the University of Chicago, to join Mott, Watson, and Fosdick on the planning committee. In January of the next year, Rockefeller began modest funding for the committee's program through the Committee on Social and Religious Surveys of the inactive I.W.M.[73]

The immediate project of the committee was to encourage and fund the completion of the survey work undertaken by the I.W.M. Rockefeller received advice from the principals in his secular philanthropies regarding the value of the research that had thus far been completed through the I.W.M. Abraham Flexner thought that much of the work was valuable, but he wondered whether any organization existed that could utilize it. Rockefeller responded that he hoped the churches would heed the results of the surveys, and that any organization he might fund would restrict its activities to research.[74]

In the wake of the I.W.M. debacle, Rockefeller's dealings with the board were extremely cautious and proceeded on the basis that Rockefeller would closely watch its work. He committed himself only to fund the completion of projects already undertaken by the I.W.M. committee. Rockefeller did, however, express a willingness to do more in the future:

> Having long shared my father's broader view of his duty as a Christian and having been looking to find some organization through which I might have a part in advancing the cause of cooperative Christianity throughout the world, I threw myself into the work of the Interchurch World Movement in the hope that it might be the very channel for which I had been looking, although at the same time recognizing its limitations and the dangers of its organization and program. The Interchurch having

73. John D. Rockefeller, Jr., to John R. Mott, 26 October 1920; Charles R. Watson to Rockefeller, 19 November 1920; Rockefeller to Ernest C. Burton, 19 November 1920; Archives: Religious Interests, box 41, folder 331.

74. Ernest D. Burton, "The Committee on Social and Religious Surveys, Minutes of First Meeting, January 5, 1921," Archives: Religious Interests, box 41, folder 328.

> not proven to be the instrument. . . some of you gentlemen feel that the time is now ripe for the establishment of a permanent instrument. . . with a representative board and a substantial endowment. . . . It may be that you are right. On the other hand, my training and experience have been along the lines of small beginnings. . . . I shall watch with eagerness and an open mind to see whether the larger field and the broader possibilities of promoting cooperative Christianity present themselves.[75]

Rockefeller's initial two hundred and fifty thousand dollar contribution to the committee served to salvage most of the projects initiated during the I.W.M. years. Rockefeller worked cautiously with the committee through 1921–1922. He had Fosdick validate the worthiness of each survey before he funded it. The committee also funded such groups as the International Missionary Council (I.M.C.); in the case of the I.M.C., it is interesting to note that Rockefeller approved a smaller amount than Mott requested. Rockefeller told Fosdick confidentially, however, that he would personally pay the difference between the committee's gift and the total actually needed by Mott for his I.M.C. project if there was indeed a shortfall. Rockefeller loved Mott's daring, but he apparently suspected that Mott was a spendthrift.[76]

Rockefeller's religious philanthropy advanced the same progressive ideals as the rest of the Rockefeller program. Among the projects that the committee funded in the early twenties, for example, was a survey of theological seminaries and religious training schools. This survey was the religious equivalent of the survey of colleges done by the G.E.B. for the purpose of promoting a comprehensive system.

An interesting episode from this period involved an application for continuation of funding from progressive economist Richard T. Ely.

75. John D. Rockefeller, Jr., to John R. Mott, Charles R. Watson, and Raymond B. Fosdick, 10 January 1921, Archives: Fosdick Papers, box 5, folder 2; in this letter Rockefeller also pledged two hundred and fifty thousand dollars. See also Harvey, "Speer versus Rockefeller and Mott," 296.

76. John D. Rockefeller, Jr., to John R. Mott, 29 April and 11 May 1921; Rockefeller to Raymond B. Fosdick, 11 May 1921; Archives: Religious Interests, box 41, folder 328. On 25 April 1924, the amount of $4,127.56 was returned to Rockefeller; Mott indeed had overstimated. Fosdick to Rockefeller, 25 April 1924, Archives: Religious Interests, box 41, folder 329.

Ely had been forced to use his own funds to continue a project commissioned by the I.W.M., and, asking for assistance, wrote bitterly to Fosdick. Fosdick wrote to Rockefeller suggesting immediate consideration of Ely's request, since he was "a very influential figure in the economic thought of America, and he holds such a place in intelligent circles that he is a dangerous man to have on the other side." Rockefeller suggested to Fosdick that the committee approve Ely's project without telling him that Rockefeller was the benefactor. Rockefeller was willing, however, to tell Ely that he had "paid for his survey" if the board was sure this would not offend him. Rockefeller saw himself as open to any criticisms of his family's legacy that the canons of modern science might provide and was attempting to avoid the appearance of influencing Ely's research.[77]

During the summer of 1922 Fosdick recommended that Rockefeller begin to support new research projects. Fosdick was impressed with the twenty-three reports that had been completed. He saw them as constituting "the first scientific approach to the problem of religious development," and he thought that they were beginning to influence the churches. He also remarked at the favorable comments that the religious press was making about the committee's work.[78] By 1923, Rockefeller was willing to fund new projects as well, including "investigations in any part of the world, and in reference to any phase of the life of society which in important ways affects or is affected by organized religion."[79] In the same year, the I.W.M. was legally dissolved, and the committee became the Institute of Social and Religious Research (I.S.R.R.).

The most notable example of research begun in the institute's first year was the Small City Study, undertaken by Robert and Helen Lynd, which culminated in the publication of *Middletown*, a ground-break-

77. Raymond B. Fosdick to John D. Rockefeller, Jr., 27 December 1920; Rockefeller to Fosdick, 28 September 1920; Archives: Religious Interests, box 39, folder 319. Fosdick to Rockefeller, 8 February 1921, Archives: Religious Interests, box 39, folder 320.

78. Raymond B. Fosdick to John D. Rockefeller, Jr., 22 June 1922, Archives: Religious Interests, box 41, folder 328.

79. John D. Rockefeller, Jr., to Raymond B. Fosdick, 18 December 1922, Archives: Religious Interests, box 41, folder 328.

ing community survey of Muncie, Indiana. In an essay on the Lynds' work, Richard Fox wrote that the I.S.R.R. was "part of Rockefeller's general effort to Christianize the American social order—in his case not a narrowly sectarian project, but a class-conscious attempt to legitimize corporate capitalism by placing it under the guidance of a morally concerned and scientifically trained elite." Fox correctly identified the I.S.R.R. as part of a wider Rockefeller program to mold society, even if Fox's description of this program was reductionistic. Although there is no evidence that Rockefeller was conscious of class or that his concern centered on a legitimization of corporate capitalism, Rockefeller certainly promoted religion in order to strengthen the social fabric.[80]

The I.S.R.R., moreover, played an important role in Rockefeller's program because it encouraged Protestants to modernize their religion so that it could serve the culture more effectively. Only a scientific approach could insure an effective ministry. In analyzing the ethos of the I.S.R.R., Fox identified two factions, each claiming to represent a "scientific" approach to ministry. One saw the task of the institute as a problem-solving enterprise on the model of modern social work. The other envisioned its work as "objective fact-finding" along the lines of an academic research institution. Each constituted an "unsettled mix" of religious and secular scientific motifs and impulses typical of "the northern Protestant intelligentsia between the 1880s and the 1930s." Only a scientific Christianity would satisfy the modern religious need—that much was sure. The debate was concerned with how to mix religion and science.[81]

As Rockefeller saw it, the right mix of religion and science would bring harmony to American society. Thus when the Lynds' research in Muncie began to stress the entrenched reality of division between the business class and the working class, the I.S.R.R. board bristled. Al-

80. Richard W. Fox, "Epitaph for Middletown: Robert S. Lynd and the Analysis of Consumer Culture," in idem and T. J. Jackson Lears, eds., *The Culture of Consumption: Critical Essays in American History, 1880–1980* (New York: Pantheon, 1983) 112. See Fosdick, *Rockefeller*, 213; see also Charles E. Harvey, "John D. Rockefeller, Jr., and the Social Sciences: An Introduction," *Journal of the History of Sociology* 4 (1982) 1–31.

81. Fox, "Epitaph for Middletown," 116.

though the institute funded the completion of the study, it did not act as publisher.[82]

Between 1923 and 1928, Rockefeller gave over one and a quarter million dollars to the institute for its research projects. Many of the studies were designed to encourage interdenominational cooperation. Local community studies, often done by Harlan Paul Douglass, invariably recommended the merger of small churches, and in 1928, Douglass published a discussion outline for churches entitled, "There Are Too Many Churches on Main Street."[83]

In 1928, Rockefeller for the first time gave the institute substantial funds for projects other than research: he channeled through the institute a gift of one and a half million dollars intended for the International Missionary Council meeting held in Jerusalem, and he made small contributions to a number of other interdenominational projects. Mott and Trevor Arnett seized on the opportunity and suggested that Rockefeller increase the 1929 budget from two hundred and fifty thousand to three hundred and fifty thousand dollars and authorize the board to make "grants in furtherance of cooperation." Rockefeller considered the proposal, but decided to retreat from implementation and return to his policy of funding research only. The board never again raised the possibility of using the I.S.R.R. for a broader effort at interdenominational cooperation.[84]

In 1930, Rockefeller made his customary contribution of two hundred and fifty thousand dollars. Among the seven projects included in the 1930 budget were the following: "Study of Representative Negro

82. Charles E. Harvey, "Robert S. Lynd, John D. Rockefeller, Jr., and *Middletown*," *Indiana Magazine of History* 79 (1983) 350–51.

83. Galen Fisher, *The Institute of Social and Religious Research, 1921–34* (New York: I.S.S.R., 1934) 28–30. John D. Rockefeller, Jr., to Raymond B. Fosdick, 5 January 1923; Rockefeller to John R. Mott, 6 February 1924; Rockefeller to Mott, 5 March 1925; Rockefeller to Fosdick, 5 January 1926; Rockefeller to Trevor Arnett, 29 December 1926; Archives: Religious Interests, box 41, folder 329.

84. John D. Rockefeller to Trevor Arnett, 20 January 1928; Willard S. Richardson to John D. Rockefeller, Jr., 14 January and 7 March 1928; John R. Mott and Arnett to Rockefeller, 16 October 1928; Arnett and Raymond B. Fosdick to Rockefeller, 18 December 1928; Rockefeller to Mott, 31 December 1928; Archives: Religious Interests, box 41, folder 329.

Churches" by Benjamin E. Mays and Joseph W. Nicholson, "Study of Movements toward Christian Unity" by H. Paul Douglass, and "Problems and Programs in Religious Education" by Hugh Hartshorne.[85] Another study initiated that year was to become the most significant in the institute's history: the Fact-finding Commission of the Laymen's Foreign Missions Inquiry, undertaken by Galen M. Fisher, H. Paul Douglass, C. Luther Fry, and Harvey H. Guy. In 1931 Rockefeller reduced the new work of the I.S.R.R. to one study, budgeted at twenty-five thousand dollars, as the institute became absorbed by the work of the Laymen's Foreign Missions Inquiry.[86]

The Laymen's Report

The Laymen's Foreign Missions Inquiry proved to be the most controversial effort of the I.S.R.R., raising again the question of Rockefeller control over one of the major ministries of American Protestantism. The impetus for the inquiry was the 1928 meeting of the International Missionary Council held in Jerusalem. The council had arisen from the epoch-making 1910 conference in Edinburgh, in which American activists spoke of the numerical and geographical conquest of the world by the Christian gospel. The 1928 Jerusalem Conference provided a sharp contrast. Gone was the easy assurance about the preaching the gospel to the world. Instead, the focus was on "the wide range of human relations—social, industrial, economic, racial, international." No longer was the battle line drawn between Christianity and pagan religions; the conference identified the crucial conflict as the one between religion and secularization.[87]

In 1928 and 1929, Mott undertook an eight-month tour of the world, during which he looked at missions through the lens of the Jerusalem Conference. Mott's report of this tour impressed Rockefeller, who called together a group of thirty-five Baptist laymen to hear from Mott in January 1930. Out of that meeting, a committee of five was

85. Fisher, *Institute*, 53.

86. John D. Rockefeller, Jr., to John R. Mott, 3 February 1930; Mott and Trevor Arnett to Rockefeller, 4 November 1930; Rockefeller to Mott and Arnett, 16 January 1931; Archives: Religious Interests, box 41, folder 329.

87. Hopkins, *Mott*, 659–61, 669–75.

appointed to consider what action might be taken pursuant to Mott's remarks. The group, headed by Albert L. Scott, a deacon in the Riverside Church, approached the Baptist Foreign Mission Society about cooperating in an audit of its missions.

Rockefeller had been having serious doubts of his own about continuing to support traditional missionary organizations. He had recently solicited the opinions of Harry Emerson Fosdick and Charles W. Gilkey, dean of the University of Chicago chapel, as to the state of the missions movement. Both responded with a clear preference for service over proselytization and confessed uneasiness about Baptist missions. Harry Fosdick wrote to Rockefeller's staff, "Whether Mr. Rockefeller will wish to tackle this situation is, of course, for you who advise him to suggest. The use of his gifts to exert pressure of this kind is necessarily a delicate matter." Rockefeller confided in Edward L. Ballard, a member of Riverside Church,

> Letters from these gentlemen seem to me so sane, so progressive and so broad. Would that this spirit could be infused into our missionary organizations, and more especially into their leaders. Perhaps, with the situation so clearly analysed and frankly stated as it has been in these letters, you and I may be able little by little to help toward that end.[88]

In Mott's discomfiture regarding missions, Rockefeller recognized both a kindred concern and an opportunity to take action. Raymond Fosdick and other members of the Rockefeller staff went to work on the logistics of the inquiry proposed by the Baptist laymen. The idea of including committees of laypersons from other denominations was investigated. Initially, Speer and Diffendorfer, secretaries of the Presbyterian and Methodist boards, raised objections to the idea of an independent agency initiating such an audit. Rockefeller responded that he thought of the lay supporters of missions as analogous to "stockholders in a business corporation," who shared an interest in the efficiency of the enterprise. Laypersons of six other denominations were recruited for the project. At a meeting of laypersons representing

88. Harry E. Fosdick to Thomas B. Appleget, 27 July 1929; Charles W. Gilkey to Appleget, 19 October 1929; John D. Rockefeller, Jr., to Edward L. Ballard, 12 November 1929; Archives: Religious Interests, box 47, folder 370.

four of the denominations, individuals agreed to conduct a "laymen's investigation" into Asiatic missions. Rockefeller offered the resources of the I.S.R.R. and promised to pay for its role in the project. He expressed to the denominational committees his desire to work "with the missionary bodies in their respective denominations" rather than to create an independent entity.[89]

A two-stage process was planned for the inquiry; this consisted of research, which was to be carried out by the I.S.R.R., and appraisal, which was to be carried out by a commission of experts from various professions. Although Rockefeller's role in the project was kept secret, he was, in customary fashion, the central force in organizing the fourteen-member commission of appraisal which toured India, Burma, China, and Japan for nine months in 1931–1932. In addition, he was the sole financial supporter of the project, with contributions that totaled three hundred and sixty-three thousand dollars.[90]

Rockefeller also took an active role in recruiting the personnel for the commission of appraisal, calling on his contacts from other enterprises. He consulted Wickliffe Rose and others in the Rockefeller philanthropic network for the names of top people in economics, public health, agriculture, and other fields in which missionaries were involved. Albert Scott, Rockefeller's friend from Riverside Church, handled the administrative affairs of the commission. James M. Speers agreed to act as its treasurer, as well as chairperson of the Presbyterian committee. William Ernest Hocking of Harvard was chosen to head the commission. Those who declined Rockefeller's invitation to join the commission included Henry Sloane Coffin of Union Theological Seminary, President Mary E. Woolley of Mount Holyoke College, President Ernest M. Hopkins of Dartmouth, Professor Richard Henry Tawney of the London School of Economics, Professor Albert R. Mann of Cornell, Charles Evans Hughes, William Mackenzie

89. John D. Rockefeller, Jr., to John R. Mott, 29 May 1930, Archives: Religious Interests, box 41, folder 329. Those denominations involved were the American Baptist, Congregational, Methodist, Episcopalian, Presbyterian Church (U.S.A.), United Presbyterian, and the Reformed Church in America.

90. Ralph Diffendorfer to John D. Rockefeller, Jr., 10 May 1930; Rockefeller to Diffendorfer, 19 May 1930; Archives: Religious Interests, box 48, folder 387.

King, and John Foster Dulles. Speers wondered whether a roster of secular experts could be sufficiently sensitive to religious motivation and was assured that a number of persons with spiritual qualifications would be added.[91]

Rockefeller chose several commission members solely on the basis of their reputation as spiritual leaders, including Quaker philosopher Rufus M. Jones; William Pierson Merrill, pastor of the Brick Church in New York; Ruth F. Woodsmall, a YWCA executive; Georgiana Sibley, president of United Church Women; and her husband Harper Sibley. Members of the commission who were chosen in part for their secular expertise included Edgar H. Betts, a businessman from Troy, New York; Arlo A. Brown, president of Drew University; Charles P. Emerson, dean of the Indiana University Medical School; Henry C. Taylor, an agricultural economist; Clarence L. Barbour, president of Brown; Frederic C. Woodward, vice-president of the University of Chicago; Henry S. Houghton, dean of the University of Iowa Medical College; and Mrs. William Ernest Hocking, founder of Shady Hill School in Cambridge, Massachusetts.

At the preparatory meetings of the commission, Rockefeller also took the lead in suggesting the philosophical approach for the appraisal. Rockefeller told the commission that it should not oppose foreign missions, but should suggest needed reforms. It should appraise "what is being done as to conduct and program and method."[92] Rockefeller believed that the purpose of mission work was "to make Christ's spirit, as revealed in his life and teachings, a vital, impelling force in the lives of the people of foreign lands."[93] The commission's job was "to see to what extent this program has drifted from the

91. Clarence L. Barbour to John D. Rockefeller, Jr., 31 December 1930, Archives: Religious Interests, box 48, folder 379. Rockefeller to Harry E. Fosdick, 25 June 1930; Rockefeller to Ernest M. Hopkins, 1 October 1930; Archives: Religious Interests, box 48, folder 387. John Foster Dulles to Rockefeller, 16 June 1931, Archives: Religious Interests, box 49, folder 389. James M. Speers to Rockefeller, 12 January 1931; Rockefeller to Speers, 16 January 1931; Archives: Religious Interests, box 48, folder 384.

92. Minutes of the meeting of the directors of the Appraisal Commission, 23 January 1931, Archives: Religious Interests, box 48, folder 386.

93. Minutes of the Laymen's Foreign Missions Inquiry, 15 May 1931, pp. 36–37, Archives: Religious Interests, box 48, folder 388.

fundamental, vital, central purpose." Rockefeller urged the commission to keep one question in mind: "Aiming always at the ideal program, to what extent should existing missionary organizations, policies, programs and personnel be continued, modified, set aside or replaced in formulating the best practical missionary program for today?"[94]

William Ernest Hocking assured Rockefeller that the commission would remain open-minded and would seek to represent those for whom missions were important. At the same time, Hocking observed that interested laypeople were already asking radical questions. He encouraged the commission members not to be "badly disturbed if there were questions on the part of the mission boards" as a result of their work.[95]

During the summer of 1931, Rockefeller and Hocking discussed the strategy for gaining the right public hearing for the report. Hocking was concerned that the report not lose its impact by appearing to be "one of the many John-R-Mott enterprises." Mott's January meeting had been a catalyst, but the doubts which Mott expressed about foreign missions were not his alone. They had already been working "in the minds of Mr. Rockefeller and others." Hocking proposed, "If we do not mention Mr. Rockefeller, and he would prefer not to be mentioned, I doubt whether we should mention any one person."[96] Rockefeller preferred to remain in the background, giving God the credit for the Laymen's Inquiry. As the commission began, he wrote, "I keep reminding myself that while the Laymen's Committee has laid the foundation for this inquiry, it is the Lord's work which the commission goes forth to do, and he will point the way and provide wisdom and strength for the task."[97]

The commission spent the autumn of 1931 in India. It nearly had to abandon its visits to China and Japan because of the Sino-Japanese War. It persevered through the collapse of Houghton's bank and the

94. Minutes of the meeting of the directors of the Appraisal Commission, 23 January 1931, Archives: Religious Interests, box 48, folder 386.

95. Ibid.

96. William E. Hocking to Ivy Lee, 25 September 1932, Archives: Religious Interests, box 48, folder 380.

97. John D. Rockefeller, Jr., to Clarence L. Barbour, 28 September 1931, Archives: Religious Interests, box 48, folder 379.

crisis in Scott's business due to the Depression. In the midst of the difficulties, the commission carried out its evaluation of American foreign missions. In a typical report to Rockefeller written from Peiping, Scott expressed disappointment at what he found. Missionaries lacked "the proper intellectual and social backgrounds to meet the needs of the present Chinese situation." Far too many of them were "of the fundamentalist type, not open to the new ideas of the day."[98]

Upon their return in August 1932, Rockefeller met the commissioners with hearty thanks and a fresh charge. They must present the truth about American Protestant missions as they saw it, "even if to do so involved a complete reversal of opinions and positions formerly held."[99] Two courses lay open to them. On the one hand, they could trim their sails to the shifting winds of public opinion in the hope of avoiding criticism, but with the assurance of subjecting themselves to the inexorable and unrelenting disapproval of the "still, small voice" within. On the other hand, they could go forward courageously, regardless of misunderstanding and criticism, confident that truth would vindicate itself.

Rockefeller assured the commission that he had every reason to expect courageous action from them, based on the early drafts of their work, which he had read "with a lump in my throat and a fervent song of praise in my heart." Rockefeller used his expression of praise for the group's efforts to remind them of the qualities he most treasured in religious discourse:

> The deep sympathy, broad grasp, keen penetration; the unquestioned faith in the fundamental, underlying, world-embracing significance of the spiritual values of true religion which these chapters reveal, coupled with the generous appreciation of all that is excellent and the courageous indication of defect and weakness, give assurance that this report if finished as it has begun is destined to have an influence not only on the religious life of the world but on civilization itself far beyond anything that has been dreamed or hoped.[100]

98. Albert Scott to John D. Rockefeller, Jr., 13 April 1932, Archives: Religious Interests, box 49, folder 393.

99. John D. Rockefeller to the Appraisal Commission, 17 August 1932, Archives: Religious Interests, box 48, folder 383.

100. Ibid.

Even before the commission reported to the denominational boards, debate was raging in the Protestant press. Between 3 October and 18 November, Ivy Lee had released the commission's findings in twenty-three installments to both the press and "five or six thousand individuals."[101] When this tactic was attacked, Lee privately conceded that he meant to insure that the public had the optimal opportunity to pass judgment on the report without the influence of denominational interpretation. Rockefeller had approved Lee's strategy, undoing the effect of his earlier expression of a desire to cooperate with the denominational boards.[102] A sampling of the headlines that appeared in the *New York Times* illustrates the impact of Lee's strategy: "Change to be Urged in Foreign Missions" (3 October), "From Sectarianism to Unity" (23 October), "Present 'Amateurish' Equipment and 'Unintelligent' Effort Not Adequate" (30 October), "Missions Advised to Befriend Reds" (31 October), "The Best or Nothing" (6 November), "Would Curb Grants to Churches in Asia" (11 November), "Many in Missions Viewed as Unfit" (14 November), and "Professor Hocking Tells Boards of Seven Denominations He Hopes They Will Accept Proposals" (19 November).[103]

The final report of the inquiry consisted of seven volumes. Hocking authored a single-volume summary called *Re-Thinking Missions*. Hocking's evaluation of American foreign missions reflected his search for a "world faith" that could wage the war against cosmopolitan secularism. In this regard, his thought paralleled Mott's reflections following the Jerusalem Conference. Predictably, his report proposed that missionaries learn to appreciate other religious traditions, as well as supporting the view that humanitarian service was a valuable part of the Christian mission. Hocking criticized the educational and medical

101. Ibid.

102. John D. Rockefeller, Jr., to Ivy Lee, 8 October 1932; Lee to James M. Speers, 31 October 1932; memorandum regarding the following up of the report of the Appraisal Commission, with Rockefeller's recommendations penciled on it; Rockefeller to Lee, 10 November 1932; Archives: Religious Interests, box 48, folder 381.

103. Press clippings, Archives: Religious Interests, box 48, folder 382; Albert Scott to John D. Rockefeller, Jr., 21 November 1932; Ralph Diffendorfer to Rockefeller, 21 November 1932; Archives: Religious Interests, box 49, folder 389.

work being done by missionaries, however, suggesting that some were justifying second-rate work because of its supposed evangelistic value. He recommended that the American missionary force be smaller and better trained.[104]

From the point of view of this study, what was striking about Hocking's report was that it treated American religion as a national expression. The report represented yet another episode in Rockefeller's program to modernize American Protestantism as a national religion. Neither Hocking nor Rockefeller thought that denominational particularity was an acceptable model for the modern religious situation. They conceived of the missionary enterprise primarily as the religious endeavor of American civilization and urged that it be reformed, not abandoned.

The commission officially completed its task with a public unveiling of its report at the Roosevelt Hotel on 13 January 1933. As usual, Rockefeller's name did not appear on the program. The extent of Rockefeller's role in the enterprise was not generally known, and he declined invitations, such as that of *Good Housekeeping* magazine, to comment on it.[105]

The task of "selling" the recommendations of the commission had only begun. Clarence Barbour devoted himself to presenting the findings of the reports to audiences at places like Broadway Tabernacle in New York, First Congregational Church of Montclair in New Jersey, and Old South Church in Boston. The brunt of the work of explaining the report, however, fell to Hocking, and Rockefeller subsequently assisted the Hocking family in their travels for this purpose.[106]

104. William Ernest Hocking, *Re-thinking Missions: A Laymen's Inquiry after a Hundred Years* (New York: Harper, 1933). See William R. Hutchison, *Errand to the World: American Protestant Thought and Foreign Missions* (Chicago: University of Chicago Press, 1987) 158–74.

105. Program, meeting of the directors and sponsors of the Layman's Foreign Mission Inquiry, New York, 18–19 November 1932; W. F. Bigelow to John D. Rockefeller, Jr., 11 October 1932; Rockefeller to Bigelow, 19 October 1932; Archives: Religious Interests, box 49, folder 389.

106. Clarence L. Barbour to John D. Rockefeller, Jr., 16 February 1933, Archives: Religious Interests, box 48, folder 379.

The denominations involved in the inquiry gave its final report a mixed review. The Congregationalists and the Methodists accepted the report and promised to act on it. The other participating denominations either wavered or opposed it. When the Presbyterians rejected the report, James Speers was placed in the uncomfortable position of mediating between his friends Rockefeller and Robert Speer, who served as head of the Presbyterian board. As Speers sought to placate the conservatives in his denomination, Rockefeller encouraged him,

> I hope you feel as well satisfied as I do with the results of the undertaking. I had expected criticism and opposition and an effort to discount the findings of the report. I had not dared to hope, however, that the report itself would be so fundamentally splendid, so fearless, so progressive and so helpful as it proved to be.[107]

Congratulations on the report came to Rockefeller from many circles. Francis Peabody at Harvard wrote to Rockefeller calling the report "an epoch-making document." Probably the most celebrated endorsement of the report was that of Pearl S. Buck. *The Good Earth*, which would garner the 1932 Pulitzer Prize, had won for Buck a place in the popular imagination as the most prominent American missionary. In a *Christian Century* article, Buck called the Laymen's Report "the only book I have ever read which seems to me literally true in its every observation and right in its every conclusion."[108]

In a subsequent speech before a Presbyterian audience, Buck caused a public controversy by calling into question traditional assumptions about Christian superiority and by affirming a more modest witness to the world. Upon learning of the Presbyterian mission board's resultant displeasure with Buck, Rockefeller wrote to Scott,

> [Buck] is the ideal type of person for the mission field from the Commission's point of view and if she is ever dropped from the

107. John D. Rockefeller, Jr., to James M. Speers, 17 July 1935, Archives: Religious Interests, box 48, folder 384.

108. Francis Peabody to John D. Rockefeller, Jr., 29 November 1932, Archives: Religious Interests, box 49, folder 389; see also Hutchison, *Errand*, 166–69; Pearl S. Buck, "The Laymen's Mission Report," reprinted in *Christian Century* 49 (1932) 3; idem, *Is There A Case for Foreign Missions?* (New York: John Day, 1932).

> Presbyterian Mission staff, I am wondering whether she could not be employed by the Baptist Foreign Board or, better yet, by the Riverside Church as its personal missionary representative in China.

Scott went so far as to show this letter to Harry Emerson Fosdick, who wrote to Rockefeller expressing his hope that the Presbyterians would relent and continue to support Buck.[109]

The public debate over the Laymen's Report, fueled by Ivy Lee and Pearl Buck, was hardly sufficient to turn the attention of the mass of Americans to the task of a renewed missionary effort against secularism. Instead, the debate became an episode in the theological controversy that led to the rupture of the Protestant mission into liberal and conservative camps. Rockefeller's effort to view the American religious mission as a whole actually served to hasten the process by which modernist Protestantism was forced to adopt a sectarian posture. Rockefeller was nonetheless pleased with the findings of the commission and decided to terminate his giving to denominational missions.

The foreign missions inquiry was the last major project undertaken by the I.S.R.R. Rockefeller asked the board in 1932 to conclude the institute's activities within eighteen months. During its history, the institute conducted or financed studies in the following areas: thirty-six studies concerning the church in North America; eighteen studies concerning the church in foreign outreach; twenty-three studies concerning education; four studies concerning race relations; and eighteen studies concerning sociological issues.[110]

Rockefeller envisioned no successor organization. In an unusually acerbic mode, Rockefeller wrote to a staff member, "It is not at all clear to me that a successor to the Institute is needed or is desired, except by those men who want to perpetuate their own employment or instrumentalities for serving their own ends, however worthy."[111]

109. John D. Rockefeller, Jr., to Albert Scott, 17 April 1933; Harry E. Fosdick to Rockefeller, 20 April 1933; Archives: Religious Interests, box 49, folder 389.

110. Fisher, *Institute*, 31–32.

111. John D. Rockefeller, Jr., to Trevor Arnett, 10 March 1934, Archives: Religious Interests, box 39, folder 329.

Rockefeller was nearly sixty, deeply committed to Riverside Church, and aware of the limits of his wealth in the wake of the Great Depression. He would personally launch no more national interdenominational crusades. The assessment of family historians seems apt:

> Somewhere along the way, one suspects Junior must have recognized that. . . the larger vision of a peaceful and harmonious world for which he believed Protestant unity was a necessary condition. . . was utopian. . . . If so, he never commented on this, nor did he express any bitterness, cynicism, or regrets, as if to suggest he knew that all he could do was to make his best effort, and beyond that the world would have its way.[112]

This kind of resignation to the way of the world was evident in 1932 when Rockefeller's abandoned another of Protestantism's great interdenominational causes—prohibition. Both Rockefeller, Sr., and Rockefeller, Jr., had been prohibitionist champions since well before the turn of the century. Yet during the 1932 campaign for repeal of the Eighteenth Amendment, which had instituted prohibition, Rockefeller announced that he no longer supported the amendment and now affirmed repeal. Although he claimed never to have "tasted a drop of intoxicating liquor," Rockefeller had come to see prohibition as a failed policy which had produced only increased drinking and widespread disrespect for the law.[113]

Although his crusading days were over, Rockefeller continued, as the following chapter will show, to contribute to the interdenominational organizations that kept alive the Protestant ethos. These organizations would themselves periodically renew the Protestant quest for a Christian America that would lead a Christian world.

112. Harr and Johnson, *Century*, 180.
113. Fosdick, *Portrait*, 256.

6

The Reborn Church

Institutions of the Protestant Establishment

Rockefeller's central role in the controversial, interdenominational attempts to treat Protestantism as a national religion should not be allowed to obscure the fact that he contributed even more, in total dollars, to the traditional Protestant structures of congregation, seminary, and denomination. After the Interchurch World Movement experiment, moreover, in addition to those projects through which he continued his own efforts toward a Christian America, Rockefeller also supported forms of interdenominational cooperation that were directed by the emerging corps of denominational professionals. Although the Federal, National, and World Councils of Churches represented an accommodation to traditional denominationalism—and thus to attitudes that Rockefeller hoped that all would transcend—these organizations were, nonetheless, major recipients of Rockefeller funds. Rockefeller was first a lover of religion and, as a result, a nurturer of its ecclesiastical forms. Rockefeller contributed more money than anyone else to the creation and support of the structures that currently embody mainline Protestantism.

One reason for Rockefeller's increased support for traditional ecclesiastical structures was that they became the locus for the rationalizing and bureaucratizing impulse within American Protestantism. During the twenties the enthusiasm for business culture which had given shape to the Interchurch World Movement seized the churches. Bruce Barton was not alone in urging the church to adopt the pragmatic attitude of business in pursuing its aims. A journal called *Church Management*, which appeared in 1923, was one of several publications created to teach church leaders the value of efficiency. Many churches hired full-time business managers, and those that could not do so packed their church boards with businesspersons. Books such as *Business Methods for the Clergy* and *The Technique of a Minister* treated the topic of the pastor as executive, and churches became service institutions which functioned week-long and were oriented to the needs of the community.[1]

The years after the First World War also witnessed the beginnings of the dramatic blossoming of denominational bureaucracies. Protestant leaders could no longer depend on a canvass of "Christian America" for support of their programs, so they turned to denominational families as a means of locating their constituencies. The religious and benevolent functions that had been carried out by ecumenical voluntary societies were rapidly absorbed by denominational apparatuses constructed according to the bureaucratic models which had been pioneered by the voluntary societies. Sociologists have pointed out that the lack of an ecclesiology that connected congregations amid American denominationalism allowed for bureaucratic development that was purposive, pragmatic, and flexible.[2]

The interdenominational impulse that had been expressed in a congeries of voluntary associations came to be embodied more and more exclusively in the Federal Council of Churches and its growing bureaucracy. First social service, then other cooperative functions such as evangelism and education became the province of the F.C.C. In 1950 the National Council of Churches incorporated into its structure a number of the remaining voluntary organizations, including the Home

1. Lunden, *Business and Religion*, 57–83.

2. William R. Garrett, "Interplay and Rivalry Between Denominations and the Ecumenical Organization," in Ross P. Scherer, ed., *American Denominational Organization: A Sociological View* (Pasadena: William Carey Library, 1980) 347–50; Gibson Winter, *Religious Identity: A Study in Religious Organization* (New York: Macmillan, 1968) 35.

Missions Council, the Foreign Missions Council, and the International Council of Religious Education.[3]

With the exception of Rockefeller's involvement in Riverside Church, Rockefeller did not take a defined leadership position in any of the organizations discussed in this chapter. By 1960, nonetheless, mainline Protestantism manifested many of the characteristics of his ideal "reborn church," and had even temporarily revived the rhetoric of a Christian America and a Christian world.

The Twilight Years of Traditional Voluntary Societies: 1920–1950

Many Protestant organizations solicited Rockefeller between World War I and the Great Depression, and Rockefeller gave modest support to several of them. The golden age of Protestant activism, however, was past. Throughout the nineteenth century, the voluntary benevolent empire had seen itself as a lay movement. With the professionalization of various aspects of the ministry, the laity of mainline Protestantism began to see their role differently. Lay experts of various kinds could minister alongside ordained persons. The untrained lay crusader, however, could no longer attract support by virtue of zeal alone.

Not all laypersons were equally attuned to these changes, and a few continued to try to operate with old models. James Speers's son, Wallace C. Speers, for example, started a group called the Laymen's Movement for a Christian World. Rockefeller participated in some of the group's activities in the forties and fifties, but accurately predicted that it would not gain the widespread support that the Laymen's Missionary Movement, in which James Speers had been prominent, had enjoyed. Although the movement was able to bring inspiration to some through its businessmen's luncheons, the vast and complex work of international Christian mission had been passed into the hands of religious professionals.[4] Laypersons like Rockefeller, however, firmly retained one task in the Protestant mission—paying the bills.

3. John A. Hutchison, *We Are Not Divided: A Critical and Historical Study of The Federal Council of the Churches of Christ in America* (New York: Round Table, 1941) 272–96.

4. Arthur W. Packard to John D. Rockefeller, Jr., 14 October 1946; Thomas J. Ross to John G. Steward, 14 March 1947; Archives: Religious Interests, box 42, folder 334. James C. Penney to Rockefeller, 3 April 1950, Archives:

Rockefeller inherited from his father an interest in a number of traditional Protestant causes. Religious education had been one of the elder Rockefeller's main concerns. He had been a founding donor to the Religious Education Association (R.E.A.) in 1903. From 1920 to 1934, the younger Rockefeller supported the R.E.A. with modest contributions totaling about forty thousand dollars. During the thirties, he also contributed annually to the International Council of Religious Education. Rockefeller's son David continued the family tradition in the early forties with his work for the New York Interdenominational Committee for Religious Education on Released Time.[5]

Rockefeller also supported the programs at the Home Mission Council. The council worked in cooperation with the Council of Women for Home Missions, the F.C.C., and the I.S.R.R. in promoting comity in the home mission field. During the twenties and thirties Rockefeller contributed one-half to one-third of the council's budget and was invited on several occasions to speak on behalf of the council. During the same period, he contributed roughly ten to fifteen percent of the budget of the Community Church Workers (C.C.W.), another organization working for the cooperation of rural churches. In 1930, when the work of Robert Hargreaves, executive secretary of the C.C.W., brought him into conflict with the C.C.W. board, Rockefeller decided to provide full support for Hargreaves, making him available as a free agent to state, county, and city councils of churches for consultation regarding both church union and the cooperation of groups promoting Christian character among youth. Hilda L. Ives of the New England Town and Country Church Commission also won Rockefeller's support for her work in promoting rural church mergers; her efforts in Rockefeller's beloved Maine especially pleased him.[6]

Religious Interests, box 42, folder 335. Weyman C. Huckabee to Dana S. Creel, 7 June 1951, Archives: Religious Interests, box 42, folder 338. Rockefeller, "Remarks at the Laymen's Movement-Harvard Review Luncheon, October 25, 1955" (Rye, NY: Wainwright House, 1956); this document can be found in Archives: Religious Interests, box 42, folder 339.

5. Records relating to religious education, 1906–60, Archives: Religious Interests, box 54, folders 425, 426, 430; and Davison II, 2. Appropriations, box 13, folder 99.

6. Records relating to home missions, Home Missions Council, 1925–42, Archives: Religious Interests, box 46, folders 360–62; records relating to

Until 1932, Rockefeller also continued to support some of the oldest efforts of interdenominational foreign missions. He regularly contributed, for example, to the International Missionary Council, of which Mott was chairperson. Rockefeller was especially interested in medical and agricultural missions in China, India, and Africa.[7]

Rockefeller's support declined, however, for other organizations which he had formerly helped. The Student Volunteer Movement (S.V.M.) caught Rockefeller's attention when he met Robert Wilder during the United War Campaign. Between 1922 and 1932, he was its largest donor, providing five to ten percent of its resources. After the Laymen's Inquiry, Rockefeller and his financial advisory board considered using the S.V.M. as a "standard-setting instrument," since it represented the "moderate progressive wing" of the missions endeavor and attracted students who wanted the movement to "go much more to the 'left.'" By this time, however, the strength of the S.V.M. was spent, and Rockefeller terminated his giving in 1934.[8] Rockefeller also declined opportunities to contribute to various phases of YMCA and YWCA work in the 1930s, even though he had given nearly fourteen million dollars to those organizations in earlier years.[9]

Rockefeller did, however, increase his giving to a few Protestant causes in the twenties and thirties. Among these causes was that of Christian internationalism. He helped pay for a conference held at Vassar in 1924, a conference that was the idea of approximately thirty women's boards of home and foreign missions which were organized

---

Community Church Workers, 1927–34, box 45, folder 355; records relating to J. Robert Hargreaves, 1930–38, box 46, folder 362; records relating to New England Town and Country Church Commission, 1930–47, box 51, folder 402.

7. Records relating to foreign missions, 1910–1919, Archives: Religious Interests, box 45, folder 357; records relating to medical and agricultural missions, 1930–52, Archives: Religious Interests, box 45, folder 353, and box 47, folder 368, respectively.

8. Arthur W. Packard, file memo, 14 February 1933, Archives: Religious Interests, box 47, folder 370; idem, Advisory Committee memo, 6 February 1934; Packard to Advisory Committee, 17 February 1933; Archives: Religious Interests, box 47, folder 370.

9. Records related to YMCA and YWCA, 1931–39, Archives: Religious Interests, box 49, folder 395.

as the Institute for a Christian Basis of World Relations. From 1935 to 1939, Rockefeller paid most of the expenses of the Movement for World Christianity, which was led by Albert Scott and Eugene Carder of Riverside Church.[10] Rockefeller, however, made very few large contributions to the traditional Protestant causes after 1920.

An Ambivalent Baptist

Even though Rockefeller harbored doubts about sectarian religious endeavor, he gave more than seven million dollars to Baptist organizations between 1917 and 1959, far more than any of his Baptist brothers or sisters.[11] From as early as 1905, Rockefeller had been convinced that the evangelical denominations needed to cooperate. By the time he gathered material for his 1917 address "The Christian Church—What of its Future?" he was toying with radical ideas about interdenominationalism. One of those whom he consulted in preparing his talk was his former pastor William H. P. Faunce, who counseled moderation. The historic American denominations, Faunce reminded Rockefeller, would not disappear overnight; in fact, they were growing. Faunce cited a study by George A. Coe, a sociologist on the faculty of Union Theological Seminary, which showed that church growth was exceeding population growth. Movements independent of the historic church, unless led by "a genius like John Wesley or William Booth," were doomed to fail, Faunce believed. There was, moreover, no need for Rockefeller to feel that he was alone in his ambivalence about being a member of a sectarian fellowship. Faunce assured Rockefeller that he knew of thirty "leading Baptists" who agreed with Rockefeller about the need for Protestant unity and suggested that these thirty might be the beginning of a movement capable of winning many others.[12]

10. Records related to Institute for a Christian Basis of World Relations Conference, 1924, Archives: Religious Interests, box 50, folder 399; Records related to Movement for World Christianity, 1930–39, Archives: Religious Interests, box 49, folder 393.

11. Creel, "Contributions," 1–12.

12. William H. P. Faunce to John D. Rockefeller, Jr., 8 November 1917, Archives: Religious Interests, box 38, folder 315.

Ernest Burton, a professor of New Testament at the University of Chicago, was also skeptical about the possibility of radical change in the structure of American Protestantism. He thought that it would not be possible to establish a "new church" and urged Rockefeller to "broaden and strengthen" those that already existed. He did suggest, however, that "possibly, in one or two central places, a new church could be established, which would stand as an example of the broadest spirit of religious tolerance."[13]

When Rockefeller delivered his speech on the future of the church to the Baptist community in December 1917, he knew that even the liberals among them would much prefer that a reborn Baptist church embody modern religious yearnings than that a new religious structure be formed. Few, however, were ready for the renovations in Baptist church practice that Rockefeller thought necessary:

> I think generally, Baptists fancy that baptism by immersion was established by Christ as the door to the church. Those who have studied those questions more deeply know that this impression is not correct. Christ was baptized; he preached baptism; He never made it a condition of church membership, nor did his disciples.

Having disposed of this shibboleth, Rockefeller then directed Baptists to their Anabaptist heritage, which included such ideas as the principles of religious equality, the freedom to study the scriptures, the right of each individual to follow his or her own reason and conscience, the doctrine of the inner light, an emphasis on the spirit of God in the individual, the universal priesthood of believers, the emancipation of women, and the church's freedom from the state. If Baptists could merely own their heritage, Rockefeller urged, then "the Baptist Church can be the foundation upon which the Church of the Living God shall be built. It can be the leader in ushering in the new era of Christian unity. What a hope! What a privilege! What a duty! In God's name I ask does any one dare let it pass?"[14] No one knew

13. Ernst Burton to John D. Rockefeller, Jr., 15 November 1917, Archives: Religious Interests, box 38, folder 315.

14. Rockefeller, "The Christian Church."

better than Rockefeller that privilege meant duty. Rockefeller's agenda for the Baptist church was fixed.

Throughout the twenties, Rockefeller continued to give to Baptist causes, even as he worked to reform the church. From 1920 to 1932, he gave three hundred thousand dollars annually to the Northern Baptist Convention (N.B.C.) as well as substantial additional gifts to the New York State Convention and the New York City Missionary Society (N.Y.C.M.S.). After the Laymen's Inquiry, Rockefeller decided to terminate his denominational giving. He made two final gifts of two hundred thousand dollars to the N.B.C. in 1933 and 1934 and concluded his giving to the state and local societies. In 1934, he wrote to the N.Y.C.M.S.:

> This will be my last gift to the regular denominational work of the Society. Hereafter such sums as I decide to devote to general religious work it is my present thought to contribute to cooperative, inter-denominational or non-denominational enterprises. If any of the work which your Society is engaged in is of that character, I shall be glad to have it brought to my attention.[15]

By 1934, Rockefeller had given up hope that the Baptist churches as a fellowship might be transformed into "the Church of the Living God." He had not, however, abandoned Burton's suggestion, that one or two strategically placed churches might serve as models for those who sought a better way. True to the Baptist tradition of congregational government, Rockefeller found that even radical changes in church life could be made in the local congregation.

Riverside Church

Around 1920, the noteworthy issues at Fifth Avenue Baptist Church were the building fund, to which the Rockefeller family made nominal contributions, and the new policy of recognizing associate and affiliate membership in the church, which had been introduced by Pastor Cornelius Woelfkin. Both were the early expressions of larger things to come.

15. John D. Rockefeller, Jr., to the N.Y.C.M.S., 26 June 1922, Archives: Religious Interests, box 8, folder 51.

In 1916, Woelfkin first proposed associate membership in order to include those who agreed with the church about "the essential elements" of the Christian faith, but who disagreed about the necessity of baptism by immersion. In a personal letter to Rockefeller, Woelfkin expressed the opinion that open membership was sure to become a widespread practice among Baptists and would present a more powerful Christian witness. He thought that "all our thinking men—laymen and preachers" were "longing for the day of a new birth of our principles." Rockefeller heartily approved the idea of broadening membership, but wanted the church to be cautious in its implementation, lest reactionaries in the congregation succeed in thwarting it altogether.[16]

Fifth Avenue Baptist moved to a new facility on Park Avenue in 1922, and the aging Woelfkin began to consider retirement. Rockefeller and James C. Colgate considered Harry Emerson Fosdick the leading candidate to succeed him as pastor. Rockefeller had long admired Fosdick and had paid to have his 1922 sermon, "Shall the Fundamentalists Win?" distributed to one hundred and thirty thousand pastors. In the fall of 1924, Rockefeller began to court Fosdick. Upon learning of Fosdick's recent preaching trip to Britain, Rockefeller volunteered, with appropriate flattery, to pay for all expenses.[17]

Rockefeller and his associates, meanwhile, discussed various possibilities for luring Fosdick from his First Presbyterian charge, including founding a new interdenominational cathedral on Riverside Drive, if the facilities on Park Avenue presented an obstacle to his acceptance. In January 1925, Fosdick declined the call to the pastorate at Park Avenue; throughout the winter Rockefeller continued to seek

16. Cornelius Woelfkin to John D. Rockefeller, Jr., draft of the proposal, 8 February 1917; Rockefeller to Woelfkin, 20 February 1917; Archives: Religious Interests, box 33, folder 263. For Rockefeller's contributions through the 1910s to Fifth Avenue Baptist, see "Systematic Contribution Plan" for various years, Archives: Religious Interests, box 33, folder 263.

17. John D. Rockefeller, Jr., to Harry E. Fosdick, 19 November 1924, Archives: Religious Interests, box 32, folder 255. One can do little to improve on Robert Moats Miller's treatment of the relationship between Rockefeller and Harry Emerson Fosdick in *Harry Emerson Fosdick: Preacher, Pastor, Prophet* (New York: Oxford University Press, 1985). The issues briefly treated here are handled more fully by Miller as cited.

property in Morningside Heights. In March, the church trustees and deacons met in Rockefeller's home and agreed to present to the congregation a plan to build for Fosdick a new church near Columbia University.[18]

Rockefeller continued to negotiate with Fosdick over a broad range of issues. During a discussion between the two in April, Fosdick averred that he did not want to be known as the pastor of the richest man in the country. Rockefeller responded, "Do you think that more people will criticize you on account of my wealth, than will criticize me on account of your theology?"[19] In May 1925, Fosdick agreed to become pastor of the congregation, which promised him a new building and the freedom to create a model modernist congregation. The call was extended with only seven dissenting votes; it appears, however, that as many as one hundred in the congregation of seven hundred actually opposed the move, but felt powerless to prevent it.[20]

Ivy Lee circulated a publication entitled, "The Call of Dr. Fosdick to Park Avenue Baptist Church," which announced that the church intended to practice open membership and receive members who had not been baptized by immersion. Not all Baptists applauded the venture. John Roach Straton suggested that the church bear a sign reading "SOCONY"—the Standard Oil Church of New York—rather than a cross, since Rockefeller's modernism denied the cross anyway. He further charged that Rockefeller had recently "tightened his grip on our denomination here in the Northland" by his large gifts to the national missionary societies.[21] With the association of Fosdick and Rockefeller, Park Avenue had moved to the center of the controversy between fundamentals and modernists in the Baptist church. At the Northern Baptist conventions, held in Seattle in 1925 and Washington in 1926, fundamentalists led several protests against the membership policies of Park Avenue and were defeated on each of the key votes. Rockefeller still valued the Baptist connection at that time, and Fosdick agreed to implement his policies slowly in order to maintain the support of the majority of Northern Baptists.[22]

18. Miller, *Fosdick*, 160–61.
19. Quoted in ibid., 162.
20. Ibid., 161–65.
21. Quoted in ibid., 165.
22. Ibid., 164–73.

As the years progressed, Rockefeller was quite content with the "taint" of Fosdick's theology. Furthermore, Fosdick, according to his most eminent biographer, succeeded in maintaining his prophetic liberty despite being Rockefeller's pastor. Fosdick, in fact, was frequently charged with being a socialist. Disagreement on social issues between the two was not frequent; Rockefeller himself was occasionally accused of socialism. The two did, however, have awkward moments early in Fosdick's pastorate. During a frank exchange over a social pronouncement that Fosdick made in the early days of his ministry at Park Avenue, Fosdick wrote to Rockefeller:

> Of course, I took it for granted that you were a liberal, and if I had not been sure of your devotion to progressive policies in industry, I never would have dreamed of taking the pastorate of a church in which you were so prominent and powerful a member. Be sure, therefore, that if ever in the pulpit I shoot off a gun on the industrial question I am thinking of you as behind the gun and not in front of it.[23]

Ralph Sockman, a prominent Methodist preacher, stated after Fosdick's retirement: "That the Rockefeller millions never muted the prophetic notes of his message is a tribute to the social insights of both Dr. Fosdick and Mr. Rockefeller."[24]

At the same time, Riverside Church itself was not an exercise in social democracy during Fosdick's years, despite its nominal congregational polity. Most Riverside trustees, including John D. Rockefeller III, Albert L. Scott, and Winthrop W. Aldrich, were related in some significant way to Rockefeller. Board meetings were held in the Rockefeller offices, and most decisions were made by the trustees, not by the deacons. It is not surprising that Rockefeller wanted to protect his investment in Riverside; his initial contributions to the structure alone totaled over ten and a half million dollars. Rockefeller was even awarded a golden key before the dedication of the edifice as "a symbol that your Father's house is open to you day and night."[25] Through

23. Harry E. Fosdick to John D. Rockefeller, Jr., 4 January 1928; see also Rockefeller to Fosdick, 19 December 1927; Fosdick to Rockefeller, 22 December 1927; Harry E. Fosdick, 1922–59; Archives: Friends and Services, box 61. Box numbers only will be given for this collection; folders are arranged alphabetically.

24. Quoted in Miller, *Fosdick*, 464.

25. Quoted in ibid., 213.

the years, Rockefeller's numerous personal gifts to the church, amounting to more than thirty-two million dollars, enabled the congregation to function without debt even during the Depression.[26]

Rockefeller contributed time and effort as well as money to the fellowship. He often invited people to attend Riverside. When Dwight Eisenhower became president of Columbia University, for example, Rockefeller offered to pick the Eisenhowers up for church on Sunday mornings. Riverside represented for Rockefeller a home church that genuinely reflected his ecumenical convictions. Fosdick, who was as strong a supporter of interdenominationalism as Rockefeller, welcomed new members to the sacrament of communion with these words:

> There are in this church many members of many denominations and many faiths. In welcoming you into our membership, we do not ask you to give up any belief or form that is dear to you but rather to bring it to us that we may be enriched thereby. We invite you not to our table or the table of any denomination but to the Lord's table.[27]

In 1934, when Rockefeller ceased giving to Northern Baptist missionary organizations, Riverside also ceased to give, stating that it would henceforth judge the worthiness of a mission organization by "the quality of its contribution to the Kingdom of God on earth, rather than its denominational affiliation."[28] At Riverside, moreover, Rockefeller could hear Fosdick proclaim,

> Once a week we preach here, but seven days and nights a week we are at work here, in practical service. Recall that ringing slogan of Charles Spurgeon's: "The God that answereth by orphanages, let him be God!" We have tried to illustrate that. The God that answereth by boys' clubs and girls' clubs, by playgrounds for children, by day nurseries and consultation on family problems—let him be God! The God that answereth by practical help to folk in trouble, by finding jobs for the unemployed, by psychiatric assistance for those inwardly distraught—let him be God! The God that answereth by Christian education,

26. Ibid., 222–23, 211–13.
27. Quoted in ibid., 214.
28. Quoted in ibid., 250.

> by friendly fellowship, by community service, by money given to causes here and around the world, let him be God.[29]

Here was a model for the "Church of the Living God." Here, at least, Rockefeller could enjoy the firstfruits of the reborn church.[30]

Seminaries

Rockefeller's contributions to interdenominational theological schools may well have been his most productive investment in the cause of unitive liberal Christianity. Rockefeller began to give to theological seminaries during the 1920s, and it was then that he and Gates formed opinions about theological education, opinions that continued forty years later to guide Rockefeller's giving. Theological education could either "increase the spirit of Jesus among men" or it could "stifle that spirit."[31] The determining factor was a school's depth of understanding of the true nature of religion, which Gates summarized in this way: "God loves Monday just as much as He does Sunday, if not more." A good theological education would not focus on a theological system; it would prepare its students for many forms of "disinterested service to humanity."[32] Gates felt in 1921 that some Baptist seminaries—such as Chicago, Rochester, Hamilton, and Crozier—and some Congregational seminaries understood the nature of true religion. Most other denominational seminaries did not. Rockefeller determined that he would send money only to those schools that promoted a broad and free inquiry into the best ways to serve God by serving humanity.

Union Theological Seminary, at which Harry Emerson Fosdick was professor of practical theology, appealed to the General Education Board in 1923 as part of a four million dollar fund-raising effort. Raymond Fosdick reported to his older brother that the board in-

29. Quoted in ibid., 248.

30. Rockefeller was also instrumental in the establishment of interdenominational churches in both of his other "homes"—the Union Church of Pocantico Hills, replete with windows designed by Chagal and Matisse; and the Mount Desert Larger Parish in Seal Harbor, Maine.

31. Frederick T. Gates to John D. Rockefeller, Jr., 25 April 1921, Archives: Gates Papers, box 3, folder 59.

32. Ibid.

tended to decline, and Harry Emerson Fosdick responded with a six-page paean to Union, stressing its unique place within American Protestantism. As a result, Rockefeller personally gave Union a million dollars, the first of many gifts which would total nearly four million dollars.[33]

After he suspended his giving to the Northern Baptist Convention, Rockefeller began to give generously to a number of interdenominational theological schools. Those to whom he gave one million dollars or more were Colgate-Rochester Divinity School, Yale Divinity School, and Harvard Divinity School. The major gift to Harvard, presented in 1954, came in response to President Nathan Pusey's public affirmation of the importance of theological education. "In the position which Harvard University and you as its president have taken, I see the dawn of a new day in the educational world," Rockefeller wrote to Pusey.[34] Harvard was able to add five prominent theological scholars to its faculty: George Buttrick, Paul Tillich, Krister Stendahl, Amos N. Wilder, and John D. Wild.

The following year, Rockefeller gave twenty-two million dollars to the Sealantic Fund, which was originally formed to benefit his home churches at Seal Harbor and Pocantico, in order "to strengthen and develop Protestant theological education."[35] The principles involved in dispensing the grant were familiar ones. The first priority was the establishment of a few model institutions. All of the schools mentioned above were among those that received grants of between five hundred thousand and one and a half million dollars. The fund also gave one million dollars or more to Vanderbilt University School of Religion, Federated Theological Faculty of the University of Chicago, and Pacific School of Religion. Rockefeller invested another ten million dollars in theological libraries, fellowships, and the promotion of cooperation among regional clusters of small seminaries. Among the cluster programs that he aided were those around Atlanta, Richmond,

33. Miller, *Fosdick*, 320; Creel, "Contributions," 10.

34. John D. Rockefeller, Jr., to Nathan Pusey, 23 December 1953, quoted in Fosdick, *Portrait*, 227.

35. John D. Rockefeller, Jr., to Sealantic trustees, 11 January 1955, quoted in Fosdick, *Portrait*, 227.

San Francisco, Rochester, and Boston. Included in the fellowship programs were three for black students. Several leaders in the civil rights movement were Sealantic fellows, including Jesse Jackson, who attended Chicago Theological Seminary. Rockefeller also gave substantial amounts to Hartford Theological Seminary and the American Association of Theological Schools.[36]

This burst of religious philanthropy from Rockefeller, then in his eighties, constituted a final variation on a familiar group of themes. Humanitarian service, cooperation, and modernization were the values that Rockefeller rewarded in his major gifts to theological education.

Religious Cooperation and Protestant Federation: 1900–1960

There was Rockefeller money behind virtually every interdenominational movement in the first half of the twentieth century. A chronicle of his giving to these movements provides a fascinating look into the various forms that the unitive impulse was taking through the years. The most significant American expression of religious cooperation in the early twentieth century was interchurch federation. Rockefeller made substantial contributions to the Federal and National Councils of Churches, as well as to the New York City Protestant Council and World Council of Churches.

Rockefeller's interest in interdenominationalism began during his early days in his father's office. As already indicated, he formed his interdenominational convictions under Gates's tutelage and was an early supporter of Mott's cooperative program.[37] As early as 1900, he had responded to an appeal from Charles Evans Hughes with a small gift from "a Baptist donor" to the National Committee on the Federation of Churches and Christian Workers. For several years, Rockefeller annually renewed this gift, which amounted to about ten percent of the group's budget.[38]

36. Harr and Johnson, *Century*, 520–21.

37. See chap. 5.

38. Charles E. Hughes to John D. Rockefeller, Jr., 21 November 1900 and subsequent years; "National Federation of Churches and Christian Workers," memo, 1 May 1908; Archives: Religious Interests, box 31, folder 246.

When the Federal Council of Churches of Christ in America was formed in 1908, Rockefeller became an immediate supporter. His initial gift constituted over five percent of the first year's expenses. Over the next four years, he followed this with annual contributions which might have been larger except for his concern that his gifts should not relieve the churches of their own responsibility. By 1913, however, Rockefeller's personal benevolence committee was questioning the effectiveness of the council, and the task of pleading the council's case to the committee fell to Secretary Charles S. Macfarlane. He tried to explain the difficulty of unifying a diverse and divided American Protestantism; it would require "a careful, thoughtful, more or less subterranean campaign of education and nurture."[39]

The Rockefeller staff was displeased over the lack of financial support that the denominations were giving the F.C.C. and sought an explanation from its usual religious counselors, including Cornelius Woelfkin, John R. Mott, and Henry F. Cope of the Religious Education Association. Their assessment of the council was that it was well intentioned but ineffective. For this reason, the Rockefellers gave nothing to the F.C.C. between 1916 and 1920.[40]

During these years, Rockefeller participated in a number of efforts to unite Protestants. In a 1917 letter to Faunce, Rockefeller mentioned that he had given a luncheon at the Hotel Astor for one hundred and seventy-five ministers who were interested in continuing the work of a recent Billy Sunday Campaign and that one minister had expressed the desire that other laity help make it possible for ministers to meet once every month or two. William P. Merrill, pastor of the Brick Presbyterian Church of Manhattan, responded by suggesting that a lay committee be established to promote interdenominationalism in New York City. Rockefeller suggested the idea to a number of pastors. A

39. Starr Murphy to Lindsley F. Kimball, 6 May 1908; Murphy to Kimball, 9 February 1910; Murphy to Kimball, 12 December 1910; Murphy to Kimball, 9 August 1911; Murphy to Charles S. Macfarlane, 6 May 1912; Murphy to Macfarlane, 14 May 1913; Murphy to Macfarlane, 2 June 1914; Willard S. Richardson to F.C.C., 1 July 1915; Macfarlane to Murphy, 28 May 1913 (regarding "subterranean activity"); Archives: Religious Interests, box 31, folder 246.

40. Willard S. Richardson to Starr Murphy, 18 June 1915, Archives: Religious Interests, box 31, folder 246.

reading of his 1917 speech at the Clergy Club of New York garnered a number of additional suggestions regarding ways to promote Christian unity.[41]

One of the ventures in which Rockefeller involved himself was the Ad Interim Committee of the Inter-Church Conference on Organic Union. The goal of this organization, which consisted of a number of prominent Protestant church leaders, was to effect the full organizational merger, under a governing council, of as many of the Protestant denominations as possible. The proposed merger would be based on a recognition of substantial creedal agreement, mutual acceptance of ordinations, and negotiated compromises on historically troublesome issues such as baptism and church government. Throughout 1919, Rockefeller corresponded with Woelfkin and Henry W. Jessup about Jessup's draft of a "Plan For Organic Union of the Evangelical Churches in the United States of America." Rockefeller was enamored with the possibility of organic church union, but asked whether the term "evangelical" might not be too narrow, suggesting instead his phrase, "The Church of the Living God." With disappointment Rockefeller watched the short-lived attempt of this group to obtain the adherence of national denominational bodies.[42]

The failure of organic union was a minor part of Rockefeller's education in denominational intransigence; the major part came through his participation in the I.W.M. disaster. Rockefeller was sorely disillusioned by what he interpreted as self-protection displayed by the major denominational bodies as they allowed the Interchurch World Movement to die. He learned an important lesson, however—any attempt to push the denominations faster or farther in the direction of cooperation than they wished to go was doomed to failure. In 1920 Robert E. Speer was elected president of the F.C.C. Rockefeller and

41. John D. Rockefeller, Jr., to William H. P. Faunce, 28 December 1917; William P. Merrill to Rockefeller, 17 July 1918; Rockefeller to John D. Adams, 29 December 1917; Fred B. Smith to Rockefeller, 9 January 1918; Rockefeller to Smith, 24 January 1918; Archives: Religious Interests, box 38, folder 315.

42. See especially John D. Rockefeller, Jr., to William H. Roberts, 12 March 1919; Henry W. Jessup to Rockefeller, 20 March 1919; Rockefeller to Jessup, 21 April 1919; Jessup to Rockefeller, 23 April 1919; Archives: Religious Interests, box 38, folder 315.

his associates were impressed by Speer, and Raymond Fosdick wrote to Rockefeller's office, recommending that Rockefeller renew his support of the F.C.C. Speer was, in Fosdick's opinion, "pretty much of a conservative," but he was also a great improvement over preceding F.C.C. leaders. Fosdick thought, moreover, that the Federal Council had "pretty well absorbed whatever impetus the Interchurch World Movement achieved" and would be improved by the infusion of energy.[43]

Rockefeller subsequently wrote to Speer, stating that he intended to support the council:

> Surely there must be many people throughout the country who have believed firmly in the principle of federation but who have not had the fullest confidence in some of the personnel, and have therefore withheld their support and cooperation. As I may perhaps have said to you, this has been our own position. Your coming into the leadership of the movement will go far toward removing that obstacle and will inspire general confidence and bring about increased support of the enterprise throughout the country.[44]

During the twenties, Rockefeller gave gifts totaling over one hundred thousand dollars to the F.C.C. Although these were not large gifts by Rockefeller standards, they were by far the largest contributions to the council during those years and constituted between five and eight percent of its budget.[45]

The officers of the council and the Rockefeller committee on benevolence regularly communicated about the council's needs and carried on philosophical discussions about "just what kind of a representative body America should have religiously."[46] On one occa-

43. Raymond Fosdick to Willard S. Richardson, 27 June 1921, Archives: Religious Interests, box 31, folder 247.

44. John D. Rockefeller, Jr., to Robert E. Speer, 4 December 1920, Archives: Religious Interests, box 31, folder 246.

45. "Federal Council of Churches of Christ in America," memo, 1 February 1934, Archives: Religious Interests, box 31, folder 247. Willard S. Richardson to Harry B. Fisher, 8 March 1923, Archives: Religious Interests, box 32, folder 253.

46. Memo of conversation between Thomas B. Appleget, Orrin Judd, and Samuel Cavert, 26 February 1929, Archives: Religious Interests, box 31, folder 247.

sion, the council office consulted Rockefeller about its policy: Edward T. Devine asked for his criticism of a draft of the statement of social ideals of the churches that was being prepared for the quadrennial meeting in 1932. The staff declined comment, Rockefeller being absent, and Fosdick expressed displeasure at Rockefeller's having been consulted: "Frankly, I do not like the idea of a statement of this kind being put up to Mr. Rockefeller or any other potential contributor for his approval."[47]

During the 1920s, Rockefeller also supported a group called "The Inquiry," which had grown out of the National Conference on the Christian Way of Life, initiated by the F.C.C. in 1922. The Inquiry promoted the use of "scientific" principles of group process developed by William H. Kilpatrick in order to resolve potential conflict in the fields of industrial, interracial, and international relations. The "Inquiry method" featured a version of situation ethics, the belief that even an intractable situation was "plastic through and through," and the assurance that conflict could be productively guided toward social growth. Principals in the group included Edward C. Carder, formerly of the International YMCA—an organization which paid special heed to Inquiry principles, and Galen M. Fisher of the I.S.R.R., with which the Inquiry shared research aims. Rockefeller contributed one third of the Inquiry's budgets for the years 1924–1932 (about twenty thousand dollars annually), although he had no direct involvement in its affairs.[48]

In 1923, Rockefeller was provided with another opportunity for ecumenical service—one that showed that Rockefeller's vision for religious unity extended even beyond that of his mentor, Gates. Episcopal Bishop William T. Manning solicited a contribution from Rockefeller for the completion of the Cathedral of St. John the Divine. Gates's bias toward low church Protestantism shone through in his counsel to Rockefeller: the Cathedral was an unfit investment on sev-

47. Edward T. Devine to John D. Rockefeller, Jr., 12 September 1929; Raymond Fosdick to Robert W. Gumbel, 17 September 1929; Archives: Religious Interests, box 31, folder 247.

48. Reprint from the "Occasional Papers of the Inquiry," September 1929; contribution records, William H. Kilpatrick, 1922–33, Archives: Religious Interests, box 47, folder 376.

eral grounds. First, it expressed "a feeling of worship and forms of worship dead to Protestants five hundred years ago" and thus did not qualify as religious art. There was, moreover, a deeper question that weighed upon true Christians. Given the suffering of millions from hunger, natural disaster, and war, why spend money on "stone and glass?" Gates pleaded that "the stones of this Cathedral will be cemented by the blood of the poor."[49]

As he would soon demonstrate bodly on Riverside Drive, Rockefeller appreciated Gothic architecture and the spiritual impulse that it represented, and so he gave half a million dollars to the Cathedral fund. He did, however, use the occasion to make a point with Bishop Manning. He accompanied his gift with a note expressing the hope that the bishop would embody his publicly expressed sentiment that the Cathedral be "a shrine of prayer and worship for all people" by allowing representatives of the Protestant communions to share in the management of the Cathedral. When Manning's private response displeased him, Rockefeller made the correspondence public. *Harper's* magazine summed up the public debate that ensued: "Rockefeller had the best of the argument, and Manning had the money; presumably, each was content."[50]

Beginning in the 1920s, Rockefeller also gave to religious charities outside Protestantism on numerous occasions. An unsolicited Rockefeller contribution to the Catholic Charities of the Archdiocese of New York was accompanied by a note that said, "In trying to meet human needs and make life happier for our fellow men, we are all of us—Catholics, Protestants, and Jews alike—serving a common cause." Rockefeller contributed a total of about one hundred and fifty thousand dollars to Catholic Charities.[51]

Jewish charitable endeavors also frequently attracted Rockefeller's support. He regularly gave, for example, to the Federation of Jewish Philanthropic Societies, and in 1927 he enclosed a note with his gift

49. Frederick T. Gates to John D. Rockefeller, Jr., 17 December 1923, Archives: Gates Papers, box 3, folder 64.

50. Ibid.; Elmer Davis, "Portrait of a Cleric," *Harper's Magazine* 203 (1926) 20.

51. John D. Rockefeller, Jr., to Cardinal Hayes, 26 April 1929, quoted in Fosdick, *Portrait*, 225. Creel, "Contributions," 3.

affirming his belief "in the work your organization is carrying on, and particularly in the cooperative spirit." Beginning in 1934, Rockefeller also made annual contributions to the work of the National Conference of Jews and Christians. He wrote to Everett R. Clinchy, the first director of the National Conference, telling him of his "profound sympathy" for the work of bringing about "fuller cooperation between men and women of all religious faiths." Rockefeller went on to state, characteristically, that civilization required "a living, vitalizing faith in religion of whatever creed."[52]

Most of Rockefeller's efforts toward religious unity, however, continued to be within the Protestant fold. He served on the Sponsoring Committee of the Federal Council's National Preaching Mission in 1936–1937 and also provided a letter of endorsement, published along with those of John J. Pershing, Senator Arthur H. Vandenberg of Michigan, William Green, president of the American Federation of Labor, and J. Edgar Hoover, director of the Federal Bureau of Investigation. Rockefeller's statement characteristically focused on the problem of social stability:

> If civilization emerges, as it must ultimately, from the period of general upheaval, strife and selfishness through which it is now passing, it will not be as a result of international treaties, diplomatic negotiations, political understandings or social or industrial panaceas. A stable, progressive, forward-moving civilization is possible only among men of integrity, high purpose and good will.

Rockefeller pointed to Christ as the model for civic virtues; Christ was the "Light of the world and the Friend and Guide of mankind."[53]

52. John D. Rockefeller, Jr., to Eli H. Bernheim, 5 December 1927, quoted in Fosdick, *Portrait*, 225. Rockefeller to Everett R. Clinchy, 24 December 1937, Archives: Religious Interests, box 32, folder 256.

Rockefeller's contributions between 1934 and 1942 were made through the Davison Fund, established by Rockefeller after he distributed a significant portion of his wealth to a trust for his children. Arthur W. Packard was the director of the fund, which had an annual budget of around three hundred thousand dollars. The Davison Fund gave the F.C.C. approximately thirty-five thousand dollars. Davison II, box 13, folder 92.

53. "Notable Letters from Well-Known Men," Laymen's Sponsoring Committee of the National Preaching Mission under the auspices of the F.C.C., New York, 1937; Archives: Religious Interests, box 32, folder 248.

With the advent of the Second World War, Rockefeller increased his giving to the F.C.C., making special gifts to John Foster Dulles's Commission on a Just and Durable Peace. During the war, Rockefeller was often asked by the Federal Council to speak on the radio as a part of the council's effort to provide a chaplaincy to the nation. Only once did Rockefeller accept the invitation, composing the following speech for the Minute of Prayer (which occurred every hour on the hour) on 1 January 1944:

> To Thee, Oh God, Father of mankind, we come in deep humility, asking forgiveness of our sins. We have too often been selfish, unkind and intolerant. May love for Thee and for our fellow men dominate and ennoble our lives! Give us to know the meaning of duty, the joy of service, the rewards of sacrifice. May even death have for us no fear so long as it be nobly met! And may we face the unknown, calm and unafraid, because of an abiding faith in Thee! Amen.[54]

In its condemnation of selfishness and intolerance and in its mention of duty, service, and sacrifice, this short prayer clearly expressed the religious ideals that Rockefeller consistently emphasized.

In the postwar period, Rockefeller, then in his seventies, continued his old ecumenical interests and added new ones. He gave annually to the F.C.C. and the Commission on a Just and Durable Peace. He supported Church World Service (C.W.S.), organized in 1946 to consolidate and oversee service agencies of the council. C.W.S. was under the direction of his old friend Harper Sibley for several years. Rockefeller also corresponded with Secretary Samuel Cavert about the affairs of the council. For example, in 1945 he wrote requesting an explanation for the council's rejection of the Universalists' application for membership.[55]

54. Henry St. George Tucker to John D. Rockefeller, Jr., 22 March 1943; Arthur W. Packard to Rockefeller, 8 April 1943; Harry P. Fish to Rockefeller, 10 August 1944; Jesse M. Bader to Rockefeller, 27 December 1943; Rockefeller to Bader, 29 December 1943; Archives: Religious Interests, box 32, folder 248.

55. Memo, "Federal Council of the Churches of Christ in America," March 1949; Dana S. Creel to Samuel Cavert, 30 March 1950; Creel to Walter Van Kirk, 16 May 1950; Archives: Religious Interests, box 32, folder 249. Cavert to Arthur W. Packard, 13 February 1945, Archives: Religious Interests, box 32, folder 248.

The postwar period also afforded Rockefeller a new opportunity to contribute to Christian unity in his home town, New York City, as the Protestant Council of New York City was established in 1946. Senior had begun giving to the council's predecessor, the Federation of Churches in New York City (later the Greater New York Federation of Churches) in the 1890s. During the twenties and early thirties, Rockefeller had become the primary supporter of the organization; his gifts accounted for about thirty percent of its income.[56]

When the federation merged into the Protestant Council, Rockefeller again became a major benefactor. He contributed two hundred and ninety-five thousand dollars between 1944 and 1961, despite his concern that the large budget of the organization might allow it act to without the cooperation of the denominations that it served. Rockefeller took special interest in the social service programs of the council.[57]

At the inaugural fund-raising dinner of the council, Rockefeller again gave his speech, "The Christian Church—What of Its Future?" Rockefeller, demonstrating characteristic consistency, reaffirmed without substantive change the principles of interdenominational cooperation that he had articulated in 1917. He had embarked on the implementation of those principles some three decades earlier and, although his strategies and tactics had changed, his goals had not. The rethinking spawned by the Depression and the war had produced the same proposal: America needed a national religion that could embody the innate religious instincts of the great mass of people. At Rockefeller's expense, the council reprinted thirty-one thousand copies of the address for distribution, and the April edition of *Readers' Digest* carried an abridged version. Nearly a thousand people wrote to Rockefeller in response. Letters from Union Churches and Larger Parishes across the United States—ecumenical congregations which were expressions of Rockefeller's philosophy—especially heartened him.[58]

56. Records related to the Federation and the Protestant Council of New York City, Archives: Religious Interests, box 51, folder 404.

57. Records related to the Protestant Council of New York City, 1890–1961, Archives: Religious Interests, box 51, folders 406, 424.

58. John D. Rockefeller, Jr., *The Christian Church, What of its Future?* (New York: Protestant Council, 1945). Related correspondence, 1945–49, Archives: Religious Interests, box 52, folders 412–16. Regarding Rockefeller's

A celebrated objection came from Episcopal Bishop James P. DeWolfe of Long Island, who urged that his communion withdraw from all councils of churches that subscribed to Rockefeller's views. DeWolfe nearly succeeded in forcing the Protestant Council to distance itself from Rockefeller's theological position until several of his fellow Episcopalians discouraged his efforts by publicly supporting Rockefeller.[59]

The greater diversity of American religion was reflected in the variety of groups participating in this new round of public debate over Rockefeller's theology. The *Jewish Ledger* pointed out that Rockefeller's characterization of Judaism in the days of Jesus as an "empty form" was not borne out by religious scholars of any persuasion. *Life* magazine ran an editorial that reflected the toughening of public theology in the neoorthodox era; it described Rockefeller's religion as "nondescript." Numerous Catholic publications held the same attitude, one even applying to Rockefeller's theology the label "ersatz Christianity." Rockefeller's staff found what it considered one of the finest interpretive criticisms of the address in the *New Age Observer*, an esoteric publication of Theodore and Corinne Heline. "More and more are coming through first hand experience to know that He can be reached without any intermediaries and prefer to make that approach direct," its review stated. Rockefeller began a friendly correspondence with the Helines. Perhaps Friedrich Schleiermacher's "religious sentiment" was relocating outside of the Protestant churches in the postwar period.[60] In addition, letters of congratulations also came from within the Protestant fold. Hocking, Rufus Jones, John Foster Dulles, Meth-

---

article in *Readers' Digest* ("That the Church May Truly Live," *Readers' Digest* 46 [1945] 25–27), see Corine Johnson to John D. Rockefeller, Jr., 15 February 1945, Archives: Religious Interests, box 52, folder 416.

59. James P. DeWolfe to the clergy of the Diocese of Long Island, 26 March 1945; related correspondence and clippings; Archives: Religious Interests, box 52, folder 416.

60. "Mr. Rockefeller on Judaism," *Jewish Ledger*, 16 February 1945, Archives: Religious Interests, box 52, folder 417. "Christianity and Creeds," *Life* 18 (1945) 28; see also Arthur W. Packard to John D. Rockefeller, Jr., "Regarding the *Life* article," 13 April 1945; "What Price Unity," *America* (5 May 1945); Theodore Heline, "The Church of the Living God," *New Age Interpreter* 6 (1945) 1; Archives: Religious Interests, box 52, folder 417.

odist Bishop G. Bromley Oxnam, and dozens of others wrote to express appreciation.[61]

Rockefeller's subsequent involvement in the Protestant Council during the forties and fifties was reflective of the revival of American Protestantism across a broad theological spectrum. The council sponsored the Billy Graham Crusade of June 1957, and Rockefeller's contribution covered about one-tenth of the expenses of the crusade and made him the second largest donor. He made this contribution despite the objections of Riverside's Robert J. McCracken, who warned that Riverside was taking a "wary and cautious" attitude toward the crusade. Because of the contribution, J. Howard Pew invited Rockefeller to a luncheon for Graham and Harold Ockenga, at which a new publication called *Christianity Today* was being unveiled. Rockefeller contributed to other public expressions of religion sponsored by the council in the fifties, including an interfaith chapel at New York's Idlewild International Airport.[62]

The birth of the World Council of Churches (W.C.C.) provided a wider arena for Rockefeller's religious benefactions. Prior to its formation, Rockefeller had made important contributions to the World's Conference on Faith and Order, the Episcopalian expression of the ecumenical impulse, and the Universal Christian Conference on Life and Work, the movement initiated by Nathan Söderblom, primate of the Church of Sweden. Rockefeller had also considered the possibility of establishing a fund for the use of William Adams Brown, the Union Seminary professor and renowned theologian of the church, in promoting the formation of a new ecumenical organization.[63]

61. Rufus Jones to John D. Rockefeller, Jr., 1 February 1945; Ernest Hocking to Rockefeller, 1 February 1945; John Foster Dulles to Rockefeller, 1 February 1945; G. Bromley Oxnam to Rockefeller, 5 February 1945; F. Ernest Johnson to Rockefeller, 9 February 1945; Archives: Religious Interests, box 53, folder 418.

62. Dana S. Creel to Yorke Allen, Jr., 27 September 1956; J. Howard Pew to John D. Rockefeller III, 3 June 1957; Archives: Religious Interests, box 53, folder 422.

63. Records related to faith and order, 1919–37, Archives: Religious Interests, box 41, folder 333; Universal Christian Council for Life and Work, 1924–44, file note dated 23 May 1934; William Adams Brown to John D. Rockefeller, Jr., 7 January 1939, Rockerfeller to Brown, 21 January 1939; Archives: Religious Interests, box 43, folder 344.

During the summer of 1939, Harry Emerson Fosdick and John Foster Dulles kept Rockefeller informed as an informal board of strategy laid plans for a world council of churches. Rockefeller immediately made himself the council's primary patron; in nineteen of its first twenty years, Rockefeller topped its list of donors. The W.C.C. represented the intersection of two of Rockefeller's long standing interests: interdenominationalism and internationalism.[64]

Several of Rockefeller's gifts to the W.C.C. were especially significant. The first of these came in 1945, at Dulles's initiative. Aware that Rockefeller was seeking a vehicle through which to aid the postwar recovery of European churches, Dulles informed Rockefeller that the Presbyterians intended to channel their aid through the incipient World Council. The war had arrested the development of the council, and the Presbyterians hoped to strengthen it by their contribution. Dulles also mentioned that the Baptists, in contrast, intended to act independently in their church relief efforts.[65]

The W.C.C. Provisional Committee was, in fact, scrambling to respond to the opportunity for Christian unity represented by the Stuttgart Declaration; in this declaration, the council of the Evangelical Church in Germany, contritely presenting itself to the W.C.C., asked for financial help. The Provisional Committee produced a nine-million-dollar program for reconstruction and interchurch aid, but was not actively engaged in any definite effort to raise the money. In a letter that reached Rockefeller the week after his discussion with Dulles, Willem Visser 't Hooft shared with Rockefeller his dream of a training center in Geneva that would prepare Christian leaders for postwar opportunities. Rockefeller subsequently learned that although one hundred million dollars was being raised for postwar reconstruction among American churches, only the World Council fund was interdenominational. He decided not to give to the Northern Baptist Convention reconstruction effort and announced his intention to make

64. John Foster Dulles to John D. Rockefeller, Jr., 30 March 1939; Roswell P. Barnes to Rockefeller, 16 May 1939; Archives: Religious Interests, box 43, folder 345.

65. John Foster Dulles to John D. Rockefeller, Jr., 27 July 1945, Archives: Religious Interests, box 44, folder 350.

a million dollar gift to the W.C.C. reconstruction program; one-half of this gift would serve to establish Visser 't Hooft's training school. Rockefeller's office assisted the Friends of the World Council of Churches, chaired by Charles P. Taft, in applying for tax exempt status in order to receive Rockefeller's contribution.[66]

Rockefeller was encouraged and amused by the notes of thanks for this gift. These letters, each written in the native language of the author, came from diverse sources, including Marc Boegner, president of the National Council of Reformed Churches in France; Ingve Brilioth, archbishop of Sweden; S. F. H. J. van der Sprenkel Berkelbac, a theologian of the Reformed Church of Holland; Eivind Berggrav, bishop of Oslo; Christophoros II, pope and patriarch of Alexandria and Africa; Germanos, archbishop of Thyatira; George Wu, secretary of the Christian National Council of China; and Martin Niemoller, recently released from Dachau.[67]

The training institute made possible by Rockefeller's gift was named the Ecumenical Institute and was originally under the direction of Heinrich Kraemer. Kraemer kept Rockefeller's staff apprised as it developed its training program for Christians in various professions. The curriculum was less explicitly theological than Rockefeller had expected, but Rockefeller decided to "keep [his] hands off." He wrote to his staff, "We have weaned the baby; it is theirs to bring up as they see fit."[68]

As favorable reports came back through the press and through friends, Rockefeller's trust for the institute was validated. By 1949, Rockefeller Foundation Director Lindsley F. Kimball was so impressed

66. Willem Visser 't Hooft, memo entitled "A Training Center," 3 August 1945; Arthur W. Packard to John D. Rockefeller, Jr., 12 September 1945; Rockefeller to Packard, 16 September 1945; Packard, memo regarding "Friends of the World Council of Churches, Inc.," 1 October 1945; Archives: Religious Interests, box 44, folder 350. For information concerning the early history of the W.C.C., see Ruth Rouse and Stephen C. Neill, *A History of the Ecumenical Movement, 1517–1948* (Philadelphia: Westminister, 1954) 714–16.

67. Letters of appreciation, 1945–46, Archives: Religious Interests, box 44, folder 350.

68. John D. Rockefeller, Jr., to Arthur W. Packard, note written on a memo dated 16 July 1948, Archives: Religious Interests, box 45, folder 352.

with the Institute that he considered breaking with the foundation's longstanding policy of avoiding religious projects in order to start a comparable institute in the United States.[69]

In 1949, Rockefeller made an additional gift of two hundred and fifty thousand dollars to the institute so that it could purchase the Chateau de Bossey, the property on which the institute had been operating.[70] Another significant Rockefeller gift—a quarter of a million dollars, given in 1955—made possible an international study and appraisal of Christian responsibility in areas of rapid social change, especially in Asia, Africa, and Latin America; other study projects in the fields of the church unity, world mission, and Christianity and war; and housing accommodations for the staff of the Ecumenical Institute. Shortly before his death, Rockefeller gave one last significant contribution to the W.C.C.: four hundred thousand dollars to be used for a new headquarters in Grand Saconnex, a suburb of Geneva.[71]

Rockefeller's gifts to the World Council greatly increased his international prestige. G. Bromley Oxnam wrote to Rockefeller reporting that Visser 't Hooft had remarked in a confidential conversation with some leaders of the World Council,

> I wish every European might have the privilege of meeting this extraordinarily able but inspiringly humble follower of our Lord Jesus Christ. Such a meeting would blot out forever the propaganda pictures of the American businessman and they would see America and its Christian leadership as it is.[72]

The primary national expression of Rockefeller's interdenominational ideals during the postwar revival was the National Council of Churches (N.C.C.). The N.C.C. was formed in 1950 as the successor

69. Lindsley F. Kimball to Arthur W. Packard, 23 June 1949, Archives: Religious Interests, box 45, folder 352.

70. Agency report of the Conference of the U.S.A. Member Churches of the World Council of Churches, 18 May 1949, Archives: Religious Interests, box 43, folder 346.

71. Draft copy of a World Council of Churches press release, 18 September 1955, Archives: Religious Interests, box 43, folder 345. Dana S. Creel to Samuel Cavert, 1 March 1957, Archives: Religious Interests, box 45, folder 346.

72. G. Bromley Oxnam to John D. Rockefeller, Jr., 29 December 1949, Archives: Religious Interests, box 45, folder 352.

to the Federal Council. The motto of its first assembly, "This Nation Under God," indicated that mainline Protestantism could return to the theme that Rockefeller had never abandoned. The N.C.C.'s first president, Episcopal Bishop Henry Knox Sherrill, elaborated its vision: "The Council marks a new and great determination that the American way will increasingly be the Christian way, for such is our heritage. . . . Together the Churches can move forward to the goal—a Christian American in a Christian world."[73]

That the N.C.C. should adopt the rhetoric of Christian conquest was appropriate, since it was the successor organization of nearly every expression of the old network of voluntary associations that had survived the Depression. The eight most active interdenominational agencies, aware that their attempts to cooperate with the growing denominational bureaucracies were increasingly inefficient, agreed to national federation with the denominations. The National Council represented the highest degree of Protestant cooperation since 1920.[74]

The N.C.C.'s rhetoric about a Christian America had softened, but the council—thanks in part to Rockefeller's support—continued to embody Rockefeller's ideals about church unity. The Interchurch Center at 475 Riverside Drive, which houses the N.C.C., was erected with a Rockefeller gift of more than four million dollars. Appropriately, the center also served as home for the national offices of the Baptist, Methodist, Presbyterian, and Congregational denominations, as well as a number of other enterprises related to mainline Protestantism. Their willingness to live in the house that Rockefeller built did not signify that those denominations ever reached the degree of unity for which Rockefeller hoped, nor were they able to provide the kind of national moral leadership that he desired. They nonetheless hired preachers trained in Rockefeller-supported institutions, used books researched on Rockefeller grants, and joined councils kept afloat by

73. Henry Knox Sherrill, "The Presidential Message," in National Council of the Churches of Christ in the United States of America, *Christian Faith in Action: Commemorative Volume: The Founding of the National Council of the Churches of Christ in America* (New York: National Council, 1951) 11.

74. Henry Knox Sherrill and Samuel Cavert, *The American Churches in the Ecumenical Movement, 1900–1968* (New York: Association Press, 1968) 203–6.

Rockefeller contributions. By 1960 the American mainline Protestant churches were not all that Rockefeller hoped they would be, but they were much stronger than they would have been without his assistance.

7

The Rockefeller Connection

The Protestant Establishment as a Personal Network

A recently published volume of essays, *Between the Times: The Travail of the Protestant Establishment in America, 1900–1960*, used the concept of an establishment to designate the way in which Protestantism functioned in American culture during these years. It defined the Protestant establishment as both a phalanx of seven powerful families of denominations and a network of relationships that reached beyond those denominations into the wider culture. According to this text, a study of this network of relationships would do much to illuminate the nature and workings of the establishment. This chapter pursues this suggestion.

If any individual emerges as the logical starting point for a consideration of the Protestant establishment, it is John D. Rockefeller, Jr. He was the most prominent lay member of one of the seven denominational groupings in question; his active career covered exactly the pertinent dates; his many-faceted philanthropy related him to nearly every development that is of interest to a study of modernist religion and its relation to modern life. If a Protestant establishment existed, Rockefeller was surely at the center of it. In his continuous effort to promote the Protestant cause, Rockefeller brought together the leaders of crusading Protestantism, the theologians of modernist Protestantism, the elites from newly developed sciences, and powerful figures from business and political life.[1]

The Rockefeller Network: Venues, Lineages, and Styles of Influence

At Rockefeller's funeral, Harry Emerson Fosdick's memorial prayer quoted words of appreciation that had been overheard by a missionary in a Siamese village: "O God, bless John D. Rockefeller, his wife and children; and bless all his buffaloes and elephants and may they all prosper."[2] Rockefeller's generosity made for him an interesting variety of friends. Indeed, one of his major functions within the leadership of American Protestantism was that of bringing people together.

Not the distant and exotic venues, but rather the familiar ones played the greatest role in establishment networks. Mount Desert Island, Maine, was one such setting. Upon receiving word from Gates about the founding of the General Education Board, Daniel Coit Gilman wrote in reply beneath his "North East Harbor" letterhead,

> If anything should bring you to the coast of Maine during the summer, I should be very glad to see you here, where you would have many friends among people personally interested in American education. President Eliot, President Low, President Seelye, Bishop Doane, and Mr. Morris Jesup are all of them nearby.[3]

Indeed, the triumvirate of Gilman, Eliot, and Doane exercised a powerful influence over the North East Harbor area of the island. Local lore has it that a visitor from the West who sought to purchase land near the harbor was put to the test in this way:

1. Hutchison, "Protestantism as Establishment," in idem, *Between the Times*, 3–13. The seven denominational groupings were the Congregationalists, Episcopalians, northern Presbyterians, white northern Baptists, white northern Methodists, Lutherans, and Disciples of Christ.

2. Miller, *Fosdick*, 318.

3. Daniel C. Gilman to Frederick T. Gates, 13 July 1905, Archives: Rockefeller Boards, box 18, folder 175. Seth Low had been president of Columbia. Laurenus C. Seelye was president of Smith College. Jesup was a New York banker and philanthropist. William Croswell Doane served as chancellor of the State University of New York.

"Do you know President Eliot?"
"No."
"Do you know Bishop Doane?"
"No."
"Do you know President Gilman?"
"No, but I am an intimate friend of President Grant."
"That makes no difference, you can't have my land."[4]

Only slightly lower in honor was Eliot's brother-in-law Francis Peabody, a Unitarian who, one island native asserted, could not "have preached better if he had the whole Trinity behind him."[5]

It was not Gates but Rockefeller who would find a second home on the island, not in North East Harbor, but in neighboring Seal Harbor. At the invitation of Union Theological Seminary professor William Adams Brown, the Rockefellers, shortly after they were married, made their first visit to Seal Harbor. Brown's family had followed Yale Professor Edward Dana to the Seal Harbor area. By 1910, the Rockefellers had decided to make the area their summer home. Rockefeller purchased a substantial piece of property on one of the summits overlooking the harbor and built roads for the use of those who wished to reach the spectacular vistas. As the years progressed, he joined Eliot and conservationist George B. Dorr in a campaign to preserve the beauty of the island through the creation of Acadia National Park.[6]

In 1918, Eliot wrote to Gates, reporting that Rockefeller had "done very well as a rich summer inhabitant of Mount Desert." He had earned the favor of year-round island inhabitants by his treatment of the local laborers and his willingness to pay high prices for certain pieces of property that enabled him to situate roads for horse and foot travel in such a way as best to open to the public the natural beauty of the island. Eliot offered, "These good works he really seems to enjoy. I never could see that he got any enjoyment out of the work of the three Rockefeller Boards in New York of which I was a member."[7]

4. This anecdote can be found in William Adams Brown, *A Teacher and His Times* (New York: Scribner's, 1940) 145.

5. Ibid., 149–52.

6. Ibid.

7. Charles W. Eliot to Frederick T. Gates, 18 July 1918, Archives: Gates Papers, box 4, folder 78.

Eliot was not the only Mount Desert neighbor who also served with Rockefeller in benevolent causes. Social gospel exponent Bishop William C. Doane was on the "millionaire's express" with Rockefeller in 1901, and Seth Low and Morris Jesup served on the G.E.B. A deep friendship developed between Rockefeller and Francis G. Peabody. His son Francis W. Peabody went to China with the Rockefeller medical effort, and in 1927 Rockefeller made a special gift to the family during the younger Francis's fatal illness.[8]

The regular summer residents could also count on visits from Protestant leaders such as the prominent Quaker preacher Rufus M. Jones, who spent a sabbatical there in the winter of 1914 cutting trails and visiting with Harvard friends, including Peabody and Eliot, as well as Draper Lewis of Haverford, Samuel Eliot and Clifford Barnes of Chicago, and the Rockefellers. Jones returned each year until 1947 to preach at the Union Church in North East Harbor. Harry Emerson Fosdick began his regular visits to the island in 1919 and became a favorite of those who lived there.[9]

At the request of an island minister, Rockefeller brought to bear the resources of the Institute for Social and Religious Research to study the religious needs of the island, and Rockefeller was the major contributor to the interdenominational institutions that resulted from the I.S.R.R.'s study. When Francis Peabody wrote to Rockefeller in 1935 to congratulate him on his interdenominational work, he could not help but wonder if "your experiences on our little island" had been formative in his interdenominational ideals. Peabody confessed that the Union Church and the Larger Parish plan had "done much to emancipate me from the ideals of denominationalism." He particularly expressed appreciation for the regular visits of Harry Emerson Fosdick and Jones.[10]

8. Fosdick, *Portrait*, 117. John D. Rockefeller, Jr., to Francis G. Peabody, 30 September 1927, Archives: Friends and Services, box 97.

9. Mary Hoxie Jones, *Rufus M. Jones* (London: Friends Home Service Committee, 1970) 43–45. David Hinshaw, *Rufus Jones: Master Quaker* (New York: Putnam's, 1951) 183. Index card file to Office of the Messrs. Rockefeller, 1889–1962, Archives: Correspondence.

10. John D. Rockefeller, Jr., to Dana S. Creel, 11 May 1927, Archives: Religious Interests, box 41, folder 329; Francis W. Peabody to Rockefeller, 29 November 1935, Archives: Friends and Services, box 97d.

The social clubs of the island brought Rockefeller into contact with the rich and famous from every sphere of life. In 1925, he helped found the Bar Harbor Yacht Club, and in 1929, he became a charter member of the Bar Harbor Club along with Edsel Ford, Henry Morganthau, and Joseph Pulitzer, as well as other celebrities too numerous to mention. Rockefeller's favorite Mount Desert Island club was the Pot and Kettle Club of Bar Harbor, which maintained lands for riding and driving around the island; he joined in 1935, and by 1944 its membership included such notables as Walter Lippmann, Harper Sibley, and Yale president James R. Angell.[11]

When he was back in the city, luncheon clubs of all kinds served to bring Rockefeller into contact with influential people. Rockefeller joined the City Club in 1902. It had been founded in 1892 with the purpose of nonpartisan political action in the Progressive mode. It worked with the Bureau of Municipal Research and became the model for "good government" clubs in most of the nation's cities. The club was instrumental in Seth Low's 1897 independent campaign for the mayoralty, and William H. Baldwin, Jr.'s reform efforts received its support. Rockefeller did not frequent the club, but he sponsored Fosdick as a member and remained a regular contributor to its work until 1935.[12]

Another civic club to which Rockefeller belonged was the Dining Club, founded in 1913 at the initiative of Manhattan borough President George McAneny. Club participants—twenty-five to thirty of the city's elite—met monthly throughout 1914 and 1915 for discussion of the public interest. Its membership list gives an indication of the connections that such a club afforded Rockefeller. Included were prominent lawyers and politicians like George Gordon Battle; Joseph Potter Cotton; Frederic Clemson Howe; Ogden Livingston Mills; William Church Osborn; Frank Lyon Polk; Charles Howard Strong; former secretary of war Henry Lewis Stimson; former U.S. Attorney General George Woodward Wickersham; former ambassador to England, Lloyd

11. Bar Harbor Clubs, 1929–60; Pot and Kettle, 1935–59; Archives: Friends and Services, boxes 19 and 22, respectively.

12. City Club of New York, 1902–51; see especially Henry H. Curran, "The City Club of New York," reprinted from *New York Herald-Tribune*, ca. 1925; Archives: Friends and Services, box 20.

Carpenter Griscom; former American consul-general in China, Willard D. Straight; U.S. District Judge Learned Hand; New York Supreme Court Justice and Tammany Hall regular Victor Dowling; J. P. Morgan executive Martin Egan; international banker Otto H. Kahn; the New York Symphony Orchestra's founding conductor, Walter Johannes Damrosch; John Lovejoy Elliott, president of the Ethical Culture Society; magazine illustrator Charles Dana Gibson; Norman Hapgood, editor of *Harper's Weekly*; architect Christopher Grant LaFarge; pioneer orthopedic surgeon Reginald Hall Sayre; *Saturday Evening Post* president Oswald Garrison Villard; and Alexis Carrel and Simon Flexner of the Rockefeller Institute.[13]

The Whitehall Club was the club most used by Rockefeller between 1911 and 1933. Rockefeller, along with Gates and Wallace Buttrick, helped found the club as a gymnasium. He managed to win a squash tournament there and paid to put in a new squash court in 1922, rendered necessary by "the crowding of squash by handball doubles." Rockefeller sponsored Fosdick as well as Everett Colby, his friend from Brown and former New Jersey state senator, as members. The charter members also included at least fifty presidents and vice-presidents of banks and other corporations with offices in the neighborhood. Rockefeller was stopped using the club when he moved his offices "uptown" from 26 Broadway to Rockefeller Center.[14]

The Broad Street Club was one that Rockefeller often visited, because it met in the building of his friend Bert Milbank and was presided over for a time by his personal attorney Thomas M. Debevoise. Nelson and Ivy Lee, Jr., also joined this club. In the thirties and forties the venerable Union Club was the scene of annual "Christmas luncheons" which Rockefeller shared with Milbank, Debevoise, and his brother-in-law William Winthrop Aldrich.[15]

Along with Jerome Greene and Ivy Lee, Rockefeller belonged to the University Club. He proposed some fifteen new members between 1908 and 1922, and his staff often used the club for meetings, as Tom Debevoise did when he met with John Foster Dulles in 1940. Rocke-

13. Dining Club, Archives: Friends and Services, box 20.

14. John D. Rockefeller, Jr., to Clarence G. Michalis, 14 November 1946; Whitehall Club; Archives: Friends and Services, box 24.

15. Broad Street Club, Archives: Friends and Services, box 19.

feller also belonged to the Recess Club with Lee and Raymond Fosdick; the Bankers Club, where he could meet with Alonzo Barton Hepburn, presi-dent of Chase National Bank, as well as the executive officers of nearly every major bank in town; Alpha Delta Phi, whose Edward Judson of Memorial Baptist Church solicited him for its New York Clubhouse; the Brown University Club; and the City Midday Club. He resigned from all of these in the 1930s and joined the Netherland Club in Rockefeller Plaza in the 1940s.[16] In Tarrytown, Rockefeller joined the Sleepy Hollow Country Club, whose advisory committee included John Jacob Astor, James C. Colgate, and Cornelius Vanderbilt. He and his children enjoyed a long relationship with this neighborhood institution.[17]

Vacation homes and social clubs represented opportunities for Rockefeller to transact the business of philanthropy, but he was not outgoing. It is not surprising that the Rockefeller network often followed family lines. Within the inner circle of Rockefeller activities were three remarkable pairs of brothers: Simon and Abraham Flexner, Jerome and Roger Greene, and Harry Emerson and Raymond Fosdick.

The Flexners were from humble origins. Their father was an itinerant peddler in Louisville, Kentucky. Young Simon failed as an apprentice plumber and went to work in a drug store. He managed to struggle through a two-year course in medicine in a Louisville school and gain acceptance to the medical program at Johns Hopkins. There the legendary William H. Welch took Flexner under his wing and, after he completed his training, brought him onto the faculty at Johns Hopkins. Flexner also joined Welch among the original members of the Rockefeller Institute for Medical Research.

In 1908, the fledgling American Medical Association persuaded the Carnegie Foundation to fund a study of medical education in America, and the Rockefeller Institute was consulted for a recommendation about who could carry out such a study. Simon Flexner recommended his brother Abraham. Abraham had been trained as an educator and experienced moderate success as an author and as founder of a private school in Louisville. The Carnegie board became convinced that he

16. University Club, Bankers Club, Midday Club; Archives: Friends and Services, boxes 23, 19, and 20, respectively.

17. Sleepy Hollow Country Club, Archives: Friends and Services, box 22.

was exactly the person to do their study, despite his having had no medical training. His epoch-making study of the country's one hundred and fifty-five medical schools fully vindicated their judgment. Frederick Gates found in the study the confirmation of all his own instincts and brought Abraham before the G.E.B. to answer the question, "What would you do if you had a million dollars with which to make a start in reorganizing medical education in the United States?" Thus began Abraham's long association with Rockefeller educational philanthropy. The Flexner brothers were Jewish, but they both married into prominent white, Anglo-Saxon, Protestant families and moved quite comfortably among the Protestant elite professionals who encircled Rockefeller.[18]

The Greene brothers were more directly linked to the American Protestant heritage. Their missionary background and its influence on Jerome's religious judgment have already been mentioned.[19] In 1911, Jerome Greene had come to the Rockefeller Institute as general manager at the recommendation of Charles W. Eliot, whom he had served as secretary. Greene's administrative ability impressed Rockefeller, and when the Rockefeller Foundation was formed in 1917, Greene became its secretary and chief administrator. When the Rockefeller team began its China mission, Jerome recruited his brother Roger, initiating the complicated relationship between Roger Greene and Rockefeller, chronicled in chapter four.[20]

The Fosdicks were the most important pair of brothers in Rockefeller's life. Gates introduced Harry Emerson Fosdick to Rockefeller, having met Fosdick in Montclair, where he served the First Baptist Church from 1904–1915. In 1908, Fosdick began his long association with Union Theological Seminary and began to have occasional contact with Rockefeller. As early as 1911, Rockefeller was sufficiently impressed with Fosdick to consider him for the job at Fifth Avenue Baptist. By this time Rockefeller had become acquainted with his brother Raymond through reform work in New York City. Gates and

18. Fosdick, *Foundation*, 11. E. Richard Brown, *Rockefeller Medicine Men: Medicine and Capitalism in America* (Berkeley: University of California Press, 1979) 135–56.

19. See chaps. 4 and 5.

20. Fosdick, *Foundation*, 21–22.

Rockefeller brought Harry Fosdick onto the foundation board in 1916. After the First World War, Raymond Fosdick began what would be a lifelong career on the Rockefeller staff. His first major assignment was to untangle the office of the I.W.M.

Harry and Raymond remained close through the years, bantering through the good times and supporting one another through the bad. The worst episode in Raymond's life came in 1932 when his manic-depressive wife fatally shot their two children and then took her own life. Rockefeller was especially loyal to the family during this time, and the Fosdicks drew on the resources of the wider Rockefeller network numerous times. Simon Flexner helped steer Harry's daughter Elinor through Johns Hopkins Medical School, and University of Chicago archaeologist James Henry Breasted, shortly after receiving a ten million dollar Rockefeller grant, guided Harry and his family on an unforgettable tour of Egypt.[21]

In many instances Rockefeller associates brought their children into the professional network. Gates's family serves as an example; his son joined Peabody's son as part of the China Medical project. During the First World War John R. Mott and Bruce Barton worked with Gates to publish the correspondence of Gates's daughter, Alice, under the title *A Red Triangle Girl in France*.[22]

Willard S. Richardson, another of Rockefeller's intimate associates, had been his closest friend during his college years. Richardson had been a senior at Brown when Rockefeller arrived and had supported the younger man in his religious convictions. The pair became traveling companions, and when Richardson was studying at Union, he also served on the staff of Fifth Avenue Baptist. When Rockefeller took control of the family philanthropy, he hired Richardson as his philanthropic advisor. Richardson's service included seats on the boards of the C.M.B. and the Davison Fund during the twenties and thirties.[23]

21. Miller, *Fosdick*, 303, 306–7, 180.

22. Alice Gates, *A Red Triangle Girl in France* (New York: George H. Doran, 1918), Archives: Gates Papers, box 1, folder 20.

23. Fosdick, *Rockefeller*, 53–54, 61–62; Harr and Johnson, *Century*, 304–5, 350, 362.

The Rockefeller staff was one of unusual stability and loyalty. The spirit of pioneering enterprise could produce strong bonds, such as the one Wallace Buttrick developed with Gates:

> For forty-five years you and I have been close friends—for over thirty years most intimate confidential friends—engaged together in exacting and stupendous enterprise, pregnant with measureless destinies, and there has never been a break between us. I hardly know where to look for a duplicate of such a record. We were built to work together just as we have, and surely it was divine Providence that placed us side by side.[24]

Although Rockefeller was sought after as a participant in numerous kinds of ventures, he was not one to do business of any kind on the basis of casual relationships. On hundreds of occasions he refused to give recommendations or make introductions because he lacked what he considered sufficient personal knowledge of those involved. Rockefeller was also slow to lend his name to causes and made it a practice not to serve on boards in which he did not exercise some real power of decision. He was also extremely reticent about giving public tributes for people beyond his close circle of friends. An amusing example of this reticence occurred in 1942 when Federal Council Secretary Walter Van Kirk made a simple request for a tribute to Frank C. Goodman, who was well known as the pioneer producer of religious radio programs.[25] In one of the many letters required to settle the matter, Rockefeller wrote a revealing letter to Harry Fosdick,

> As you know from your own experience, I am often asked to write letters of this character and frequently asked to write letters of endorsement for men who are seeking admission to clubs. Such friendly service I am always more than glad to render when I know the person well enough so that I can speak with personal knowledge and genuine sincerity. In the case of Mr. Goodman, while I know well of the important service he has rendered, that knowledge has come to me second hand and I am not even sure that I ever personally met him. . . . If, in the light

24. Wallace Buttrick to Frederick T. Gates, 23 October 1923, Archives: Gates Papers, box 1, folder 7.

25. Walter Van Kirk to John D. Rockefeller, Jr., 13 April 1942; Janet M. Warfield to Van Kirk, 15 April 1942; Harry E. Fosdick to Warfield, 28 April 1942; Archives: Religious Interests, box 32, folder 256.

> of the above, you still feel that a letter from me in this instance is important and would be willing to suggest two or three sentences covering what Mr. Goodman has done that I might have knowledge of without a personal acquaintance with him, I shall be glad to undertake to incorporate such sentences in a personal letter.[26]

Fosdick responded with a suggested letter replete with enough expressions like "so my friends tell me," "those who know of your contribution," and "I am glad to join with these friends," to satisfy his scrupulous parishioner.[27]

Rockefeller was equally reticent to be honored himself. His response to the idea of an honorary dinner suggested by the National Conference of Christians and Jews was characteristic and sincere:

> Some years ago I attended [such a] gathering. While I greatly appreciated the spirit that prompted the gracious and laudatory remarks which were made, I was so embarrassed thereby that I have not since been able to bring myself to again accept the public adulation of my fellow citizens, deeply as I appreciate the regard which it reflects.[28]

Rockefeller often chose to work behind the scenes, which sometimes led to suspicions of conspiracy.

The Rockefeller Network: Form and Substance

Rockefeller was quite willing to use his personal influence when he was convinced of the cause and the cast of characters. He orchestrated a continuous effort to modernize and promote Protestantism during the first sixty years of the twentieth century. During this period the Protestant church in America changed from a broad church into a divided one, from a place of commanding broad public support into a place of embodying a limited constituency. These evolutions

26. John D. Rockefeller, Jr., to Harry E. Fosdick, 1 May 1942, Archives: Religious Interests, box 32, folder 256.

27. Harry E. Fosdick to John D. Rockefeller, Jr., 4 May 1942; Rockefeller to Frank C. Goodman, 24 April 1942; Rockefeller to Fosdick, 7 May 1942; Archives: Religious Interests, box 32, folder 256.

28. John D. Rockefeller, Jr., to Everett R. Clinchy, 10 January 1955, Archives: Religious Interests, box 32, folder 256.

can be illuminated by considering the interconnected careers of persons brought together under Rockefeller auspices.

We can adumbrate four spheres that were brought together in service of the Protestant cause and under Rockefeller's orchestration: the leaders of traditional Protestant movements, the modernist theologians at Rockefeller-funded institutions, the elites of scientific professions with whom Rockefeller was acquainted through the broader world of Rockefeller philanthropy, and powerful Protestants involved in business and politics. Rockefeller's influence and orchestration within each of these groups was significant. He was, moreover, uniquely able to bring together individuals from within different groups in order to mold and promote the Protestant cause. Rockefeller mediated the influence of modern scholarship on traditional Protestant institutions, brought Protestant resources into the modernist camp, used business and political contacts to further religious ends, and brokered the interaction of the four groups in dozens of other ways in which no one else could have.

Within the first of these groups—the leaders of traditional Protestantism—the foremost member was John R. Mott. An account of the relationship between Rockefeller and Mott suggests the kinds of changes that the old benevolent empire was undergoing through the century. Rockefeller first met Mott at Brown in 1895, when Mott visited as a promoter of the Student Volunteer Movement for Foreign Missions. Mott reported that a "great revival" had broken out during his time at Brown and that one of his hosts had been Rockefeller, "the only son of the great business man who is worth probably two hundred million dollars. He is an industrious, levelheaded fellow—with good habits." Soon thereafter, Mott became general secretary for the foreign department of the YMCA and successfully solicited several hundred thousand dollars from Rockefeller over the next decade.[29]

29. John R. Mott to Elmira Dodge Mott, 27 January 1895, quoted in Hopkins, *Mott*, 116. Correspondence between John D. Rockefeller, Jr. and Mott, September and October 1900, cited in Hopkins, *Mott*, 220. Rockefeller to Mott, 25 April 1901, quoted in Hopkins, *Mott*, 238. Also see Hopkins, *Mott*, 237–38, 253. Rockefeller to James L. Barton, 17 April 1902; Frederick T. Gates to P. S. Benson, 11 April 1905, Archives: Religious Interests, box 1, folder 1.

In the early years of the twentieth century Mott was the undisputed leader of the crusade for "the evangelization of the world in this generation," in part because of Rockefeller's support for his ministry.[30] One incident illustrates the way in which Rockefeller money, when in the hands of a master promoter like Mott, could serve as a powerful catalyst. As he traveled the world, Mott kept a list of the needs of International YMCA facilities; by 1908, these needs totaled over a million dollars. His fund-raising efforts flagging in the wake of the panic of 1907, Mott approached Rockefeller, requesting that he give seven hundred and twenty thousand dollars for forty-three buildings around the world. Rockefeller dispatched Ernest D. Burton to survey the situations described by Mott in the Ottoman Empire, India, China, and Japan, and he decided to make the contribution. Mott then called President Taft and persuaded him to address a meeting of approximately two hundred distinguished guests in the East Room of the White House; at this time, Mott would announce the Rockefeller gift, along with several others. Emboldened by the occasion, Mott declared to the gathering that he was raising his financial goal to a million and a half dollars. Within a few months he had raised over two million.[31]

Mott's 1911 effort to secure an endowment of a million dollars for the purpose of unifying Western missions, as well as the subsequent Rockefeller Foundation grant of nearly half a million for this purpose, were discussed in chapter five. This episode marked the beginning of Rockefeller's efforts to promote the unification of American Protestantism. Mott's role in the formation of the China Medical Board was noted in chapter four. The Rockefeller China mission was a cause through which Rockefeller brought together Protestant leaders—such as Mott—and American scholars—such as Charles W. Eliot—who otherwise would have had little to do with each other.

30. See John R. Mott, *The Evangelization of the World in This Generation* (New York: Student Volunteer Movement, 1905). For a discussion of the slogan "the evangelization of the world in this generation," see Hutchison, *Errand*, 118–21.

31. Hopkins, *Mott*, 321. Frederick T. Gates, memo regarding John R. Mott's appeal, 13 June 1910, Archives: Gates Papers, box 4, folder 77.

Both the disillusionment brought on by the war and the subsequent I.W.M. debacle severely damaged the credibility of the interdenominational crusading that Mott epitomized. Mott had been closely associated with the I.W.M., and his reputation was tarnished by its failure. Undaunted, Rockefeller joined a small number of wealthy Protestants in funding the Committee on the Work of John R. Mott "to make possible the leadership you are giving to these several great world movements." Rockefeller considered it "a privilege to help" Mott in this way and, through five-year commitments, personally gave a total of two hundred and fifty-four thousand dollars to the Mott committee. In the postwar years, Rockefeller also gave over two million dollars to the YMCA, appointed Mott chairperson of the board of the I.S.R.R., and conceived the Laymen's Commission in response to Mott's concerns. He continued to support Mott as Mott turned his primary efforts in the direction of ecumenism in the thirties and forties.[32]

Rockefeller's support enabled Mott to act as a free agent, unfettered by the more cautious constituencies of the major denominational bodies, long after Mott could trust the general public to support his own endeavors adequately. A major factor in the influence of the Protestant establishment during the early years of the twentieth century was the money made by Protestants in an earlier era. It could still translate into power long after that era had passed.

Billy Sunday, another long-time friend of the Rockefeller family, represented a different dimension of traditional evangelicalism—revivalism. William G. McLoughlin, in his biography of Sunday, argued that the Rockefellers and other powerful Protestant businessmen used Sunday as a "a police measure—as a means of keeping the lower classes quiet." He cited as evidence the claim of contemporaries that Sunday's 1914 Colorado crusades turned that state's attention from the coal miners' strike to the campaign for prohibition.[33]

32. John R. Mott, 1928–56, Archives: Friends and Services, box 95. Harvey, "Speer versus Rockefeller," 298 n. Creel, "Contributions," 4. Hopkins, *Mott*, 455, 573, 596, 664, 691. Hopkins notes (p. 573) that Mott's sympathetic biographer, Basil Mathews (*John R. Mott, World Citizen* [New York/London: Harper, 1931]), chose not to mention Mott's extensive relationship with the I.W.M.

33. "Topics of the Times: Facing the Future with Calm," *New York Times*, 20 May 1916, p. 10, quoted in William G. McLoughlin, Jr., *Billy Sunday Was*

There is no evidence that Rockefeller encouraged Sunday to go to Colorado, but Rockefeller did serve as a member of the executive committee for Sunday's 1917 crusade in New York City. The crusade was held in the early days of the war against "infernal Prussian militarism,"[34] and Sunday served up a potent mixture of religion and nationalism. Rockefeller's motivation for supporting the crusade was suggested in what he told his Bible class just before the campaign: "Our churches do not lay hold of the masses of the people. If [Sunday] can touch them, there is just one place for me, and that is at his back."[35] The social control that Rockefeller sought was real, if indirect: he wanted all classes to make a commitment to the spirit and teachings of Jesus and was confident that social harmony would result. Rockefeller, who had met Sunday at the station when he arrived for the crusade, hosted a luncheon for Sunday and a contingent of guests including Colonel Theodore Roosevelt. Rockefeller defended Sunday against charges of financial irregularity and opened his own home for an intimate evangelistic meeting. At the conclusion of the campaign, Rockefeller expressed appreciation for its interdenominational influence and stated that it had exceeded "the most enthusiastic expectations of those who invited him here."[36]

Rockefeller sought Sunday's support for the I.W.M. in 1920, but Billy could not fully endorse the movement because of the involvement of "liberalists, higher critics," and "those who teach the New Theology as advocated by Rauschenbusch. . . and the Bushnellian theory—salvation by character."[37] Two letters related to the I.W.M. show the warm side of the relationship between Sunday and Rockefeller, Sr. Sunday penned this postscript on a letter to Rockefeller: "Give my love to your good father. I like him—he always treats me like a son."[38] Another letter to Rockefeller that same month, this one handwritten, dropped a friendly hint:

His Real Name (Chicago: University of Chicago Press, 1955) 237, see also 242–54.

34. Ibid., 56, 210.

35. Ibid., xviii.

36. McLoughlin, *Billy Sunday*, xxi–xxii, xxvi, 114, 196, xxviii.

37. Billy Sunday to Starr E. Taylor, 5 May 1920, Archives: Religious Interests, box 38, folder 318.

38. Billy Sunday to John D. Rockefeller, Jr., 19 May 1920, Archives: Religious Interests, box 38, folder 318.

> I came near writing you or your good father asking for a loan to buy the old farm at Ames, Iowa where I was born and where my mother, brother, sister, uncles, aunts, and grand parent are buried in the old grave yard on the farm. I have been waiting thirty-five years for the farm to be for sale but the man wants $450 per acre—that would take $72,000 as there are 160 acres in the farm. I felt if I owned that farm it would be all I would need in this world, but I didn't know when I could pay you back so I didn't write.[39]

There is no evidence that Senior took the hint. Sunday, moreover, did not share the same warmth with Junior, especially after Rockefeller delivered his modernist statement about the future of the Christian church six months after the New York crusade. The fracture of the broad Protestant consensus was at hand. Not until the fifties did Rockefeller again lend major support to a revivalist.

In the meantime, Rockefeller's support gravitated to speakers who shared his theology. For example, Rockefeller met E. Stanley Jones, the popular exponent of liberal views of the Christian mission, through the National Preaching Mission in 1937 and came to deeply appreciate Jones's work for the advancement of Christianity and the promotion of cooperation among the churches. The Davison Fund sent Jones a gift the following year.[40]

Rockefeller used his financial assistance to encourage the ministry of lesser-known Protestant workers who, for reasons that appealed to him, developed independent opinions or sought to work outside denominational structures. An example of this practice was the case of J. Robert Hargreaves. Hargreaves was released in 1930 by Community Church Workers because of his innovative methods of encouraging mergers between small churches in rural locations. When Hargreaves applied to Rockefeller for funds so that he could carry on his work under the general oversight of the Baptist Home Missions Council, Rockefeller's staff regarded him "a genius. . . with a heap of common sense and tremendous working capacity." Rockefeller supported him

39. Billy Sunday to John D. Rockefeller, Jr., May 1920, Archives: Religious Interests, box 38, folder 318.

40. John D. Rockefeller, Jr., to James M. Speers, 24 March 1937; E. Stanley Jones to Rockefeller, 25 July 1937; Archives: Religious Interests, box 32, folder 252.

for four years as a roving consultant to state, county, and city councils of churches that were forced by the Depression to consider complicated church mergers.[41]

The I.W.M. had encouraged a number of major religious leaders to work independently, at least for a time. During the movement's crucial months in 1920, Dr. Starr Earl Taylor was torn between retaining the directorship of the I.W.M. and returning to his post at the head of Methodist missions. He agreed to stay with the movement only after Rockefeller arranged a "golden parachute" in the form of funds that were available so that Taylor could continue nonaligned religious work should the I.W.M. fail.[42]

Abram E. Cory, another executive of the I.W.M., caught Rockefeller's attention while serving as business manager of the movement's promotional tour. Rockefeller took a special interest in his career and suggested that, in light of Cory's service as a China missionary, the China Medical Board should consider making him their permanent American representative in China. Vincent reported that nothing could be gained by such a position, and Rockefeller dropped the idea and subsequently gave Cory a personal gift of twenty-five thousand dollars to cover a bad investment and to get settled into parish work. Rockefeller considered Cory, as well as I.W.M. executives Daniel A. Poling and Ralph E. Diffendorfer, for the position of Secretary of the Laura Spelman Rockefeller Memorial. He also suggested to Fosdick and Mott a plan to hire I.S.R.R. Board member Charles R. Watson for the memorial and the I.S.R.R. simultaneously, an offer that Watson declined.[43]

41. Willard S. Richardson to John D. Rockefeller, Jr., 28 August 1933, Archives: Religious Interests, box 46, folder 362.

42. Starr E. Taylor to Abram E. Cory, 17 April 1920; Cory to Taylor, 19 April 1920; Taylor to John D. Rockefeller, Jr., 13 May 1920; Rockefeller to Taylor, 20 May 1920; Taylor to Rockefeller, 25 May 1920; Archives: Religious Interests, box 38, folder 318. Robert Gumbel to Rockefeller, 18 June 1920, Archives: Religious Interests, box 38, folder 319.

43. John D. Rockefeller, Jr., to George W. Perkins, 19 April 1920, Archives: Religious Interests, box 38, folder 318. Rockefeller to Raymond B. Fosdick, 16 July 1920; Fosdick to Rockefeller, 13 July 1920; Rockefeller to Fosdick, 17 July 1920; Archives: Religious Interests, box 39, folder 319. Abram E. Cory to Rockefeller, 28 February 1921; Rockefeller memo, 28

A year later, Rockefeller used his influence to assist Arthur Bestor, head of the Chautauqua Institute and teacher of the Fifth Avenue Baptist Men's Bible Class, after Bestor had acted as financial chairperson of the I.W.M. fund-raising drive. Bestor, feeling the need for a change, had taken a leave of absence from Chautauqua. Rockefeller wrote to Ernest Burton, who was preparing to chair a commission heading for China on behalf of the International Missionary Council, asking him to consider taking Bestor along as business manager. "Please regard the matter in an entirely cold-blooded, impersonal way and give it no consideration unless it commends itself to you as of real help and value in the work of your commission." Burton responded that, although too many Baptists were already on the commission, he would arrange it.[44]

Rockefeller also maintained influential relationships with denominational executives. Until 1932, Rockefeller was a pillar of support for the Baptist missionary effort at home and abroad. Presbyterian leaders Robert E. Speer and William Adams Brown worked with Rockefeller in their areas of mutual concern, as did Methodist leaders such as Starr Earl Taylor.

Wallace Buttrick was one notable example of an important pattern—the denominational executive who became a Rockefeller administrator. Buttrick was educated at Rochester Theological Seminary and served as a Baptist pastor for twenty years. During his pastorate he became a member of the American Baptist Education Board, where he met Gates. His relationship with the Rockefellers was strengthened during his tenure as secretary of the American Baptist Home Mission Society, and in 1902 he was appointed executive secretary of the G.E.B., where he served for two decades as an affable and tolerant implementer to Gates, who was a blustering, strategic genius. His career with the Rockefeller philanthropies also included service on the boards of the Rockefeller Foundation (1917–1926) and the China

March 1921; Rockefeller to Cory, 2 May 1922; Archives: Religious Interests, box 39, folder 320. Fosdick to Rockefeller, 6 May 1921, Archives: Religious Interests, box 41, folder 328.

44. John D. Rockefeller, Jr., to Ernest Burton, 17 January 1921; Burton to Rockefeller, 27 January 1921; Archives: Religious Interests, box 46, folder 365.

Medical Board. Rockefeller regularly recruited denominational executives for the family's secular philanthropies because he believed that these new trusts should assume some of the functions previously performed by Protestant denominations.[45]

The second group of leaders with whom Rockefeller was linked in religious work were those who provided the theological and ideological underpinnings for modernist Protestantism. Rockefeller's preference for modernism rather than more conservative theological principles was, in the opinion of his conservative opponents, one of the greatest factors in modernism's success. Rockefeller was certainly modernism's primary financial supporter. He promoted it both within Protestant circles and as a candidate for America's common religion.

Rockefeller's network extended to his own pastors. During Rockefeller's youth and adolescence, William H. P. Faunce enjoyed a ten-year pastorate at Fifth Avenue Baptist Church. Faunce came to Fifth Avenue as a young graduate of Newton Theological Seminary and was responsible for leading the church away from the old style of Baptist piety. Members were no longer to be called "brethren" and "sisters," the pastor "elder," or a revival "drops of mercy." The Rockefellers became religious liberals under Faunce's guidance. Faunce also steered Rockefeller to his alma mater, Brown, and later returned there himself two years after Rockefeller's graduation. He served as president of Brown for the next thirty years, and remained an outspoken proponent of modernism.[46]

Rockefeller relied on Faunce for counsel on industrial relations, interchurch union, and a host of other subjects. Faunce was a moderate social gospeler. In a 1920 letter to Rockefeller, which Rockefeller carefully marked, Faunce insisted against the premillennialists that "the church has a stake in creating physical and social and industrial conditions that make Christian life possible." At the same time he counseled Rockefeller against taking public stands on particular issues: "The

45. "Doctor Wallace Buttrick; A Minute," recorded in November 1926 by five Rockefeller Boards, Archives: Friends and Services, box 51.

46. Eugene C. Carder, "The Riverside Church: One Hundred Years of Historical Background, 1841–1941" (New York: Riverside Church, 1941) 7–8; this document can be found in Archives: Religious Interests, box 68, folder 517.

silences of Christ are most significant. He said nothing about slavery, nothing about unjust taxation. . . but quietly enunciated principles which overthrew injustice."[47] In 1923, Faunce also wrote to the Rockefeller office with glee over an incident at the National Convention during which John Roach Straton embarrassed even his fundamentalist friends by seeking to bar Faunce's speech: "Your friend James C. Colgate, after listening to Dr. Straton, said he always had some difficulty with miracles, especially with the miracle which tells us that Balaam's ass was about to speak—but he was now prepared to believe, because he himself had heard him." Faunce served on the I.S.R.R. board and, until his death in 1930, continued as a major adviser to Rockefeller.[48]

Cornelius Woelfkin, pastor of Fifth Avenue from 1911 to 1926, also became a prominent exponent of modernism. Rockefeller brought Woelfkin to Fifth Baptist from Rochester Seminary, where he had taught homiletics after a successful career as a revivalist and denominational executive. Woelfkin baptized all of Rockefeller's children and presided over Senior's funeral. In 1916, with Rockefeller's support, Woelfkin led Fifth Avenue to adopt associate membership on a broad basis, thus taking its first step toward interdenominationalism. Woelfkin counseled and encouraged Rockefeller during the furor over his 1917 address and through the I.W.M. fiasco. As a result of Woelfkin's modernism, fundamentalists attempted to prevent the seating of the Park Avenue delegation at the Northern Baptist Convention in 1924. Woelfkin was a great admirer of Harry Emerson Fosdick and a strong supporter of the church's efforts to obtain him as the next pastor.[49]

The connection between Rockefeller and Fosdick has been much commented upon by historians. Even before Fosdick became Rockefeller's pastor in 1926, the alliance between Rockefeller's money and

47. William H. P. Faunce to John D. Rockefeller, Jr., 23 July 1920, Archives: Friends and Services, box 60.

48. Rockefeller read with appreciation William H. P. Faunce's 1920 speech, "The Church and Social Reconstruction," Northern Baptist Convention, 21 May 1919, printed by order of the convention; John D. Rockefeller, Jr., to Faunce, 8 July 1920; Faunce to Edward L. Ballard, 24 May 1923; Archives: Friends and Services, box 61.

49. Carder, "The Riverside Church," 10–11. Obituary for Cornelius Woelfkin, *New York Times*, 7 January 1928, Archives: Friends and Services, box 123.

Fosdick's theology had already resulted in the distribution of Harry D. Fosdick's 1922 challenge, "Shall the Fundamentalists Win?" to every pastor in the United States. During his twenty years at Riverside Church, Fosdick became one of modernism's most influential teachers.[50]

Equally important for the present study is the way in which the connection between Rockefeller and Fosdick extended into the theological world around Union Seminary, where Fosdick taught between 1915 and 1934. Fosdick's biographer has found evidence of Fosdick's close collegial relationships with such faculty members as James Frame, Julius Bewer, Arthur Cushman McGiffert, John Knox, Cyril Richardson, John Baillie, Ernest Scott, Eugene Lyman, and Reinhold Niebuhr. Among those who counted Fosdick as a mentor were Samuel Cavert, Ralph Sockman, John C. Bennett, and Mary Ely Lyman. Fosdick, representing the seminary's case to Rockefeller on numerous occasions, secured a million dollar grant for the seminary in 1923, negotiated the Rockefeller gift that brought Paul Tillich to Union in 1933, and defended Reinhold Niebuhr against charges of social radicalism which Rockefeller raised in 1944. Rockefeller was a major donor to Union under the tenure of four presidents: Francis Brown, Arthur Cushman McGiffert, Henry Sloane Coffin, and Henry Pitney Van Dusen. In all, he gave the seminary almost four million dollars. Among those Union students who were referred to Rockefeller and who carried on their research with the use of Rockefeller funds were psychologist Anton T. Boisen and sociologist Robert S. Lynd.[51]

In his essay on Robert and Helen Lynd, Richard Fox illustrates the way in which the Rockefeller network orchestrated the careers of bright young scholars. Lynd attended Union Theological Seminary, where he studied under Fosdick and William Adams Brown. When he was at Union, Lynd did mission work at Elk Basin, Wyoming, where he wrote a muckraking study of Rockefeller oil interests and in the process met Fosdick's brother Raymond. Thus, on the recommendation of several Rockefeller associates, Lynd was offered a job with the I.S.R.R. after his graduation.[52]

50. Miller, *Fosdick*, 204–13, 116, 165.
51. Ibid., 319–32, 225; Creel, "Contributions," 9.
52. Fox, "Lynd," 109–13.

As was discussed in chapter six, Rockefeller also contributed substantial amounts to other university-related schools of divinity and religion, including Colgate-Rochester Divinity School and the University of Chicago Divinity School.[53] Rockefeller ties to Rochester went back to Senior's relationship to Augustus H. Strong, who was professor of systematic theology and president of the seminary for forty years (1872–1912). When Junior was a child, the two families vacationed together and Strong's daughters Mary and Kate were Junior's playmates. Augustus Strong's eldest son Charles married Rockefeller's oldest sister Bessie. Another son, John Strong, was Rockefeller's lifelong friend, who, incidentally, organized a fishing trip during which Rockefeller became acquainted with Cornelius Woelfkin, resulting in Woelfkin's service at Fifth Avenue Baptist.[54]

During the late nineteenth century, Strong operated Rochester Divinity School on a broad consensus among Baptists around the moderate conservatism represented by his *Systematic Theology*. Strong freely conceded the validity of evolution and progressive revelation, but stood firm regarding the doctrine of divine inspiration. The Bible was a "human composition," but it was also "in all its parts the work of God." Strong was worried that younger scholars would accept the historical-critical method which seemed to him to deny the possibility of divine inspiration.[55]

Strong enjoyed the support of the elder Rockefeller during the 1880s, when Senior presided over the New York Baptist Union for Ministerial Education, a group that oversaw the affairs of Rochester Seminary. Had Strong not lost Rockefeller's support during the negotiations that led to the founding of the University of Chicago, Rockefeller money might have continued to aid moderate conservative causes rather than modernist ones. In the 1880s, Strong had written frequently to Rockefeller, Sr., about a plan to build the great Baptist "University of the Future" in New York. When Rockefeller decided to build such a

53. Creel, "Contributions," 1–12.

54. Fosdick, *Portrait*, 28, 35–36; John D. Rockefeller, Jr., to Cornelius Woelfkin, 6 June 1911; Eugene H. Paddock to Rockefeller, 9 June 1911; Archives: Friends and Services, box 114.

55. Augustus H. Strong, *Outlines of Systematic Theology* (Philadelphia: Griffith & Rowland, 1908) 59–60, xi.

university, however, he accepted the Chicago plan in which William Rainey Harper was the central figure.

In December 1888, when Strong's daughter came home on holiday break from Vassar, where Harper was teaching, Strong read her notebook for Harper's class in Old Testament history. He was greatly alarmed, and on Christmas Day he sent a threatening letter to a fellow Vassar trustee—John D. Rockefeller, Sr. In Strong's opinion, Harper had "departed from the sound faith as to inspiration and prophesy, and is no longer to be trusted in his teachings." Harper held the same views that forced the Baptists to "dismiss Dr. Toy from the University of Louisville." Senior suspected that the real reason for Strong's sudden concern over Harper's orthodoxy was that Senior had announced two weeks earlier that he favored Chicago over New York for the site of the Baptist university.[56]

Harper was able to secure adequate assurance for Senior that his Baptist fellows supported him theologically. Senior cared little about such matters; his choice of Chicago over New York was based on financial, rather than theological, considerations. Strong's concerns were well founded, however, regardless of his unfortunate timing in voicing them. Under Harper's leadership, the Chicago theological method developed in precisely the way that Strong had feared. The Chicago theologians declared that all doctrinal statements, including those of the Bible, were reflections of historical circumstance and ought to be seen as transient rather than permanent. Harper, Shailer Mathews, George Burman Foster, and Gerald Birney Smith became the theological avant-garde.

A second aspect of the University of Chicago negotiations was even more significant in insuring that Rockefeller money would go toward the promotion of a theology more radical than that of Strong. Through these negotiations, Senior met Gates, who was a graduate of Rochester Divinity School, where Strong was professor and presi-

56. Augustus H. Strong to John D. Rockefeller, Sr., 25 December 1888, as well as other related correspondence, Archives: Educational Interests, box 100, 1886–90 folder. See also Grant Wacker, *Augustus H. Strong and the Dilemma of Historical Consciousness* (Macon, GA: Mercer University Press, 1985) 51, 54–55.

dent.[57] Years after graduation, Gates wrote mockingly of his seminary days, expressing scorn for Strong's systematic theology:

> God was analyzed, mapped, and discussed with extreme detail. His thoughts, purposes, methods, and unseen activities were all accurately classified, named, and described, and the plan of salvation was reduced to a logical, coherent, and exact system. . . . It is a pleasure to add that in recent years the course of study in the Rochester Theological Seminary, and in many other seminaries north of the Ohio River, has been progressively changed in the right direction.[58]

Although he was not so disdainful of Strong during the events of 1888, even then Gates expressed his support for Harper's bold scholarship, his remorse for Strong's tactic, and his own doubts about the nature of divine inspiration of the Old Testament.[59]

Senior's immediate affection for Gates was based on Gates's business acumen, not his theological posture. Gates's liberalism, however, had a major impact on Junior and on the subsequent direction of Rockefeller religious giving. In addition to Gates, William Faunce, who arrived at Fifth Baptist in 1889, also drew Rockefeller, Jr., in the direction of theological liberalism. For these reasons, the years 1888 and 1889 represented a theological watershed for Rockefeller religious philanthropy.

Even with the growth of Chicago, Rockefeller ties with Rochester remained strong. Not only Gates, but also Wallace Buttrick and Ernest Burton had graduated from the venerable Baptist seminary. Clarence Barbour's presidency at Rochester from 1915 to 1929 also strengthened the Rockefeller connection. Barbour was a graduate of both Brown and Rochester. Before returning to his seminary as professor of homiletics and later as president, he served as Mott's associate at the International YMCA. While president of Rochester, Barbour kept up a frenetic pace as a visiting speaker on liberal religious topics; between January and March 1926, he spoke at twenty-one colleges, churches,

57. See correspondence in Archives: Educational Interests, box 102, 1889 folder; regarding the Strong-Harper-Rockefeller relationships, also see Archives: Rockefeller, Sr., box 45, folder 338.

58. Gates, *Chapters*, 74–76.

59. Frederick T. Gates to William R. Harper, 5 January 1889, as well as other related correspondence, Archives: Educational Interests, box 102, 1889 folder.

and schools, including Williams, Vassar, and Andover Seminary. In part, he kept up this pace in order to make enough money to repay a loan Rockefeller had given him to rescue his financially insolvent son. In 1929, Barbour accepted the presidency of Brown, where he continued the liberal religious tradition. Brown's convocation speakers during Barbour's seven years as president included Rufus Jones and Harry Emerson Fosdick. Barbour also served on the Laymen's Foreign Missions Inquiry and afterwards remained active in missions reform.[60]

As for the Strong family, although Augustus Strong was never fully reconciled to the Rockefellers, his children remained Rockefeller, Jr.'s good friends. John Strong's career at Rochester stretched into the fifties, and the friendship that he and his wife Lide shared with John and Abby Rockefeller was strengthened by vacations together and the exchange of numerous gifts. Strong would remain his father's son, conservative enough to be published in the forties and fifties in *Christianity Today* and *His* magazines. He continued to try and win Rockefeller, Jr., to a conservative position:

> I am venturing to send you under separate cover a paper of mine entitled, "Oneness with Christ." You may not like it. It may seem to you technical, abstruse, and theological. And yet, who knows? Something may appear in it to interest and to challenge you. That would make me happy.[61]

His efforts with Junior, however, were no more successful than his father's had been with Rockefeller, Sr.

Rockefeller's promotion of theological liberalism through these associations and others was well known in the twenties and thirties. Among those most interested in keeping a scorecard on Rockefeller's modernist philanthropy were its fundamentalist opponents. William Bell Riley warned, "When one man can control the financial world, the educational world, and practically the religious world, it looks as though the day of the Anti-Christ is not far distant."[62] The Baptist Bible Union saw Fosdick's call to Riverside Church as "obviously

60. Clarence Barbour, 1923–46, Archives: Friends and Services, box 46.

61. John Strong to John D. Rockefeller, Jr., 29 September 1957, as well as other related correspondence, 1911–60, Archives: Friends and Services, box 114. The article was published by John Strong, "Oneness with Christ," *Christianity Today* 2 (1957) 13–15.

62. Quoted in Miller, *Fosdick*, 165.

part of a plan to extend to the whole Baptist denominational life the influence of the Rockefeller Foundation, which already has succeeded in converting nearly all our educational institutions into hotbeds of modernism."[63] Ernest Gordon devoted an entire chapter of his diatribe against ecumenism, *An Ecclesiastical Octopus*, to the Rockefeller modernist network.[64] The conservatives were right. Rockefeller was carrying on a many-faceted campaign to promote modernism. His efforts seemed particularly diabolical to conservatives, who called into question the traditional American Protestant role of cultural guardianship. By the standards of premillennialists, Rockefeller's program could only be seen as the work of the Antichrist, whom they thought of as seeking to bring everything and everyone under the control of one world government.

Rockefeller's philanthropy and religious work led to a third network of relationships—those he formed with research scientists and university scholars. Through his philanthropy, Rockefeller came in contact with the finest minds in the developing fields in the medical sciences, the other natural sciences, and the social sciences. Rockefeller's biographer mentioned Simon Flexner, George E. Vincent, and Wickliffe Rose as having been particularly strong influences on Rockefeller's intellectual development. Of course, not all of the scholars in Rockefeller's network were Protestants. Rockefeller conceived of their work, however, in religious terms and was in a unique position to bring their services to the Protestant cause.

The trust that Rockefeller placed in such specialists was illustrated by an incident related to the building of the two-hundred-inch telescope at the Palomar Observatory, paid for by six million dollars, which the Rockefellers had given to the International Education Board. Junior had declined Rose's suggestion that he act as a trustee of the board when the family created it with a twenty-two million dollar gift in 1923, "because it is a technical field and I have no qualifications as an advisor."[65] When the board was considering the large, experi-

63. Quoted in ibid.

64. Ernest Gordon, *An Ecclesiastical Octopus: A Factual Report on the Federal Council of the Churches of Christ in America* (Boston: n.p., 1948) 115–47.

65. Raymond Fosdick, "Introduction," in George W. Gray, *Education on an International Scale: A History of the International Education Board, 1923–1938* (New York: Harcourt, Brace, 1941) x.

mentally designed telescope, Rose asked Raymond Fosdick to inquire with Rockefeller, since the proposed expenditure was so large. In what Fosdick termed a "characteristic" reply,[66] Rockefeller responded,

> I have no competence in the field of astronomy. Six million dollars *is* a large sum of money, but I have complete confidence in Dr. Rose and the trustees, and if after careful investigation they decide that it is the wise thing to do, there certainly will never be any criticism from me.[67]

George E. Vincent, the first president of the Rockefeller Foundation and one of Rockefeller's most trusted advisors, was a scholar trained at the University of Chicago. He received his doctorate there and served as dean of the faculty of arts and sciences before coming to the Rockefeller offices. Vincent was an electrifying circuit speaker, having cut his teeth on the Chautauqua circuit, of which his father was a cofounder. Vincent brought a scholar's mind and temperament to Rockefeller's right hand. His urbane, witty skepticism served as an important counterbalance to Gates's forceful dogmatism in setting the tone and direction for the foundation in its early years.[68]

Rockefeller family ties were, of course, especially strong with many scholars at the University of Chicago, not the least of whom was William Rainey Harper. Harper had begun his career at Denison College where he formed a lifelong friendship with Elisha Benjamin Andrews. In 1879, he went to the Baptist Union Theological Seminary of Chicago. Senior was a patron of the seminary, but the two did not meet until 1886. At that time Harper was being courted by Yale, and Rockefeller was enlisted to try and deter him. Harper, nonetheless, went to Yale in the fall of 1886, where he developed a friendship with Wallace Buttrick, who was serving as pastor of the First Baptist Church of New Haven.[69]

A year later, Strong drew Harper into his plan to found a Baptist university with Rockefeller's backing. Strong argued that the United States had no research university like those of Europe, that the Bap-

66. Ibid.

67. Ibid.

68. Fosdick, *Portrait*, 123; Harr and Johnson, *Century*, 147.

69. Thomas Wakefield Goodspeed, *William Rainey Harper: First President of the University of Chicago* (Chicago: University of Chicago Press, 1928) 57, 59, 95.

tists ought to seize the initiative in founding one, and that New York was the best city in which to do so. Strong was a believer in sectarian education. He lamented every sign of departure from the Baptist fold at colleges like Brown and Vassar. Strong seemed to feel that the best way to handle modern scholarship was to domesticate it under Baptist auspices before making it available to America's youth. He labored to persuade Harper to support the plan for a Baptist university rather than succumb to Yale's offer to build a modern department of Near Eastern studies with Harper at its center.[70]

By the time Rockefeller was convinced to move forward, Gates, not Strong, was the broker, and Harper emerged as the scholar capable of creating a university faculty. When Chicago was chosen over New York, Harper suggested calling the school the "University of the West." In 1890 he was made president with initial gifts from Rockefeller totaling four million dollars.[71]

Before leaving Yale, Harper grabbed his favorite student, James Breasted, by the lapels and said, "Breasted, if you will go to Germany and get the best possible scientific equipment, no matter if it takes you five years, I will give you the professorship of Egyptian studies in the new University of Chicago." Breasted did indeed return, and proved to be a uniquely gifted scholar and popularizer who received more than his share of Rockefeller money through his career. Vincent once jokingly accused him of "digging not in Egypt but Wall Street."[72] The distinguished Chicago faculty also included John Dewey, Albion W. Small, and George Herbert Mead.[73]

Rockefeller was made a trustee of the university as soon as he entered his father's office; he served with Gates in negotiating the family's ongoing interest in the university. Harper struggled in the early

70. Augustus Strong to John D. Rockefeller, Sr., 4 January 1887; Strong to Rockefeller, Sr., 22 March 1887, with a thirteen page outline; Archives: Educational Interests, box 100, 1886–90 folder. Strong to Rockefeller, Sr., 18 August 1888, Archives: Rockefeller, Sr., box 45, folder 338. Goodspeed, *Harper*, 81–83.

71. Correspondence among Frederick T. Gates, William Rainey Harper, and John D. Rockefeller, Sr., 1886–90, Archives: Educational Interests, box 100, 1886–90 folder.

72. Goodspeed, *Harper*, 116; Fosdick, *Portrait*, 360.

73. Hudson, *Religion*, 277.

years of the university to meet the fiscal demands of the Rockefeller staff, who for a time refused to give further gifts until costs were brought under control. By 1905, Harper had succeeded in obtaining a surplus of twenty-six dollars and thus won the resumption of Rockefeller support, but his untimely death in 1906 prevented him from enjoying the more prosperous days that followed. The addresses at his funeral were given by William H. P. Faunce, Elisha Benjamin Andrews, and Harry Pratt Judson, one of Harper's Chicago colleagues.[74]

A long line of University of Chicago presidents maintained the Rockefeller connection. Harry Pratt Judson, who succeeded Harper, had come from the University of Minnesota in 1892 to chair the history department and act as dean of the college. Judson was instrumental the following year, much to Rockefeller's satisfaction, in the financial restructuring of the National Baptist Convention. Charles Evans Hughes had been asked to chair the convention session, and when he declined, Shailer Mathews presided over what he called in his autobiography the "Reconstruction of a Denomination."[75] Judson led the Rockefeller China commission of 1911 and was a charter member of the board of the foundation, serving until 1924.[76]

Ernest DeWitt Burton, Judson's successor, had a common mentor with Rockefeller, having come under the spell of Elisha Benjamin Andrews at Denison in the 1870s. He attended Rochester Theological Seminary where Gates was two years ahead of him and Wallace Buttrick was a year behind. Upon graduation he became professor of New Testament Greek at Newton Theological Institution; there Shailer Mathews was a colleague and William H. P. Faunce a student. Burton also cultivated a close friendship with William Rainey Harper during the 1880s, and in 1892 Harper persuaded Burton to come to Chicago as head of the New Testament department. He would serve there for thirty-three years.

Burton was especially influential in Rockefeller's theological development. In 1908, Burton went to China for Rockefeller and thereafter maintained an interest in education there. He returned to China

74. Goodspeed, *Harper*, 81–82, 95, 116, 194, 215.

75. Shailer Matthews, *New Faith for Old* (New York: Macmillan, 1936) 106. Rockefeller's role in this consolidation was discussed in the second chapter.

76. Goodspeed, *Harper*, 124.

with Rockefeller and the China Medical Board in 1921, and in that year he also accepted a position on the board of the I.S.R.R. Burton received Rockefeller's million dollar gift to Chicago's Divinity School in 1923.[77]

In the early years of Rockefeller philanthropy, another important counselor from the academic community was President Charles W. Eliot of Harvard. Eliot was a cosmopolitan Unitarian who was attracted to Rockefeller philanthropy because of its scientific spirit. Eliot first became involved with the Rockefellers in 1908 through the Rockefeller Institute for Medical Research. He was an early defender of Rockefeller, Sr., feeling that the public wrongly condemned Senior for carrying on business earlier in his career according to the ethics of his day. He felt that Senior had changed with the times and that by 1914 his ethics were as good as anyone's. Eliot was an outspoken member of the G.E.B. and the International Health Board as well as the board of the foundation. Eliot served as the primary academic counselor when Rockefeller and Gates studied the question of how best to introduce Western science into China. The Rockefeller China endeavor brought Eliot together with evangelical Protestants, with whom he would not have worked otherwise.[78]

Eliot encouraged Rockefeller with a visit during the 1915 Walsh hearings on industrial relations,[79] and as Rockefeller became a visible labor relations spokesperson, Eliot urged him to support profit-sharing and other progressive ideas. Even after he resigned from the Rockefeller boards in 1917, Eliot continued to correspond with Rockefeller, keeping him abreast of progress toward a National Park for Mount Desert Island, and urging on him benefactions to places like Roxbury Latin School and Smith College.[80]

Other university presidents who served as Rockefeller trustees and became personal friends included E. A. Alderman of the University of Virginia, Ray Lyman Wilbur of Stanford, James Rowland Angell of

77. Thomas Wakefield Goodspeed, *Ernest DeWitt Burton: A Biographical Sketch* (Chicago: University of Chicago Press, 1926) 11, 15–16, 23–26, 33, 76.

78. Charles W. Eliot, 1914–34, Archives: Friends and Services, box 59.

79. See chap. 2, p. 47.

80. Charles W. Eliot, 1915–34, Archives: Friends and Services, box 59.

Yale, and Ernest M. Hopkins of Dartmouth.[81] Hopkins especially enjoyed Rockefeller's trust. Two of Rockefeller, Jr.'s sons, John and Nelson, attended Dartmouth, and Hopkins stayed in the Rockefeller home and spoke at Park Avenue Baptist Church. Throughout 1927 and 1928 Rockefeller urged Hopkins to leave Dartmouth to assume the presidency of the reorganized Rockefeller Foundation.[82]

Rockefeller's 1941 tribute to Hopkins on his twentieth anniversary as president of Dartmouth indicated that Rockefeller's unchanging ideas about what a college should be were based on his Brown experience. What Rockefeller admired about Hopkins was his commitment to "the adequate training of his students for useful living."[83] Rockefeller valued the modern tools promoted by educational experts such as Abraham Flexner, but the key to a quality college was, in his mind, a caring mentor like Elisha Benjamin Andrews or Ernest Hopkins.

Countless universities were recipients of Rockefeller funds. For example, in 1919, the General Education Board made available fifty million dollars in matching grants to endow faculty salaries in two hundred and three colleges and universities, including public, private secular, and religious schools.[84] Needless to say, with this kind of monetary power Rockefeller could direct careers within the academic establishment. An example was the career of Henry S. Houghton. The Peking Union Medical College took over the work of the struggling Harvard Medical School of China, an endeavor begun in 1911 by Harvard graduates, but without formal ties to Harvard University. As part of the merger, the Harvard Medical School's young director, Henry Houghton, became part of the P.U.M.C., serving as its director until 1927, when, with Rockefeller's recommendation, he left to become dean of the Medical School of the University of Iowa. Houghton went to the University of Chicago as a result of his travels with University Vice-President Frederick C. Woodward, which took place in connection with the Laymen's Commission. In 1934, when Rockefeller relieved Roger Greene of executive responsibilities in the P.U.M.C.,

81. Fosdick, *Portrait*, 122–24.

82. Ernest M. Hopkins, 1923–52, Archives: Friends and Services, box 70.

83. John D. Rockefeller, Jr., *Ernest Martin Hopkins* (Hanover: Dartmouth, 1941), Archives: Friends and Services, box 70.

84. Bass, "Ministry on the Margin," 54.

Houghton was asked by Rockefeller to leave Chicago and return to China. He agreed, "their long-time friendship making it difficult for him to refuse."[85]

Rockefeller was able to recruit from this network of scholars and rely on its expertise in the task of molding Protestantism along modern lines. Examples abound. Thomas W. Salmon, the Columbia psychiatrist whose ideas about counseling shaped the ministry of Fosdick, was a Rockefeller Foundation employee. The committee whose consultation facilitated the consolidation of medical missions in China into the Peking Union College brought together Presidents Eliot of Harvard and Judson of Chicago with religious leaders such as John R. Mott and Robert E. Speer. In 1912, University of Chicago president Ernest Burton studied the international work of the YMCA and YWCA for Rockefeller. As discussed in chapter five, the many surveys of the I.S.R.R. constituted a sustained effort by Rockefeller to promote religious work that was conceived along the lines of secular principles of research and carried out by university-trained social scientists.[86]

Relations were not always cordial between the religious and educational leaders brought together by Rockefeller projects. Mott was especially objectionable to some of the university elite. Eliot found Mott

> one of the worst "blowers" I have ever met, or read about. He thinks in millions of men and money, and aspires to a world-conquest, not of the German kind, to be sure, but a conquest equally fantastic and unattainable. . . . He lacks the rational and scientific quality which should characterize all the work of the Rockefeller Foundation.[87]

Jerome Greene also received a negative report about Mott from Anson Phelps Stokes, who called into question Mott's integrity because of Mott's practice of working with fundamentalists as well as liberals.[88]

85. Mary Ferguson, *China Medical Board*, 102. Clarence Barbour to John D. Rockefeller, Jr., 21 November 1933, Archives: Friends and Services, box 46.

86. Miller, *Fosdick*, 260.

87. Charles W. Eliot to Frederick T. Gates, 6 November 1914, Archives: Gates Papers, box 1, folder 21.

88. Jerome Green to John D. Rockefeller, Jr., 23 July 1913, Archives: Religious Interests, box 46, folder 365.

The Laymen's Foreign Missions Inquiry is perhaps the clearest example of Rockefeller's conjoining the expertise of his scientific associates as well as the theological posture of his modernist seminarians with the traditional crusades of his friends in Protestant leadership. The Commission of Inquiry assembled by Rockefeller included two college presidents, one college vice president, two professors of philosophy, two deans of medical schools, one agricultural economist, two specialists in women's religious work, the founder of an experimental school, three businessmen, and only one clergyman. Nearly all had long-standing relationships with Rockefeller, and most of them owed their livelihood to institutions that benefited from Rockefeller philanthropy.[89]

At least half of the commissioners were personal friends of the Rockefellers. Georgiana and Harper Sibley were recruited for the commission after a stimulating summer luncheon with Abby and John at Seal Harbor.[90] Reflecting on Rockefeller's financial assistance to his family, Clarence Barbour wrote to Abby Rockefeller, "Did ever anybody have better friends than you and Mr. Rockefeller?"[91] While the commission was traveling in Asia, the Houghton family was left destitute by the failure of the Bank of Iowa City, so Abby and John began to support Houghton's college-aged daughters. Rufus Jones's participation in the commission closely followed Rockefeller's funding of the publication of his *Preface to Christian Faith in a New Age*. Although Jones failed to secure from China the stone gateways he had promised for Abby's Seal Harbor garden, that he had carried this assignment into the teeth of the Sino-Japanese War indicates the depth of their friendship.[92]

Rockefeller's business connections were also important in the work of the Commission of Inquiry. His brother-in-law Winthrop Aldrich,

89. Evidence for relationships was drawn from Index card file to Office of the Messrs. Rockefeller, 1889–1962, Archives: Correspondence.

90. John D. Rockefeller, Jr., to Georgiana Sibley, 3 October 1930, Archives: Religious Interests, box 48, folder 385.

91. Clarence Barbour to Abby Rockefeller, 2 October 1931, Archives: Religious Interests, box 48, folder 379, and box 49, folder 391.

92. Rufus Jones to John D. Rockefeller, Jr., 28 February 1932, Archives: Religious Interests, box 49, folder 390. See also Index card file to Office of the Messrs. Rockefeller, 1889–1962, Archives: Correspondence.

who was president of the Chase Manhattan Bank, arranged with Chase Manhattan and American Express offices in India, Burma, China, and Japan for the financial needs of the group.[93]

The commission viewed the cultivation of a healthy economy as integral to religious mission. Albert Scott of the engineering firm Lockwood Greene, Inc., was the commission's expert on the relation of missions to industry. He also became the commission's chairperson. Scott was a close Rockefeller associate who served as president of the board of Riverside Church for many years and joined Raymond Fosdick in 1933 on the Rockefeller-funded Liquor Control Commission. Scott was a graduate of Brown and served on its board of trustees, as well as on the board of trustees of the University of Chicago and Spelman College.[94]

James M. Speers was among the businesspersons who served on the commission. Speers, who was twelve years older than Rockefeller, had been omnipresent in the array of Protestant lay movements at the turn of the century. Speers was born in Ireland and came to the United States at the age of eighteen. He gained the presidency of McCutcheon Linens while serving as an exemplary Presbyterian layman. During the missions heyday before the First World War, he was vice president of the Presbyterian Board of Foreign Missions, chairperson of the Laymen's Missionary Movement, and treasurer of the Student Volunteer Movement. After the war, he and Rockefeller served in the New York Billy Sunday campaign, the I.W.M., the YMCA, and the F.C.C.'s National Preaching Mission. Rockefeller helped Speers through a business crisis during the Depression. In 1940, Speers decided to try to revive the Laymen's Missionary Movement. Speers, moreover, passed the crusading spirit along to his son, Wallace C. Speers, who launched the Laymen's Movement for a Christian World. The old crusades were still very much alive in the hearts of laity like the Speers.[95]

93. John D. Rockefeller, Jr., to Winthrop Aldrich, 15 September 1931, Archives: Religious Interests, box 49, folder 393; Rockefeller to Aldrich, 25 September 1931, Aldrich Papers, box 156, Baker Library, Harvard University.

94. Obituary for Albert Scott, *New York Times*, 3 March 1946, Archives: Friends and Services, box 112.

95. James M. Speers to John D. Rockefeller, Jr., 22 October 1940 and 13 May 1941, and other related correspondence, Archives: Religious Interests,

Rockefeller's ideas about the meaning of lay participation in religious mission had changed, even if those of the Speers had not. In bringing together secular professionals thoroughly imbued with the modern scientific world view for his missions inquiry, including experts in the fields of medicine, agriculture, and philosophy, Rockefeller was responding to the altered relationship between religious endeavor and the lay community. The lay role was that of "appraisal," carried out by specialists presumed to be qualified for an authoritative evaluation according to scientific canon. The driving force behind the appraisals that Rockefeller inspired was not a desire to destroy the Protestant crusade, but a zeal to remodel it according to modern standards. The commission's conclusion—that a Protestant American mission to the world ought to continue, but under drastically changed guidelines—was a sincere one.

The new model by no means diminished Rockefeller's sense of his own role; indeed, the major component of Rockefeller's self-understanding remained the civic-minded Christian layman. He was always most comfortable with business associates like Tom Debevoise, Bert Milbank, and Winthrop Aldrich. Raymond Fosdick pictured Rockefeller as formal in all his relationships.[96] To be sure, Rockefeller was awkwardly formal with Fosdick himself. With the inner circle of his fellow Christian professionals, however, he was quite informal. This 1948 note from Rockefeller to Debevoise catches the flavor of the relationship among the four mentioned above:

> On Wednesday, December 22d, at seven-fifteen at my apartment, I am looking forward to having you and Winthrop dine with me for another of our good talks. I have just written Bert that we three could not think of having the Christmas luncheon without him and that we were, therefore, abandoning it for this year confident that next year he would be with us.[97]

Debevoise was attorney for both Rockefeller and all the Rockefeller boards in the twenties and thirties. Whatever daily involvement

---

box 44, folder 334. Wallace C. Speers to Rockefeller, 28 April 1947, Archives: Religious Interests, box 42, folder 336; Index card file to Office of the Messrs. Rockefeller, 1889–1962, Archives: Correspondence.

96. Fosdick, *Portrait*, 421.

97. John D. Rockefeller to Thomas Debevoise, 10 December 1948, Archives: Friends and Services, box 57.

Rockefeller maintained with investments, business ventures, and private trusteeships was likely to have been handled with Debevoise's assistance. Tom took his family to stay in Rockefeller's Pocantico home during their travels. Rockefeller and Debevoise corresponded constantly, exchanging thoughts on war, peace, and the state of the world in general, spicing their letters with quotations from the likes of Henry M. Wriston, Friedrich August von Hayek, and Winston Churchill.[98]

Bert Milbank was a schoolmate from the Browning School. He became a member of the law firm Masten and Nichols, and he brought Rockefeller in as a client. The firm merged with Murray, Aldrich, and Webb in 1931 when Winthrop Aldrich left the latter to become president of the Chase National Bank. The weight of Milbank's association with Rockefeller brought him to the head of the list in the combined firm of Milbank, Tweed, Hope, and Webb. Milbank and Aldrich shared numerous financial interests, including the funding of the German war debt, which represented at least one motivation for the support of peace groups; Milibank, Aldrich, and Rockefeller all participated in supporting these groups during the thirties.[99]

Abby's brother Winthrop Aldrich was one of Rockefeller, Jr.'s most trusted associates. Their many-faceted relationship included mutual interests in business, politics, and religion. Aldrich served on the boards of the foundation and the G.E.B., as well as that of Riverside Church, where he was a major source of counsel for Rockefeller. Aldrich acted as treasurer for the Laymen's Commission. He was also a director in Rockefeller's Industrial Relations Counselors, sent Rockefeller the latest research or opinion about relations between union and

98. See John D. Rockefeller, Jr., to Thomas Debevoise, 27 July 1933, when Rockefeller was preparing to go on vacation; Rockefeller to Debevoise, 31 October 1942; Rockefeller to Debevoise, 22 July 1941; Archives: Friends and Services, box 57. Henry M. Wriston, a foreign relations expert, was president of Brown. Friedrich August von Hayek was a conservative Austrian economist. The British prime minister Winston Churchill was a perennial favorite of Rockefeller.

99. Harr and Johnson, *Century*, 314; Bert Milbank to Henry Stimson, 19 July 1931, Archives: Friends and Services, box 57; Aldrich Papers, box 66, Baker Library, Harvard University.

management, and kept Rockefeller in touch with events at the Economics Club.[100]

In this circle of close friends, Rockefeller discussed and carried out his relatively scant political activity. He was a loyal moderate Republican, although he could be influenced on some policy matters by Democrats like Raymond Fosdick. From 1920 onward, Rockefeller regularly made gifts to various Republican committees—gifts as large as twenty-five thousand dollars in a presidential election year. Often Aldrich or Debevoise acted as the intermediary. Rockefeller would never have supported a Democratic presidential candidate and remained unreconciled to the New Deal and its legacy. By far his largest political gift, over one hundred thousand dollars, went to Alf Landon in 1936. In that same year Rockefeller had to defend his modest gifts to the Maine Republican Committee. Unpleasant incidents such as this one kept Rockefeller from major campaign giving in most other years. His celebrated 1933 reversal on the prohibition issue came at the urging of Debevoise and Aldrich. On other occasions, he seemed guarded, even with them, about his political judgments. When his children John III and Nelson developed political interests, Rockefeller referred them to "Uncle Winthrop" for counsel.[101]

Despite Rockefeller's relatively limited political activity, there were many important ways in which his political connections reinforced his religious work. Rockefeller regularly recruited politicians as celebrities in his various religious crusades, most notably the I.W.M.'s "friendly citizens campaign." One of those whom Rockefeller contacted for the I.W.M. was his predecessor as Bible teacher at Fifth Avenue Baptist, Charles Evans Hughes. Hughes was then serving as a Rockefeller Foundation trustee, having resigned from the U.S. Supreme Court in 1916 for an unsuccessful run for the presidency. Rockefeller continued to solicit Hughes's support for religious projects while Hughes served as secretary of state (1921–25): Hughes returned to the Supreme Court as chief justice of the United States (1930–41).

100. Aldrich Papers, box 156, Baker Library, Harvard University.

101. Various contributions are discussed in Aldrich Papers, box 66, "Debevoise" folder. John D. Rockefeller, Jr., to Winthrop Aldrich, 17 June 1932; John D. Rockefeller III to Aldrich, 8 May 1930; Aldrich Papers, box 156, Baker Library, Harvard University. Harr and Johnson, *Century*, 398.

Numerous favors passed between the foundation and the United States government in times of international crisis. For example, the foundation and the State Department worked together closely to insure the welfare of those Rockefeller staff members imprisoned during the Japanese occupation of the P.U.M.C. Mary Ferguson, the P.U.M.C. board secretary who spent a year in a concentration camp, gave extremely valuable information to the State Department upon her return.[102]

Of particular interest to this study is the way in which Rockefeller worked with powerful Protestants in government in order to influence the direction of national policy. One member of the Rockefeller network whose political career has been seen as an expression of Protestant principles is John Foster Dulles. The paths of Rockefeller and Dulles crossed in interesting ways that allowed the power of one to reinforce that of the other. The first such case surrounded the controversy over Harry Emerson Fosdick's ministry in a Presbyterian pulpit during the twenties. Fosdick's sermon "Shall the Fundamentalists Win?" published by Rockefeller, made him a target of fundamentalist Presbyterians, who questioned his right to a Presbyterian pulpit. Dulles emerged as Fosdick's champion in the 1924 General Assembly, standing firmly against William Jennings Bryan's opposition of Fosdick.[103]

During these same years, Dulles was asked by Robert Speer to serve on the F.C.C.'s newly formed Commission on International Justice and Goodwill. Throughout the twenties and thirties, Rockefeller made special gifts to this commission. Rockefeller asked Dulles to serve on the Laymen's Commission in 1930, and although Dulles declined, this began a close association which continued for thirty years. The two corresponded frequently during the thirties on a variety of topics related to religion and foreign policy. In 1935, Dulles became a trustee of the Rockefeller Foundation and the G.E.B., and he later served for two years as chairperson of the board of the foundation. In 1939, Dulles invited Rockefeller to participate in a church peace conference

102. Raymond B. Fosdick to John D. Rockfeller, Jr., 18 January 1950, Archives: Rockefeller Boards, box 13, folder 112.

103. Mark G. Toulouse, *The Transformation of John Foster Dulles from Prophet of Realism to Prophet of Nationalism* (Macon, GA: Mercer University Press, 1985) 17–21.

in Geneva, and Rockefeller sent copies of Dulles's 1939 book, *War, Peace, and Change*, to friends.[104]

The friendship grew during the Dewey campaign in 1940; through Dulles, Rockefeller funneled contributions to the Republican candidate and met with Dewey and Dulles for lunch in the spring of 1940. In 1941, Dulles became the chairperson of the F.C.C. Commission on a Just and Durable Peace. The commission included Reinhold Niebuhr, John R. Mott, and Raymond Fosdick, and its inner circle included Edwin E. Aubrey of Chicago Divinity School, John C. Bennett, and William Ernest Hocking. Its purpose was to construct a systematic prophetic program through which the constituents of the F.C.C. could work toward implementing a Christian moral order. Rockefeller lent his support to the group by paying for the 1943 publication of Dulles's "Six Pillars of Peace," which argued that American Christians held a "special responsibility" to translate their beliefs into reality until "the Kingdom of world becomes the Kingdom of Christ."[105] Dulles sent Rockefeller a confidential memo in March 1943 that summarized a conversation with President Franklin D. Roosevelt.[106] Rockefeller also sponsored a luncheon for New York's leading citizens so that Dulles could present his program, and Rockefeller served on the sponsoring committee of a mass meeting held at the Cathedral of St. John the Divine. He also wrote to Dulles that year with appreciation for Dulles's article "A Righteous Faith," asking how he could obtain copies for distribution. After the war, Rockefeller continued to support the Commission on a Just and Durable Peace, as well as the Commission on Policy of the Department of International Justice and Goodwill.[107]

In 1947, Dulles sent Rockefeller a gift subscription to *Christian Century* in 1947.[108] This is a noteworthy symbol; the vision that in

104. Ibid., 62–67. John D. Rockefeller, Jr., to John Foster Dulles, 10 January 1939, Index card files to Office of the Messrs. Rockefeller, 1889–1962, Archives: Correspondence.

105. John Foster Dulles, "Conference on the Basis of Peace," *Federal Council Bulletin* 25 (1942) 9, quoted in Toulouse, *Dulles*, 67.

106. Index card files to office of the Messrs. Rockefeller, 1889–1962, Archives: Correspondence.

107. Archives: Religious Interests, box 31, folder 247.

108. Index card files to office of the Messrs. Rockefeller, 1889–1962, Archives: Correspondence.

1900 led the founders of the publication to name it "Christian Control," lived on in both Dulles and Rockefeller. The vision of the kingdom of God and its realization in America remained a powerful undercurrent in American public policy throughout the first half of the twentieth century, in part because of Rockefeller's money.

Both within and beyond the borders of the Protestant churches, Rockefeller translated his money into influence. The extensive network of relationships around Rockefeller, taken alone, constitute sufficient justification for the claim that a powerful establishment existed within American Protestantism in the years from 1900 to 1960. This establishment transformed institutions such as the Christian college, the sectarian seminary, the revival meeting, and the mission station into forms suitable for the modern world, and through them, this establishment continued the quest for a Christian America.

8

Conclusion

Secularization and Common Religion

America was no longer a Protestant nation in the years between 1900 and 1960, but the families, the institutions, and the resources that bolstered Protestantism at the turn of the century did not disappear overnight. Rather, they constituted an important part of the core culture during and after the modernization of America. A powerful establishment within Protestantism, including Rockefeller, continued to carry on the quest to establish its version of the kingdom of God in America. These realities bear on our understanding of two concepts prominently related to discourse about religion in America: secularization and common religion.

American culture certainly became more secular during Rockefeller's lifetime. At the beginning of this period, Rockefeller heard his pastor worry aloud over the possible impact of Sunday newspapers and motor cars on religious observance. At the midpoint of this period, he heralded the death of Protestant America's favorite crusade, prohibition. He lived into the decade that announced the very death of God. Along the way, his modernist theological outlook allowed him to contribute, intentionally and unintentionally, to secularization in many ways. Nevertheless, Rockefeller remained religious. Until the end of his life, he continued to pray to God daily, as his parents had taught him.

Throughout his life he sought to maintain and advance the cause of "a Christian America."

Perhaps Rockefeller's religious activity can be seen as an instance of cultural lag. Just as more tolerant sectarian Protestants begat liberals in the 1880s, perhaps Protestant liberals begat secularists in the 1920s,[1] and then lived out the remainder of their lives as the last exemplars of a dying breed.

This, however, does not seem to have been the case. Liberal Protestants not only survived in the twentieth century; they flourished—as, of course, did sectarian Protestants! Protestant power continued to be a major factor in American culture, as each generation of Billy Sundays found its Rockefellers. Any model of American religious life in the years between 1900 and 1960 must account for the existence of a variety of expressions of Protestantism within American culture, expressions that coexisted with aspects of modernity in a variety of ways. America became more secular, but powerful Protestants were by no means a mere anachronism.

If it is not true that America was becoming wholly secularized during Rockefeller's lifetime, it is certainly true that the nation was becoming more religiously diverse. Yet, while many Protestants, like Rockefeller himself, welcomed new religious *forms*, they were, nonetheless, anxious to maintain a common religious *substance* in order to insure a harmonious society. While, for most of these years, conservatives generally chose to retreat into a subculture to await the second coming of Christ, it was liberals who often endeavored to maintain a common religion. In the words of Martin Marty, they opted for an "ordering faith rather than a saving faith."[2] One can easily make associations between such faith and rather unspiritual desires for social control. The fact remains, however, that, along with fellow mem-

1. For a discussion of the nurture of late nineteenth-century liberals, see William R. Hutchison, "Cultural Strain and Protestant Liberalism," *AHR* 76 (1971) 386–411. William Sims Bainbridge and Rodney Stark give evidence ("Sectarian Tension," *Review of Religious Research* 22 [1980] 105–24) that second-generation sectarians seek to lessen the tension between their religious beliefs and the larger culture.

2. Martin Marty, *Religious and Republic: The American Circumstance* (Boston: Beacon, 1987) 65.

bers of the Protestant establishment, Rockefeller thought that the "spirit and teachings of Jesus" constituted a sufficiently broad platform for public religion. Given the program of this establishment, it was no accident that Will Herberg could still detect a common faith in America in 1955.[3]

Many Americans, of course, found Rockefeller's formulation too confining. By 1960, liberal Protestantism had become merely one religious expression among many cultural expressions—religious and nonreligious. Protestantism's long guardianship over America had ended. The kingdom had not come to America.

The religious instinct that a group of people cannot live peaceably together without a common assent to transcendent principles, however, may well be a perennial one. Many within the Protestant establishment continued to act on this premise long after the demographic, philosophical, and material realities of American culture rendered problematic any conception of a common religion. In the years since 1960, the same instinct has been expressed in the programs of persons as diverse as Wilfred Cantwell Smith, Richard John Neuhaus, and Jerry Falwell.[4] In this context, Rockefeller's promotion of a religion of good deeds, which was embodied in his extensive investment in human welfare, represented not only an attempt to perpetuate a dying hegemony, but also the expression of an undying religious aspiration.

3. Will Herberg, *Protestant, Catholic, Jew* (Garden City, NY: Doubleday, 1955) 102.

4. See Wilfred Cantwell Smith, *Towards a World Theology* (Philadelphia: Westminster, 1981); John Richard Neuhaus, *The Naked Public Square* (Grand Rapids, MI: Eerdmans, 1984); Jerry Falwell, *Listen, America!* (Garden City, NY: Doubleday, 1980).

Index

Abbott, Lyman, 43, 72
Acadia National Park, 199, 227
Aldrich, Nelson, 17, 23
Aldrich, Winthrop W., 177, 202, 230, 232–34
Alderman, Edwin A., 70, 71, 227
American Association of Religion in Universities and Colleges, 83
American Association of Theological Schools, 181
American Board of Commissioners for Foreign Missions, 33, 42, 56, 127
Anderson, Martin, B., 37
Andrews, Elisha Benjamin: at Brown, 16, 19–22; at Denison College 223, 225–27; influence on Rockefeller, 28, 49, 87; educational philosophy, 70–71
Angell, James R., 201, 227
Armour, Alexander W., 147
Arnett, Trevor, 154
Astor, John Jacob, 139, 203

Baldwin, Roger N., 144
Baldwin, William H., Jr., 71–76, 201
Baptist societies: Bible Union, 222; City Mission, 34; Education Society, 37, 214; Board of Foreign Missions, 35, 37–38, 123, 125–27, 156, 164; Home Mission Society, 35, 37–38, 73, 104, 123, 213–15; New York State Convention, 34, 174; Northern Baptist Convention, 35, 174, 176, 180, 193, 225; Social Union of New York, 30, 121
Barbour, Clarence L., 158, 162, 221, 229–30
Barton, Bruce, 27, 168, 205
Barton, James L., 33, 56, 127
Bestor, Arthur, 137, 139, 146, 214
Betts, Edgar H., 158
Bliss, William D. P., 34
Bowers, L.M., 48
Breasted, James Henry, 205, 224–25
Brown, Arlo A., 158
Brown, William Adams, 53, 130, 192, 199, 214, 218
Brown University, 16–23, 28, 215, 221, 224
Browning, John A., 15–16

Bryan, William Jennings, 19, 235
Buck, Pearl S., 163–64
Bureau of Municipal Research, 44, 201
Bureau of Social Hygiene, 87
Burton, Ernest DeWitt, 225–26; and cooperative Protestantism, 150, 173; and foreign missions, 97, 209, 214, 228; influence on Rockefeller, 54; at Rochester Seminary, 220
Buttrick, Wallace, 214–15; and China Medical Board, 104–5; and Frederick T. Gates 206, 214; and the General Education Board, 35, 73, 75, 76; and William Rainey Harper, 224; at Rochester Seminary, 220, 226; and Rockefeller, 202

Carnegie Foundation, 80, 98, 203
Carnegie, Andrew, 78, 80, 140
Cathedral of St. John the Divine, 186
Catholic Charities, 23, 186–87
Cavert, Samuel, 189
Chicago, University of, 36, 46, 58, 82, 228, 230; founding, 16, 37, 219–20, 223–25; Divinity School, 52, 56, 173, 179, 180, 181, 218, 226
China Medical Board, 97–120, 126, 140, 213, 215, 226
Christian Century, 147, 163, 236
Clinchy, Everett R., 187
Cochrane, Thomas, 112–14, 118–19
Coe, George A., 172
Coffin, Henry Sloane, 157, 217
Colgate, James C., 35, 137, 175, 216
Colgate-Rochester Divinity School, 12, 37, 180, 218, 219, 226. See also Rochester Theological Seminary
Colorado Fuel and Iron Company, 45, 48–49, 81, 210–11
Community Church Workers, 170, 212
Conroy, Joseph, P., S.J., 57–58
Cory, Abram E., 139, 149, 150, 213
Council of Women for Home Missions, 170
Crozier Seminary, 77
Curry, James L. M., 75–76

Debevoise, Thomas M., 115–17, 202, 232, 233
DeWolfe, James P., 190
Diffendorfer, Ralph, 149, 150, 156, 213
Doane, William C., 71, 198–99, 200
Dodge, Cleveland H., 56, 137
Dorr, George B., 199
Douglass, Harlan Paul, 154, 155
Dulles, John Foster, 158, 188, 191, 192–93, 202, 234–36

Eisenhower, Dwight, 178

Eliot, Charles W., 226–27; and China 98, 102, 109, 209, 228; educational philosophy, 74; and Frederick T. Gates, 40; and Jerome Greene, 204; and John R. Mott, 229; and Rockefeller, 55, 61, 198–200
Ely, Richard T., 19, 151–52

Faunce, William H. P.: at Brown, 56; at Fifth Avenue Baptist, 13, 16, 18, 34, 42–43, 50, 215; influence on Rockefeller, 172, 216, 220; and Rockefeller network, 182, 225, 226
Federal Council of Churches of Christ in America: and the Interchurch World Movement 130, 135, 146, 148; and labor, 50, 144–45; Preaching Mission, 187, 231; Rockefeller support for, 167–68, 170, 181–85
Federation of Jewish Philanthropic Societies, 187
Ferguson, Mary, 234
Fifth Avenue Baptist Church, 13, 14, 23, 130; and Harry E. Fosdick 174–75, 204, 216, 218; prominent members 35, 137, 205, 215, 216, 218; Young Men's Bible Class, 24–28, 34, 211, 214
Fisher, Galen M., 155, 185
Fiske, John, 28, 29
Flexner, Abraham, 203–4, 227
Flexner, Simon, 41, 85–86, 105–6, 150, 202, 203–4, 205, 222
Fosdick, Harry Emerson: and cooperative Protestantism, 192, 200; influence on Rockefeller, 60, 61–62, 64, 88–89, 91, 156, 164; pastor of Riverside Church, 13, 175–79, 222; Professor at Union, 180, 217; and Rockefeller network 4, 198, 203–6, 217–18, 221, 234–35
Fosdick, Raymond B.: Institute for Social and Religious Research, 149–52, 156; Interchurch World Movement, 140–41, 145–46, 184; counsellor to Rockefeller, 44, 50, 184, 185; Rockefeller Boards, 115–17, 223; Rockefeller network, 81, 201, 202, 203, 204–5, 213, 218, 230, 232–33, 235; secularism of, 81–82, 88–89
Foulkes, William, 139
Franklin, James H., 99
Fry, C. Luther, 155

Gates, Frederick L., 105
Gardiner, Henry B., 19
Gates, Frederick Taylor: and education, 78–81, 97; influence on Rockefeller, 23, 29, 31–44, 51, 55, 61–62, 181; and modern science, 84–87, 99, 101, 103, 104; religious convictions, 39–41, 123, 186,

220; and Rockefeller Boards, 67–70, 73, 74, 77–81, 124–27; Rockefeller network, 198, 199, 202, 204, 205, 215, 226; University of Chicago, 223–25
General Education Board, 29, 67, 98; founding of, 71–73; and racism 73–77, 140; and religion, 78–81, 180; and the Rockefeller network, 35, 198, 200, 204, 215, 226, 227
Gilkey, Charles W., 156
Gilman, Daniel Coit, 198, 199
Gladden, Washington, 33, 34
Goodchild, Frank, 55, 56
Goodman, Frank C., 206–7
Graham, Billy, 191
Greene, Jerome, 100, 114–18, 126–27, 129, 202, 203, 204
Greene, Roger, S., 101, 102, 106, 109–18, 203, 204, 228
Guy, Harvey H., 155

Hankey, Donald, 121
Hargreaves, J. Robert, 170, 212–13
Harper, William Rainey: counsellor to Rockefellers, 16, 18; 34, and the University of Chicago, 37, 82, 219–20, 223–26
Hartford Theological Seminary, 56, 181
Hartshorne, Hugh, 155
Harvard Medical School of China, 106, 228
Harvard University, 46, 56; Divinity School, 180; Medical School, 106
Hawkins, F.H., 112
Hayes, Egbert M., 112, 113, 119
Heline, Theodore and Corinne, 190
Hocking, Ernest William, 119, 157, 159, 161, 162, 191, 235
Home Mission Council, 170
Hopkins, Ernest M., 157, 227
Houghton, Henry S., 109, 116, 118, 158, 159, 228, 230
Hughes, Charles Evans, 24, 137, 139, 157, 181, 225, 234

Industrial Relations Counselors, Inc., 50
Institute for Social And Religious Research, 148–55, 170, 185, 200, 213, 216, 218, 226, 228
Inter-church Conference on Organic Union, 183
Interchurch World Movement, 129, 130–48, 151, 152, 168, 183–84, 205, 210, 211, 213; Industrial Relations Department, 142, 143–44; United Simultaneous Financial Campaign, 136–40, 214, 234
International Council of Religious Education, 170
International Education Board, 81, 86, 223
International Missionary Coun-

cil, 151, 154, 155, 171, 214
Iowa, University of, 80, 83
Ives, Hilda L., 170

Jesup, Morris, 71, 198, 200
Jessup, Henry W., 183
Jones, E. Stanley, 212
Jones, Rufus M., 158, 191, 200, 221, 230
Judson, Edward, 12, 40, 203
Judson, Harry Pratt, 35, 36, 101, 225, 228

Kilpatrick, William H., 185
King, Martin Luther,Jr., 77
King, William Lyon Mackenzie, 32, 44–51, 57
Kraemer, Heinrich, 193

Laura Spelman Rockefeller Memorial, 68, 87, 138, 213
Laws, Curtis Lee, 56, 57
Laymen's Foreign Missions Inquiry, 59, 155–64, 174, 210, 228, 229, 230, 233, 235
Laymen's Missionary Movement, 56, 169, 231
Laymen's Movement for a Christian World, 169, 231
League of Nations, 89, 138
Lee, Ivy Ledbetter, 45, 56, 129, 145–46, 161, 164, 176, 202, 203
Li, C.F., 119
Lippmann, Walter, 47, 48, 51, 201
London Missionary Society, 105, 109, 112
Low, Seth, 198, 200, 201
Lynd, Robert S. and Helen, 152, 153, 217, 218

MacFarlane, Charles S., 182
Manning, William T., 186
Mathews, Shailer, 56, 64, 219, 225, 226
Mays, Benjamin E., 155
McConnell, Francis J., 143
McCormick, Cyrus, 140
McCracken, Robert J., 191
Men and Religion Forward Movement, 148
Merrill, William Pierson, 158, 183
Milbank, Bert, 202, 232–33
Millar, William B., 56
Mott, John R.: and China Medical Board 98–100, 105, 113; cooperative Christianity, 123–29, 150, 151, 154, 171, 181, 182; and Interchurch World Movement, 130, 133, 137, 138; Laymen's Foreign Missions Inquiry, 155, 156, 159, 161; missiology, 59, 98, 161; Movement for World Christianity, 172; and Rockefeller network, 4, 33, 205, 208–10, 213, 221, 228–29, 235
Murphy, Starr, 124, 127, 149

National Council of Churches, 167, 168, 169, 181, 195
National Conference of Jews

and Christians (Christians and Jews), 187, 207
Niebuhr, Reinhold, 217, 235
New England Town and Country Church Commission, 170
Nieh, Chichen, 108
New York Interdenominational Committee for Religious Education on Released Time, 170

Ockenga, Harold, 191
Ogden, Robert, 71, 72
Oxnam, G. Bromley, 191, 194

Park Avenue Baptist Church, 63
Peabody, Francis G., 56, 163, 199, 200
Peabody, Dr. Francis W., 101, 200
Peking Union Medical College, 90, 105–20, 228, 234
Perkins, George W., 52, 137
Pew, J. Howard, 191
Poling, Daniel A., 149, 150, 213
Presbyterian Board of Foreign Missions, 99, 127, 163, 164, 231
Princeton University, 45, 89
Protestant Council of the City of New York, 30, 181, 189, 190, 191
Pruitt, Ida, 108
Pusey, Nathan, 180

Rauschenbusch, Walter, 22, 42, 53
Religious Education Association, 170, 182
Richardson, Willard S., 116, 205
Riverside Church, 77, 164, 191; founding of, 13, 174–79, 186; prominent members of, 156, 172, 233; Rockefeller's participation in, 165, 169, 217, 222
Rochester, University of, 37, 179
Rochester Theological Seminary, 12, 37, 218–19. See also Colgate Rochester Divinity School
Rockefeller, Abby (daughter), 60, 61
Rockefeller, Abby Aldrich (wife), 17, 23, 24, 60, 61, 62, 221, 229–30
Rockefeller, Alta, 10, 11
Rockefeller, Bessie, 10, 218
Rockefeller, David, 60, 61, 170
Rockefeller, Edith, 10, 11
Rockefeller, John D., Sr.: and education, 71, 77, 97; and modern philanthropy, 34–36, 38, 67, 81, 84; and muckrakers, 29, 33, 34, 42, 226; and religious giving, 123, 124, 138, 139, 170, 189, 211–12; religious life, 7, 8, 10, 15, 23, 69, 165, 216; and Rockefeller, Jr., 12–13, 32, 51, 62, 135; and the Rockefeller network, 218, 220, 224; and Standard Oil,

9, 26; and University of Chicago, 16, 36, 37, 82. 223–24
Rockefeller, John Davison III, 60, 61, 111, 113, 116, 227, 234
Rockefeller, Laura Celestia Spelman, 7, 8, 9, 10, 11, 12, 24
Rockefeller, Laurance, 60, 61
Rockefeller, Nelson, 60, 61, 202, 227, 234
Rockefeller, Winthrop, 60, 61
Rockefeller Foundation, 49, 88; founding of 38, 65–68, 204; International Health Board, 86, 226; and medical work, 84–87, 101–2; Oriental Education Commission, 97; and religious work, 126–29, 194, 209; and the Rockefeller network, 199, 204, 209, 223, 227, 228, 229, 233, 234, 235
Rockefeller Institute for Medical Research, 29, 67, 85, 203, 226
Rockefeller Sanitary Commission, 73, 86
Rose, Wycliffe, 81, 86, 97, 157, 223, 222
Ruml, Beardsley, 87

Sanger, Margaret, 87
Scott, Albert L., 156, 157, 160, 163, 164, 172, 177, 230
Sealantic Fund, 180, 181
Sheldon, Charles, 22, 134
Sherrill, Henry Knox, 195
Shields, Randolph, T., 100
Sibley, Georgiana and Harper, 158, 188, 201, 229
Smith, Wilton Merle, 139
Smock, C. Mckay, 57
Sockman, Ralph, 177
Speer, Robert E.: and the China Medical Board, 99–101, and cooperative Protestantism, 127–30, 148, 149, 150, 184; on labor, 50, 144–45; Laymen's Foreign Missions Inquiry, 156, 163; and the Rockefeller network, 214, 228
Speers, James, 138, 139, 141, 146, 157–58, 163, 169, 230–31
Speers, Walter C., 169
Spelman College, 77, 230
Spelman Seminary, 72
Spelman, Lucy (aunt), 10
Spelman, Lucy Henry (grandmother), 18, 72
Straton, John Roach, 176, 216
Stron, Sydney, 57
Strong, Augustus H., 12, 218–21, 224
Strong, John, 218, 221
Stuart, John Leighton, 107, 111
Student Volunteer Movement for Foreign Missions, 128, 148, 171, 208, 231
Sunday, Billy, 123, 137, 182, 210–12, 231

Tarbell, Ida, 29, 33

Taylor, Henry C., 158
Taylor, Starr Earl, 135, 137, 139, 140, 146, 148, 213, 214
Tillich, Paul, 180, 217
Trevor, John B., 144, 145
Tsu, Y.Y., 108–11

Union Theological Seminary of New York, 52, 53, 128, 144, 172, 180, 192, 204, 217, 218
United War Work Campaign, 52, 132, 171
Universal Christian Conference on Life and Work, 191

Vincent, George, E., 114, 116, 118, 223, 222
Visser 't Hooft, Willem 193, 194

Ward, Henry F., 144
Washington, Booker T., 74, 76
Watson, Charles R., 150, 213, 214
Welch, William H., 105, 203
Wilder, Robert, 171
Willard, Frances E., 12
Wilson, George, 22
Woelfkin, Cornelius, 55, 130, 174, 175, 182, 183, 216, 217, 218
Woodsmall, Ruth F., 158
Woodward, Frederic C., 158, 228
Women's International League for Peace and Freedom, 90
World Council of Churches, 167, 181, 191, 192, 193, 194
World Missionary Conference (Edinburgh, 1910), 123, 128
World's Conference on Faith and Order, 191

Yale, 16, 37; Divinity School, 180
Young Men's and Women's Christian Associations, 52, 158, 185, 221, 231; Rockefeller contributions to, 83, 123, 171, 208, 209, 210, 228; Rockefeller participation in, 18, 28